Practice Informed Research Methods
for Social Workers

Teresa Morris, M.S.W. Ph.D.
Professor
School of Social Work
California State University, San Bernardino
5500 University Parkway
San Bernardino CA 92407
Phone (909) 537 5561
Fax (909) 537 7029
http://socialwork.csusb.edu/facultyStaff/morris.htm

Preface

In my first book on Social Work Research Methods (Morris, 2006) I introduced the idea that social workers can carry out research in a more liberated fashion than is usually outlined in most research methods text books. I gave a philosophical, theoretical, historical and practical foundation for implementing research from four alternative perspectives: positivism, post positivism, critical theory, and constructivism. As well as introducing these paradigms, I integrated research methodologies with social work practice by translating the steps of the generalist, social work, practice model (engagement, assessment, planning, implementation, evaluation, termination and follow up) into the research process (research focus, design, data collection, data analysis, data interpretation, and communication and dissemination of findings). I divided that book into four parts according to each paradigm with a fifth part that addressed cross cutting issues such as ethics, diversity, politics, and technology.

This book updates and reorganizes these ideas and methods so that the flow of the discussion more closely parallels the flow of the research process. Instead of being organized according to the paradigms, it is organized according to the stages of research. After an introductory chapter it has the structure outlined below in Figure 1. Also, to assist with instruction on this new organization, there is a web based resource that contains power point slides, full text of example student studies using these approaches, test questions, the manuscript of my first book and other supplementary materials. This can be accessed by contacting me at tmorris@csusb.edu

I have made these changes because, after using my first book for a few years, I realized that starting with positivism and ending with constructivism has left students who are keen to learn about critical theory and constructivism "cooling their heels" for half of the course. Now, when I integrate the four paradigms throughout the course, I offer a continual comparison of those approaches as we learn about each stage of generalist research methods. Having tried this with drafts of this book, I can honestly say that classroom discussion has become more lively….and demanding.

Figure P1
Structure of Book

Part One: Assessment and Engagement (Developing the Focus)
- i. Positivism
- ii. Post Positivism
- iii. Critical Theory
- iv. Constructivism
- v. Important Cross Cutting Issues
  1. Ethical Issues
  2. Political Issues
  3. Diversity Issues
  4. Technology

Part Two: Planning (Design)
- i. Positivism
- ii. Post Positivism
- iii. Critical Theory
- iv. Constructivism
- v. Important Cross Cutting Issues
  a. Diversity
  b. Technology

Part Three: Implementation (Data Gathering)
- i. Positivism
- ii. Post Positivism
- iii. Critical Theory
- iv. Constructivism
- v. Important Cross Cutting Issues
  a. Diversity
  b. Technology

Part 4: Evaluation (Data Analysis)
- i. Positivism
- ii. Post Positivism
- iii. Critical Theory
- iv. Constructivism
- v. Important Cross Cutting Issues
  a. Diversity
  b. Technology

Part 5: Termination and Follow up (Ending the Study and Developing the Dissemination Plan that Translates Findings into Evidence for Social Work Practice)
- i. Positivism
- ii. Post Positivism
- iii. Critical Theory
- iv. Constructivism
- v. Developing the Dissemination Plan

I am ending this preface with something I say when students get frustrated with the constant switching between paradigms that this new organization of the materials introduces.

> "Look at that tree outside the window. Now, if you are a positivist you see something with dimensions that can be measured quantitatively. If you are a post positivist you see something that can be described in words but can never be fully understood. If you are a critical theorist you see something that needs to be protected from exploitation and, if you are a constructivist, you understand that what you see is different from what the poet sees or the timber mill owner sees or the farmer sees or the child sees."

References

Morris, T. (2006) *Social Work Research Methods: Four Alternative Paradigms* Thousand Oaks CA: Sage

Introduction

Contents

Introduction

A note to Instructors

The goal of this book is to introduce social work students to practice-informed research by integrating research methods into professional practice and introducing alternative, approaches to the research process. This methodology is guided by three CSWE standards that address B.S.W. and M.S.W. curricula, specify generalist practice, define professional practice as a recognized change process at various levels of intervention and note the link between practice experience and scientific inquiry.

These standards are (my italics):

- "The *BSW* curriculum prepares its graduates for generalist practice through mastery of the core competencies. The *MSW* curriculum prepares its graduates for advanced practice through mastery of the core competencies augmented by knowledge and practice behaviors specific to a concentration". (Introduction to accreditation standard 2)"

- "Professional practice involves the dynamic and interactive processes of *engagement, assessment, intervention, and evaluation at multiple levels.*" (Educational Policy 2.1.10)"

- "Social workers use practice experience to inform research, employ evidence-based interventions, evaluate their own practice, and use research findings to improve practice, policy, and social service delivery. Social workers comprehend quantitative and qualitative research and understand scientific and ethical approaches to building knowledge. Social workers

  - *use practice experience to inform scientific inquiry and*

  - *use research evidence to inform practice."*

(Educational Policy 2.1.6)

With these standards in mind, we redefine the steps of the Generalist Intervention Model –Engagement, Assessment, Planning, Implementation, Evaluation, Termination and Follow Up – as stages of the research process. We also introduce four alternate approaches to micro (individuals, families, and groups) and macro (organizations and local, national, and international communities) practice research. These are positivism, post positivism, critical theory and constructivism.

A Generalist Approach to Social Work Practice Research

Kirst-Ashman and Hull (2012) suggest the following definitions of the steps of a generalist planned change process.

1. Engagement: "the initial period where you orient yourself to the problem at hand and begin to establish communication and relationships with others who are also addressing the problem." (page 36)

2. Assessment: "the investigation and determination of variables affecting an identified problem or issue..." (page 37)

3. Planning: "specifies what should be done: work with client, prioritize problems, translate problems to needs, evaluate levels of intervention for each need, establish goals, specify objectives, specify action steps, formalize contract.." (page 40)

4. Implementation: " the actual doing of the plan" (page 43)

5. Evaluation: "proof that intervention has been effective" (page 43)

6. Termination: a process of disengagement and stabilization (page 43)

7. Follow up: "Reexamination of client's situation at some point after the intervention" (page 44)

These authors note that generalist practitioners have the knowledge, values, and skills, to intervene at the micro and macro levels of social organization, while acknowledging the interlocking influences of all those levels on the target of the social work intervention. The same is true for practice-informed researchers. They too have the knowledge, values, and skills, to intervene with clients at both micro and macro levels of social organization to gather knowledge scientifically and, in some cases, to take action based on that knowledge. We can therefore adapt the steps of the generalist planned change model to parallel those that a social work practice informed researcher must implement.

1. Assessment and Engagement:

   a. Developing an understanding of the research question or problem statement or problem focus; and

   b. Identifying and utilizing strategies for gaining entrée to the research setting;

2. Planning:

   a. Deciding on the design of the study;

   b. Deciding who will be in the study; and

   c. Deciding how study participants will be selected;

3. Implementation:

    a. Gathering quantitative and/or qualitative data;

4. Evaluation:

    a. Analyzing quantitative and/or qualitative data;

5. Termination and Follow up:

    a. Reporting on findings;

    b. Developing and implementing a dissemination plan for transforming findings into evidence based practice;

    c. Exiting the research setting; and

    d. Identifying and implementing any plans for any further communication with the research site.

These five steps of practice-informed research are the central organizing theme of this book. In addition, within each of these steps we introduce four alternative paradigms and their associated methodologies.

Four Alternate Research Paradigms

There are as many ways of intervening with clients at the micro and macro levels of practice as there are social workers carrying out the interventions, Given the complexities of the social problems, client groups, and settings in which social workers intervene, not only do we need this range of practice strategies we also need a range of research strategies that can provide evidence for practice. How do we acknowledge the diversity of practice and also validate our client interventions using research methods whose intellectual traditions are accepted by our professional communities? To stay true to practice and scientific inquiry we can acknowledge that there is more than one way to do social work practice research. According to Guba (1990), there are four[1] paradigms or world views for approaching research, and they all have rigorous intellectual traditions. These are positivism, post positivism, critical theory, and constructivism described below with a summary of assumptions in table I.1 For a more detailed discussion of the scholarship supporting these world view see Morris (2006)

- Positivism

---

[1] Recently Lincoln, et al (2011) noted the emergence of a fifth, participatory, paradigm. This paradigm stresses a reality created jointly by study participants and researchers, a critical theory approach, and action that is developed collaboratively. However, in this book, the original four paradigms have been modified to incorporate the participatory approach into critical theory and constructivist research

- **Nature of Reality**: There is an objective reality that can be methodically studied. This world view is based on philosophical assumptions and theories about probability and sampling that call for gathering data to addresses research questions in which the regulatory mechanisms of the human experience are measured and manipulated in numerical form.

  - **Role of Researcher**: The researcher takes a neutral position and does not affect the implementation of the research project.

  - **Nature of Data**: Quantitative data is the only data that can meet the requirements of the assumptions of the positivist paradigm.

- **Post Positivism**

  - **Nature of Reality:** There is an objective reality but adherence to the strict methodological prescriptions of the positivist paradigm results in data gathering, analysis and findings that cannot always capture the complexity and richness of the human experience. Reality cannot be methodically studied and manipulated but can only be found in naturalistic settings, i.e. settings where people are living out the focus of the study.

  - **Role of Researcher:** The researcher tries to stay neutral but can have an influence on the implementation of the project. The researcher must, therefore, learn to be aware of and control that influence.

  - **Nature of Data:** Qualitative data is the only data than can meet the requirements of the post positivist paradigm.

- **Critical theory**

  - **Nature of Reality:** There is an objective reality but it can never be known because it is always viewed through the prism of an ideology (e.g. racism, feminism, neo-Marxism)

  - **Role of Researcher:** The researcher acknowledges the ideology with which he or she is viewing the focus of the study and makes explicit statements about power relationships. Also, the researcher takes action to empower those who are oppressed by those power relationships.

  - **Nature of Data:** Quantitative and qualitative data is gathered to document the impact of an ideology on a particular population and to identify and evaluate action steps that aim to empower those who are oppressed by that ideology.

- **Constructivism**

o **Nature of Reality:** All reality is subjective,

o **Role of Researcher:** The researcher partners with study participants to build a shared understanding of the human condition.

o **Nature of Data:** Qualitative data that is an accurate representation of study participants' constructions of the focus of the study.

Table I.1 Overview of Assumptions of Four Paradigms

	Positivism	Post Positivism	Critical Theory	Constructivism
Assumption about the nature of reality	Objective with observable regulatory mechanisms	Objective with observable regulatory mechanisms	Objective with observable regulatory mechanisms that our often viewed in a distorted manner because of the influence of ideology	Subjective, there are no observable regulatory mechanisms only a combination of individual points of view which combine to create understanding.
Assumption about the relationship between the researcher and those being researched	Separation between observer and observed	No separation between observer and observed but the observer must try to control biases	No separation between observer and observed, the observer bust state biases	No separation between observer and observed, each have valid perspectives
Research Methods	Study is designed before data gathering begins. Quantitative data (numerical data analyzed using statistics)	Qualitative data (words and/or observations) collected in naturalistic settings	Qualitative data (words and/or observations) mostly, could include some quantitative data on nature of oppression. Action research	Qualitative (words and/or observations), unless someone can only explain their perspective using numbers. Action research
Goal of research	Passive development of knowledge	Passive development of knowledge	Development of knowledge and action	Development of knowledge and action
Generic question	What causes this?	How does this happen?	Why does this oppression happen and what should we do about it?	What is everyone's understanding of what is happening and what should we do about that understanding?

We can see the potential to expand knowledge about social work practice when we consider alternate paradigms. Practice-Informed researchers, when considering their own research projects, can choose one paradigm and then implement each step of the approach accordingly, as summarized in table I.2. They can develop a question, focus, or statement depending on the chosen paradigm. They can develop a design and decide on the sampling plan for including participants in the study. They can decide which quantitative or qualitative data they wish to collect and analyze and they can develop appropriate termination and follow up procedures as well as dissemination plans for converting research findings into evidence for social work practice.

Table I.2 Practice-Informed Social Work Research Methods

	Positivism	Post Positivism	Critical Theory	Constructivism
Assessment and Engagement	Development of Question, Literature Review, Development of Theoretical Orientation	Development of Focus, Literature Review, Development of Theoretical Orientation	Development of Statement, Literature Review, Development of Theoretical Orientation	Development of Statement, Literature Review, Development of Theoretical Orientation
Planning	Design of study and sampling plan	Design of study and sampling plan	Design of study and sampling plan	Design of study and sampling plan
Implementation	Methods for collecting quantitative data	Methods for collecting qualitative data	Methods for collecting qualitative data	Methods for collecting qualitative data
Evaluation	Quantitative Analysis	Qualitative Analysis	Qualitative Analysis	Qualitative Analysis
Terminations and Follow Up	Plan for disengagement and Dissemination Plan	Plan for disengagement and Dissemination Plan	Plan for disengagement and Dissemination Plan	Plan for disengagement and Dissemination Plan

To sum up, this book offers a novel approach to practice-informed research methods that applies the generalist change model to the research process and offers four alternate ways to carry out research. The book is divided into five sections:

1. Assessment and Engagement

2. Planning

3. Implementation

4. Evaluation

5. Termination and Follow up

Within each section there are four chapters:

i. Positivism

ii. Post Positivism

iii. Critical Theory

iv. Constructivism

Throughout the book, we review examples of real students' studies (full texts available as a web based resource for this book), as well as questions and learning assignments intended to give practical guidance on implementing practice-informed research.

Instructors and practitioners will recognize that the above explanation gives the impression that each step of practice-informed research is separate and can be followed in a linear fashion and that each paradigm is completely separate from the others. However, as in social work practice, when we carry out a research project there is often overlap between the stages of the research process, and frequently we go back and visit stages again. The differences between the research paradigms sometimes lie more in the world views they bring to the research process than in specific differences in methodologies. This will become clearer as we develop our understanding of practice-informed research.

A note to students

When you decided to be a social worker you probably saw yourself as someone working with people who need help. The personal statement you wrote when you applied to your social work program surely described that vision; however, being a researcher was probably not part of that picture. When you thought about helping people, you may have thought about talking to them and their families and applying intervention skills that would improve their situations. You probably thought that in your social work program you would learn about these skills and how to implement them. Now that you are in your social work program you may have wondered about these skills, asking yourself, how do we decide which interventions we should use in social work and how do we know if they are effective? Well, the answer is research. If we are to be effective social workers, we need to at least know what the research literature says about the interventions we are implementing but, more importantly, be able to carry out our own research projects. Indeed our professional code of ethics notes that:

> "(a) Social workers should monitor and evaluate policies, the implementation of programs, and practice interventions.

> (b) Social workers should promote and facilitate evaluation and research to contribute to the development of knowledge.

> (c) Social workers should critically examine and keep current with emerging knowledge relevant to social work and fully use evaluation and research evidence in their professional practice."

(Section 5.02 Evaluation and Research)

How do we carry out research that gives us useful information about our social work practice with individuals, families, groups (micro practice) and communities at the local, national and international levels (macro practice)? The answer is *practice-informed* research. If you intend to be a professional social worker, then practice-informed research will be at the core of your work. To keep up with "best practices" you will read and understand research that others have done but, more importantly, to monitor your impact on clients and/or solve problems you will also carry out your own research projects. This book shows you how to do this. Is shows you how to integrate research skills with practice skills so that you can become a proficient social worker.

Accredited social work programs use a generalist practice model as the foundation for teaching students about the knowledge, values, skills, and competencies needed to intervene at the micro and macro levels of human organization. One definition of this generalist planned change process is offered by Kirst-Ashmand and Hull (2012) who suggest that when a generalist social worker intervenes, he or she should follow these steps.

1. Engagement: "the initial period where you orient yourself to the problem at hand and begin to establish communication and relationships with others who are also addressing the problem." (page 36)

2. Assessment: "the investigation and determination of variables affecting an identified problem or issue..." (page 37)

3. Planning: "specifies what should be done: work with client, prioritize problems, translate problems to needs, evaluate levels of intervention for each need, establish goals, specify objectives, specify action steps, formalize contract." (page 40)

4. Implementation: "the actual doing of the plan" (page 43)

5. Evaluation: "proof that intervention has been effective" (page 43)

6. Termination: a process of disengagement and stabilization (page 43)

7. Follow up: "Reexamination of client's situation at some point after the intervention" (page 44)

This process can be aligned with the generic steps of the research process identified in most research texts. For example Neuman and Kreuger (2003) list the following steps of the research process

1. Choose Topic

2. Focus Research Question

3. Design Study

4. Collect Data

5. Analyze Data

6. Interpret Data

7 Inform Others

(page 12)

These steps are aligned with the generalist change model in Table I.3 so that we can see how we can integrate research into our practice.

Table I.3
Comparison of Generalist Practice and Research Processes

Steps of the Process	Generalist Practice	Research
Engagement and Assessment	The initial period where you orient yourself to the problem at hand and begin to establish communication and relationships with others who are also addressing the problem. The investigation and determination of variables affecting an identified problem or issue.	Choose Topic Focus Research Question
Planning	Specifies what should be done: work with client, prioritize problems, translate problems to needs, evaluate levels of intervention for each need, establish goals, specify objectives, specify action steps, formalize contract	Design Study
Implementation	the actual doing of the plan	Collect Data
Evaluation	proof that intervention has been effective	Analyze Data Interpret Data
Termination and Follow Up	a process of disengagement and stabilization Reexamination of client's situation at some point after the intervention	Inform Others

When we combine the two approaches described in Table 1.3 we can identify the following research process:

1. **Assessment and Engagement:**

    e. Developing an understanding of the research question or problem statement or problem focus; and

    f. Identifying and utilizing strategies for gaining entrée to the research setting;

2. **Planning:**

    a. Deciding on the design of the study;

    b. Deciding who will be in the study; and

    c. Deciding how study participants will be selected;

3. **Implementation:**

    a. Gathering quantitative and/or qualitative data;

4. **Evaluation:**

    a. Analyzing quantitative and/or qualitative data;

5. **Termination and Follow up**:

    a. Reporting on findings;

b. Developing and implementing a dissemination plan for transforming findings into evidence based practice;

c. Exiting the research setting; and

d. Identifying and implementing any plans for any further communication with the research site.

Having seen how we can integrate research into practice we now need to accommodate the need for diverse approaches. Such diversity is illustrated in our daily lives. Every day we get up, assess our situations, engage the people we meet, gather data about how things are going, analyze that data to decide what we need to do and then go ahead and do it. That's how we make it through the day, whether we're grocery shopping, driving the car, crossing the street, or simply appreciating the weather. The way we do this depends on our personal history and the world view we have developed over time. Some of us are guided by impressions and emotions, while others by facts and figures. There are as many ways of approaching our daily research as there are people on this planet. When we shift from a personal to a professional role, however, our approach to research needs to have intellectual traditions accepted by our professional communities. This is often the point at which social work students (not you of course) become alienated from the research process because they cannot see or feel a connection between their personal approach to problem solving and the professional approach to research that they learn about.

To address this alienation, let us consider some alternatives. Guba (1990) identified four paradigms[2], or world views, that offer alternate ways to carry out research and they all have rigorous intellectual traditions. These are positivism, post positivism, critical theory, and constructivism. **Positivism** is the approach to research that most of us think of when we think about research methods. A question and hypothesis is developed and then quantitative data, i.e. data in the form of numbers, is gathered and analyzed using statistics. **Post Positivism** rejects the idea of gathering quantitative data instead assumes that the only way to gather valid data about the human condition is to go into naturalistic settings where the focus of the study is being lived out and interview and observe people. Qualitative data is therefore collected and analyzed in the form of words rather than numbers. **Critical Theorists** reject the assumptions of both positivism and post positivism and take a world view that says we all view human situations influenced by an ideology such as racism, feminism, or neo-Marxism. We, therefore, need to identify that ideology and the power relations it suggests and take action to empower those who are oppressed by the impact of that ideology. Finally, **constructivists** disagree with all of the other approaches and assume that the only way we can understand any human condition is to study the

---

[2] Recently Lincoln, et al (2011) noted the emergence of a fifth, participatory, paradigm. This paradigm stresses a reality created jointly by study participants and researchers, a critical theory approach, and action that is developed collaboratively. However, in this book, the original four paradigms have been modified to incorporate the participatory approach into critical theory and constructivist research

subjective perspectives of the people living out that human condition. They acknowledge the influence of the researcher's perspective on the study and rely on the collection of qualitative data via interviews and observations.

With these four paradigms in mind we can think of some very interesting possibilities for carrying out practice-informed research. For example, imagine we are interested in studying social work interventions with homelessness in a particular region. As Table I.4 shows us, each paradigm will have its own over-arching question and its own research goal and therefore each will gather a different kind of knowledge about micro and macro social work practice with the homeless population.

Table I.4
Alternate Approaches to Research on Social Work Interventions with the Homeless

Paradigm	Question/Focus/Statement	Goal of Research
Positivism	**Micro Practice**: Which intervention is most effective with homeless families in this region, self help groups or parent training? **Macro Practice**: Which program works best with homeless families in this region, a shelter based set of services or an income assistance program with no services?	To test effectiveness of interventions with and programs for homeless families
Post Positivism	**Micro Practice**: How do we intervene with homeless families in this region? **Macro Practice**: How does this community respond to the homelessness problem in this region?	To build micro and macro practice theories of intervening with the homeless population
Critical Theory	**Micro Practice**: What action must be taken within homeless families experiencing spousal abuse to empower the mothers to seek help? **Macro Practice**: What action must be taken in this region to address poverty and thus empower the homeless community?	To collaboratively empower the homeless to understand their oppression and what action needs to be taken to address that oppression.
Constructivism	**Micro Practice**: How do the members of this homeless family and other key informants understand their situation and what needs to be done about it? **Macro Practice**: How do the key stakeholders in the issues of homelessness in this region understand homeless families and the interventions they need?	To engage family members and key homelessness stakeholders in building a joint understanding of homelessness and what action needs to be taken to address homelessness.

What we see here is a gradual building of knowledge about social work practice with homeless families from different perspectives using both quantitative and qualitative research methods. The positivist paradigm will give us knowledge about whether intervention programs works. The post positivist paradigm will give us knowledge about the process of intervening with homelessness at the micro and macro levels or practice. The critical theory paradigm will give us knowledge about how to

17

empower the homeless. The constructivist paradigm will give us knowledge about how everyone involved with homelessness understands that phenomenon and what we should do about it.

Combining these alternate paradigms with the generalist research process allows us to define practice-informed research as shown in Table I.2. We can see here that we can choose a paradigm for our research project and then implement the five stages of research accordingly. There is one more thing to understand about practice-informed research. Given the description above, you might think that we follow a linear process where we begin with step 1 and end with step 5 of the generalist approach. You might also think that you can choose one paradigm and then ignore the content of the book that refers to any of the other paradigms. This is not quite true. There is often overlap between the stages of the research process, and frequently we go back and visit stages again as we implement our research project. Also, the differences between the paradigms sometimes lie more in the way we carry out specific tasks than there being different tasks for each paradigm. For example, regardless of your paradigm you are most likely to gather data using interviews. However, your approach to those interviews will vary according to the paradigm that you choose. If you are carrying out a critical theory study, you may well read about how to carry out an interview in the post positivist chapter but in the critical theory chapter you will learn how to integrate interviews into a critical theory teaching-learning process. You will be alerted to the need to read from different sections throughout the book.

Research Ethics

Before we move on to learning about practice-informed research, we need to consider ethical issues associated with carrying out research. The NASW code of ethics states that:

"(d) Social workers engaged in evaluation or research should carefully consider possible consequences and should follow guidelines developed for the protection of evaluation and research participants. Appropriate institutional review boards should be consulted.

(e) Social workers engaged in evaluation or research should obtain voluntary and written informed consent from participants, when appropriate, without any implied or actual deprivation or penalty for refusal to participate; without undue inducement to participate; and with due regard for participants' wellbeing, privacy, and dignity. Informed consent should include information about the nature, extent, and duration of the participation requested and disclosure of the risks and benefits of participation in the research.

(f) When evaluation or research participants are incapable of giving informed consent, social workers should provide an appropriate explanation to the participants, obtain the participants' assent to the extent they are able, and obtain written consent from an appropriate proxy.

(g) Social workers should never design or conduct evaluation or research that does not use consent procedures, such as certain forms of naturalistic observation and archival research, unless rigorous and responsible review of the research has found it to be justified because of its prospective scientific, educational, or applied value and unless equally effective alternative procedures that do not involve waiver of consent are not feasible.

(h) Social workers should inform participants of their right to withdraw from evaluation and research at any time without penalty.

(i) Social workers should take appropriate steps to ensure that participants in evaluation and research have access to appropriate supportive services.

(j) Social workers engaged in evaluation or research should protect participants from unwarranted physical or mental distress, harm, danger, or deprivation.

(k) Social workers engaged in the evaluation of services should discuss collected information only for professional purposes and only with people professionally concerned with this information.

(l) Social workers engaged in evaluation or research should ensure the anonymity or confidentiality of participants and of the data obtained from them. Social workers should inform participants of any limits of confidentiality, the measures that will be taken to ensure confidentiality, and when any records containing research data will be destroyed.

(m) Social workers who report evaluation and research results should protect participants' confidentiality by omitting identifying information unless proper consent has been obtained authorizing disclosure.

(n) Social workers should report evaluation and research findings accurately. They should not fabricate or falsify results and should take steps to correct any errors later found in published data using standard publication methods.

(o) Social workers engaged in evaluation or research should be alert to and avoid conflicts of interest and dual relationships with participants, should inform participants when a real or potential conflict of interest arises, and should take steps to resolve the issue in a manner that makes participants' interests primary.

(p) Social workers should educate themselves, their students, and their colleagues about responsible research practices.

(5.02 Evaluation and Research)

The document at the core of our professional practice gives us a clear directive to pay attention to the ethics of our research projects. Not only do we have a professional code that requires ethical treatment of people involved in research but we also have international codes, federal legislation and national reports that require ethical research practice. The Helsinki agreement drawn up in 1975, to address human rights and fundamental freedoms, enjoins us to follow basic humanitarian practices. The Belmont report, drawn up in 1979, offers ethical principles to guide research decisions: respect for persons, beneficence, and justice. Such codes and guidelines instruct us to be informed about current thinking and, when carrying out research, to follow guidelines for ethical practice. Other federal mandates include:

- The code of federal regulation – The common rule (56FR28003, June 18, 1991)

- The health insurance portability and accountability act of 1996 (HIPPAA), Title 11)

- The family educational rights and privacy act (FERPA), revised 1997

These directives have become necessary because of a history of abuse associated with carrying out research on human beings. Reamer (2006) reminds us that social work and other human service professions' commitment to ethical research grew out of the horrors revealed at the Nuremburg trials in 1945 that exposed the inhumane experiments carried out by Nazi doctors and the Human Rights movements of the sixties that gave us the consciousness and vocabulary to understand and protect the rights of participants in research projects. Specific examples of abusive practices that proved the need for ethical oversight include the Tuskegee syphilis study (Jones, 1981) begun in the 1930s but only publicized in the 1970s, that allowed poor black men who were diagnosed with syphilis to remain untreated so that the natural progression of the disease could be studied. Also, there was the Willowbrook (Krugman et al, 1962) study that similarly studied the natural progression of another disease, infectious hepatitis, in a group of children suffering from mental retardation who were intentionally infected with that disease. So, throughout this book reminders about the ethics of how we plan to implement our research project will be offered.

To sum up, practice-informed research takes the generalist model and applies it to four alternate research paradigms. This gives us rigorous scientific approaches that accommodate the diversity of social work perspectives. Throughout the book you will see examples of real students' studies as well as questions and learning assignments that will help you apply what you are learning. The book is divided into five parts:

1. Assessment and Engagement

2. Planning

3. Implementation

4. Evaluation

5 Termination and Follow up

Within each part there are five chapters:

i. Positivism

ii. Post Positivism

iii. Critical Theory

iv. Constructivism

v. Important Cross Cutting Issues (e.g. diversity, ethics, politics, technology)

References

Guba, E. G. (1990). The Paradigm Dialog. Newbury: Sage.

Jones, J. H. (1981). *Bad Blood: The Tuskegee syphilis experiment.* New York: Free Press.

Kirst-Ashman, K. K. Hull, G.H. (2012) Understanding Generalist Practice. Florence, KY: Cenage.

Lincoln, Y.S., Lynahm, S.A. & Guba, E. G. (2011) *Paradigmaatci Controversies: Contradictions and Emerging Confluences Revisited.* In, Denzin, N.K., & Lincoln, Y.S. (Eds) The Sage Handbook of Qualitative Research (pp 97-128) Thousand Oaks, CA: Sage

Krugman S, Ward R, Giles JP.(1962) The natural history of infectious hepatitis. *Am J Med;* 32: 717-28.

Lincoln, Y.S., Lynahm, S.A. & Guba, E. G. (2011) *Paradigmaatci Controversies: Contradictions and Emerging Confluences Revisited.* In, Denzin, N.K., & Lincoln, Y.S. (Eds) The Sage Handbook of Qualitative Research (pp 97-128) Thousand Oaks, CA: Sage

Morris (2006), *Social Work Research Methods: Four Alternative Paradigms.* Thousand Oaks: Sage

Neuman, W.L. and Kreuger, L.W. (2003) *Social Work Research Methods: Qualitative and Quantitative Applications.* Boson: Allyn and Bacon.

Reamer, F.G. (2006) *Social Work Values and Ethics*. New York: Columbia University Press

Part 1

Assessment and Engagement

Problem Statement, Literature Review, Theoretical Orientation

---

Contents

> *Part 1 discusses Assessment and Engagement in relation to positivism, post positivism, critical theory and constructivism. Each paradigm is discussed in a separate chapter and important cross cutting themes are discussed in the final chapter:*
>
> > *Chapter I: Positivism*
> > *Chapter II: Post Positivism*
> > *Chapter III: Critical Theory*
> > *Chapter IV: Constructivism*
> > *Chapter V: Important Cross Cutting Issues*
>
> **However, there is some overlap between the paradigms. Where an overlap is noted, there are links to the shared information.**

Assessment is the development of an understanding of the research topic, while Engagement is initial contact with key players at the research site. Assessment and Engagement consists of three tasks:

1. the development of the research question, problem statement, or problem focus;

2. the development of the literature review; and,

3. the development of the theoretical orientation.

All these tasks must be completed regardless of the paradigm that we choose or the level of practice that we are studying. However, the way we carry out each of these tasks, will depend on our paradigm. Sometimes one of these tasks is the first thing we do, while at others that same task may well be the last. Sometimes we do each task separately in a linear fashion, while at other times each task affects the others and we circle back to change our research focus, literature review or theoretical statement. And sometimes we complete these tasks alone while at other times we engage gatekeepers at the research site and study participants in them. These differences are shown in table 1.1

Table 1.1
Assessment and Engagement tasks for each paradigm

	Development of research question, problem statement, or focus.	Development of the Literature Review	Development of the Theoretical Orientation
Positivism	A question is developed by the researcher with input from the study site but not engagement of the study site. The question does not change once the study has begun	Is carried out by the researcher.	Is carried out by the researcher
Post Positivism	A problem focus is developed by the researcher and is increasingly clarified through engagement with the study site. The problem focus can change during the study as a result of engagement with the study site	Is carried out by the researcher and is then further developed as a result of engagement with the study site.	Is carried out by the researcher but it can change during the study as a result of engagement with the study site
Critical Theory	A problem statement emerges completely through engagement with the study site. The problem statement can change during the study as a result of engagement with the study site.	Is carried out by the researcher and is then further developed as a result of engagement with the study site	Is carried out by the researcher as a result of engagement with the study site
Constructivism	A problem statement emerges from a partnership between the researcher and the research site and it will change during the study as a result of engagement with the study site.	Is carried out by the researcher and is then further developed as a result of engagement with the study site.	Is carried out by the researcher as a result of engagement with the study site

Each of the following chapters discusses: development of the problem question, focus or statement; development of the literature review; and development of the theoretical orientation. In addition ethical, politics and diversity, issues associated with each paradigm at the Assessment and Engagement stage are reviewed.

The positivist worldview assumes that an objective reality exist outside of personal experience that has demonstrable and immutable laws and mechanisms. Some authors refer to this worldview as the traditions of rationalism and empiricism (McCarl-Neilson, 1990). Positivist researchers suppose that one can identify the laws and mechanisms of human behavior and therefore reveal cause and effect relationships. Finding these causes and correlations is the goal of positivist research. This worldview assumes that, "it is both possible and essential for the inquirer to adopt a distant, non-interactive posture. Values and other biasing and confounding factors are thereby automatically excluded from influencing the outcomes. If we decide to adopt the positivist paradigm for our research project then we state research questions, and hypotheses about the answers to those questions, before we begin the study. We might ask social work practice questions about how things work such as "How did this intervention program affect clients' depression?" or "How did refugee adaptation improve after the introduction of focused resettlement programs?" Or we might ask social work practice questions about the connection between things such as, "What is the link between poverty and child abuse?" or "What is the link between an individual's self-esteem and coping mechanisms?"

Developing the Research Question

We develop the **research question** with minimal engagement of the research site. We may begin with a vague interest in a topic, for example poverty. Then, we might narrow the focus of the study to "interventions with poverty." We would then consider interventions at the micro (individuals, families, and groups) and macro (organizations and local, national, and international communities) levels of human organization. At the micro level these inventions might be employment and work training programs, benefit programs, and ancillary substance abuse and or mental health services if needed. At the macro level they could be organizational such as the Temporary Assistance for Needy Families (TANF) administrative divisions, and communities of recipients of TANF. We then decide whether to investigate current interventions with poverty or initiate and evaluate innovative programs. This decision leads us to the identification of the research question(s). At this point we need to decide whether we are asking a **causal** or a **correlational** question: is the research question addressing explanations of events or describing patterns of events? Questions associated with these two purposes are illustrated with examples in Table I.1.

Table I.1
Causal and Correlational micro and macro practice research questions

	Causal (Explanatory)	Correlational (Descriptive)
Micro Practice (target is individuals, families or groups)	What is the differential effectiveness on TANF clients of two approaches to employment training where one group receives training and the other receives no training and is simply placed immediately into a job?	How does the family assessment device (FAD[1]) assess families from three different ethnic groups?
Macro Practice (target is organizations or communities)	What is the impact uptake of county mental health services where one county has neighborhood mental health clinics and the other has a central mental health clinic?	How do the contrasting supervisory styles in two departments of children's services affect staff retention rates for social workers?

In Table I.1 the causal micro practice question targets individuals, the correlational micro practice question targets families, the causal macro practice causal question targets communities, and the correlational macro practice question targets organizations. The target of the question is not only the level of practice to be addressed but also the **unit of analysis**. The unit of analysis is the category of people about whom we will make assertions arising from the findings of our study.

Now that we have developed research questions, as positivist researchers our next step is to develop proposed answers to the questions, that is, hypotheses. **Hypotheses**, in positivist research, are based on current knowledge found in the scholarly literature. Thus for our example questions, the proposed answers might be:

1. The TANF recipients who receive *work training* are more likely to gain *permanent employment* than those who do not

2. The *FAD* is more likely to assess Anglo *families* as functional than Japanese-American and Hawaiian American[2] *families*.

3. The county with neighborhood *mental health clinics* will experience a higher *up-take of services* than the county with a central *mental health clinic*.

4. The organization where *supervision* offers encouragement and support is more likely to have a high *staff retention rate* than the organization where *supervision* offers assessment and direction only.

---

[1] The Family Assessment Device (FAD) was developed by Epstein and Bishop (1981). For a study of its sensitivity to diversity see Morris (1990)

[2] Hawaiian families are being referred to as Hawaiian-American here to distinguish this identity from the native Hawaiian identity.

By developing theses hypotheses we have become more specific about what we intend to study. We have redefined an idea or concept as an actual activity or entity that can be measured. This is called **operationalization**, which is when the concepts within our research question are changed into variables (in italics) with identified dimensions. The hypotheses facilitate a clear statement of the relationship between the variables that we intend to test. They narrow down the focus of the study and clarify exactly who and what the study is about. This is illustrated in Table I.2.

Table I.2
Operationalization of concepts and variables

Concept/Variable	Operationalization	Dimension
Approaches to work training (i.v.)	Provision of a training program or placement directly into employment with not training.	Range has two values, Training=1 No training=2
Permanent Employment (d.v.)	Presence or absence of paid employment that lasts for six months or more	Range with 2 values unemployment=1 employment=2
FAD (d.v.)	Specific Family Assessment Device created by Epstein and Bishop (1981)	Scores from 1 to 4 on each item of assessment device 1=strongly agree, 2=agree, 3=disagree, and 4=strongly disagree
Families (i.v.)	Families from three ethnic groups: Anglo, Japanese-American, Hawaiian-American	Range with 3 values Japanese American=1 Anglo=2 Hawaiian American=3
Mental Health Clinics (i.v.)	A county system of providing mental health services to the community either by providing one large central clinic or a number of smaller neighborhood clinics	Range with 2 values Centralized=1 Neighborhood=2
Uptake of Mental Health Services(d.v.)	Rates of usage of mental health services as a proportion of rates of mental health problems such as depression, suicide, and schizophrenia.	Percentage of eligible population in county using mental health services.
Supervision (i.v.)	A style of staff management that ranges from authoritarian and directive to supportive and facilitative	Range with values from 1 to 5 with 1 and 5 being the anchors at each end of the scale 1=authoritarian and directive 5=supportive and facilitative. Subjects are asked for scores between 1 and 10.
Staff Retention Rate (d.v.)	The rate at which social workers leave the organization per year	The percentage of staff that leave each year.

We are now ready to state our hypotheses in terms of relationships between variables:

1. For TANF recipients, the higher the score on approaches to work training, the lower the score on permanent employment.

2. For families, the higher the score on ethnicity of families, the higher the score on the FAD.

3. For counties, the higher the score on mental health clinics the higher the score on up take of mental health services

4. For the organization, the higher the score on supervision the lower the score on staff retention rate.

So now we have stated the direction of the relationship of the variables in the hypotheses that we anticipate. The first relationship is **negative**; that is, as one variable increases, the other decreases. The second relationship is **positive**; that is, both scores increase or decrease together. The third relationship is also positive and the fourth is negative. In addition we have identified two different types of variables, dependent and independent (identified with a d.v. or i.v in Table I.2). The **dependent variable** is the variable we think will change; it is usually the focus of our study. The **independent variable** is the variable we think will cause, or correlate, with the change. Put more precisely, the dependent variable shows the effect and the independent variable is the cause. In our examples, the dependent variables are permanent employment, scores on the FAD, up-take of mental health services, and staff retention rates. The independent variables are approaches to training, families, mental health clinics and supervision. We can see that such questions and hypotheses will require the collection of **quantitative data**, i.e. data gathered in the form of numbers that facilitate measurement of variables. The procedures for gathering and analyzing such data will be discussed later, however before we get to that we need to move on to developing the literature review.

Developing the Literature Review

As we are developing our research question we are also reviewing the literature. Our hypotheses about causal or correlational relationships rely on assumptions based on established knowledge in the academic literature about regularities and mechanisms in human interaction. The scholarly literature (scholarly journals, books, dissertations, reports and presented papers) is the primary source of literature for any research project. Neuman and Kreuger (2003) offer us useful advice on techniques for, carrying out a literature review. They suggest that the first step is to narrow the research topic. For example a topic such as "refugee resettlement" is too broad. However, "South East Asian refugees' experience of welfare" sharpens the focus of the search.

The next step is to make a plan for searching the literature given the time that we have and the types of materials we need to access. To carry out a thorough search of the academic literature on our research topic, we need access to a library and we have access to university libraries and electronic sources of scholarly journals that are very easy to use. The search page on these library web sites is about as simple as any other search engine. Here is one example http://www.lib.csusb.edu. In recent years, these sources have increased their subscriptions to social work journals and access to full-text versions of articles. Other services are abstracting services (Social Work Abstracts, Psychology Abstracts, Social Science Citation Index), which are also available online through the search page at any university library. From these sources citation information is available and an option to search online for a full text version of the cited article is usually offered at the click of a button. Dissertations are a good source for more recent research, and we can search them by accessing "Dissertation Abstracts International" at http://www.umi.com/en-US/catalogs/databases/detail/dai.shtml and if the university library does not have the government documents option, we can access them through sources such as the federal digital system at http://www.gpo.gov/fdsys. Using the internet we can also track down authors of presentations and conference papers we would like to review via posted email addresses. When carrying out these searches, we need to make sure we try several key words, since not all databases understand words in the same way. The university library web site will be a source for searching the library catalogue and other libraries' catalogues for books. It is also a good idea to look at the references or bibliography of our sources, to see whether there is something there we might want to look up.

Having found the sources of our literature, we must make a decision. How will we read and synthesize all this information? We check out all the books, print the full text articles and reports, and photocopy hard-copy sources. Now we have a big pile of books and paper that makes us feel like we have achieved something. We take it home and there it is– this overwhelming stack of information. We circle it, leave the room, come back and sit down, but where to begin? The best idea, as for any project, or life, is to take it one step at a time. We need to have a simple way of summarizing each article or book and have a system of recording and indexing based on the information we need to glean from each source.

Berg (2008) offers an approach to this task by developing citations that are organized by both topic and author. A citation should contain all or most of the following.

- Author, Year, Title, and journal source or publisher; all the citation information you will need for your reference list.

- The abstract of the article, or a summary of the overview of the book given in the book's preface (or perhaps the table of contents for the book), or the executive summary of the report.

- Specific Quotes from the body of the source that illustrate points you want to make about the topic, including page numbers.

- If it is a publication describing a research study, the research question, hypotheses, measurement of concepts, design (sample and data collection strategies), and major findings.

Berg calls his referencing system the "two card" system. This is a reference to using an old-fashioned paper system of index cards, but it works in word processing programs too. The first card refers to citations organized by topic. When we searched for out literature we used words and phrases that described aspects of our research interest likely to be used in information search engines and indexes. For example, in a review of literature on immigrants and refugees words and phrases that we might use include:

- Characteristics of a particular refugee or immigrant group such as South East we Asian Refugees in the United States or African immigrants in the United Kingdom

- Historical Context of their status

- The experience of transition to the Host County

- Typical welfare services available to them

- Resettlement experiences (divided into women, men, old and young, or other relevant sub groups)

- Mental Health Issues for Immigrants and Refugees

We can now use these concepts as headings for organizing our indexing system. This is a "topic index," We put the topic at the top of a page and then reproducing verbatim quotes on that topic with associated authors' names as illustrated in Figure I.1. where we have one page of a series of sources and quotes on mental health issues for immigrants and refugees.

The second parallel indexing system is the "author index," which lists the author(s) and all citation materials on one reference "card"—or one page of a word processing document. This is the system we can see in figure I.2. In this system we can search and sort entries alphabetically using the search and find function of the word processing program.

Figure I.1
Citations organized topic

Mental Health Issues for immigrants and Refugees

Developing Preventive Mental Health Interventions for Refugee Families in Resettlement

Stevan Merrill Weine M.D.

Family Process 50:410–430, 2011

Mental disorder prevention among resettled refugees must address the fact that refugee youth and parents are at risk for a range of possible negative mental health outcomes that go along with poverty, discrimination, and other forms of social adversity, including other mental disorders (e.g., depression), substance abuse disorders, negative behavioral outcomes, early pregnancy, and HIV/AIDS risk behaviors (Blake, Ledsky, Goodenow, & O'Donell, 2001; Fenta, Hyman, & Noh, 2004; Hankins, Friedman, Zafar, & Strathdee, 2002; Lustig et al., 2004). Page 410

Mental Health Service Utilization of Somali Adolescents: Religion, Community, and School as Gateways to Healing

B. Heidi Ellis, Alisa K. Lincoln, Meredith E. Charney, Rebecca Ford-Paz, Molly Benson, Lee Strunin,

Transcultural Psychiatry Vol 47(5): 789–811. November 2010

Given the prevalence of mental health problems among refugee youth, and the growing presence of refugee youth within the US, mental health service systems must rise to the challenge of providing culturally appropriate, accessible, and effective services. Research suggests, however, that refugee youths' access to mental health services lags far behind the need. It is well documented that children, particularly ethnic minority children, underutilize mental health services (Coard & Holden, 1998; Kataoka, Stein, & Jaycox, 2003; Takeuchi, Bui, & Kim, 1993). Page 790

The mental and physical health difficulties of children held within a British immigration detention center: A pilot study

Ann Lorek, Kimberly Ehntholt, Anne Nesbitt, Emmanuel Wey, Chipo Githinji, Eve Rossor, Rush Wickramasinghe,

Child Abuse & Neglect, Vol 33 Issue 9, September 2009 Pages 573-585

The study assessed the mental and physical health of children held within a British immigration detention center. 24 detained children (aged 3 months to 17 years) were assessed with their parents or career after being referred by a registered legal charity. Thirteen were seen by a pediatrician alone, 4 by a psychologist alone, and 7 by both professions using semi-structured clinical interviews. The psychologist also used standardized self-report questionnaires to measure psychopathology. Of the 8 children aged 1–4 years old seen by pediatrician and/or psychologist, all mothers raised concerns about their children's development or behavior, including frequent crying or withdrawn behavior (8), food refusal (3), refusal to feed self (1), back in nappies day and night (3), and a 4-year-old regressed to bedwetting (1), plus day time soiling by a 3-year-old (1). Page 573

Morris, T. (2005). Social Work Professional Education and Workforce Development: A Ladder of Learning. In Professional Development: The International Journal of Continuing Education. 8(Vols. 2 and 3) pp. 108-115.

This article suggests that university based social work programs can collaborate with work place based academies to create a new model of social work professional education providing lifelong learning from high school to the Doctoral level. A "ladder of learning" is proposed linking educational levels, competencies, work place requirements and organizational change. It is suggested that such a framework gives social work a conceptual tool to identify, discuss and promote educational and work place reform.

This paper suggests a "ladder of learning" for social work professionals that begins in High School and continues until the doctorate. This ladder includes levels of education and/or training, job skills that accompany those levels of learning, and various funding and technology needs that would support such a ladder of learning.

"In the workplace there is a trend towards introducing generalist practice by challenging organizational barriers between, for example, TANF, Child Welfare, Mental Health and Adult and Aging Services. Such practices suggest philosophies that make the client the focus of services and interdisciplinary teams the obvious intervention strategy"

Current commitments to service learning and community volunteerism in high schools make social work perfectly positioned to encourage certificate training that could lead to a paid position as an "apprentice" human service worker. Such certificate training could be carried out in the high schools in collaboration with training sites and county employers.

Having indexed our readings we can now prepare to write our literature review. For this we need to go to the citations organized by topic. This is because, when we write the literature review, we will be synthesizing our understanding of the literature, not writing an annotated bibliography. The biggest mistake students make when writing the literature review is to give a list of brief abstracts of each source without discussing common threads in the readings or how the sources relate to the research topic. The author index is for finding authors and articles; it should not guide the structure of the literature review. To give an idea of what this means, below is the beginning of a good literature review from a student study authored by Brown, L. (2011). It begins with a listing of topics that will be covered and then a discussion of what each author said about the first topic listed.

...This literature review will focus on key findings in the areas of child welfare practice and outcomes with African American families, the role of cultural competence and the development of culturally competent practices in child welfare, relevant cultural needs and strengths for African American families, the role of spirituality/religion in research regarding factors relevant to child welfare practice, and finally the theoretical assumptions and concepts underlying the constructivist approach and methodology used in this study.

Child Welfare and African American Families

The involvement of public child welfare in the lives of African American families is a fairly recent occurrence. Prior to the 1950's public child welfare did not include services to African American families and children (Smith & Devore, 2004). Services to children and families, including public assistance, child protection, foster care, and adoption services were offered to African American children through both formal and informal networks in the African American community which included church sponsored agencies and services, non-profit African American agencies and organizations, and formal and informal networks of family and kin (Smith & Devore, 2004).

Since their full inclusion in the public child welfare system in the 1950's, there has been a steady increase in the involvement of African American children in the child welfare system, and more disturbing, in the removal of African American children from their homes. In their book 'Children of the Storm', Billingsley and Giovanni (1972) describe this increased inclusion in the child welfare system as being the result of three contributing factors: "(1) large numbers of black families migrating to the North; (2) the civil rights movement and the national focus on integration; and (3) decreasing poverty among white children and the formal system increasingly caring for poor minority children". According to Smith and Devore (2004), by the 1970's African American children were becoming the most overrepresented group in child welfare.

Currently, African American children are among the most disproportionately overrepresented group in the child welfare system nationally. Annually, data regarding child maltreatment is collected from child welfare agencies in all 50 states, the District of Columbia (Washington, DC) and Puerto Rico as part of the National Child Abuse and Neglect Data System (NCANDS) and reported in an annual Child Maltreatment report. The Child Maltreatment 2009 report indicates that of all children with alleged and substantiated reports of maltreatment; ....(page 13)

Having developed our research question and completed our literature review, we have one more task to carry out at this stage of the study and that is to recognize our theoretical orientation.

Developing the Theoretical Orientation

Often, when students are asked which theory underlies their research project, a panicked blank look comes over their faces. This discussion aims to get rid of that look. To start with, we need to carefully distinguish between a paradigm and a theory. According to the Merriam Webster dictionary, a *paradigm* is "a philosophical and theoretical framework of a scientific school or discipline within which theories, laws, and generalizations, and the experiments performed in support of them, are formulated." Merriam Webster defines a *theory* as "the analysis of a set of facts in their relation to one another" or "a plausible or scientifically acceptable general principle or body of principles offered to explain phenomena." Payne (2005) defines theory as "an organized statement of ideas about the world" (p. 5). He notes that social work theory covers three possibilities:

- perspectives, which "express values or views of the world which allow participants to order their minds sufficiently to be able to manage themselves while participating" (p.5);

- explanatory theory which, "accounts for why an action results in or causes particular consequences and identifies the circumstances in which it does so" (p.5); and

- models, which "describe what happens during practice in a general way, in a wide range of situations and in a structured form, so that they extract certain principles and patterns of activity which give practice consistency" (p.50).

In this book we have been discussing Payne's *perspectives* in terms of our four paradigms. In this section on theory, we will be talking about what he refers to as *explanatory theory* and *models*.

Since we do not live in a vacuum and we have several years of life experience plus a few months of graduate education to work with, we will more than likely be approaching our research project with either an implicit or an explicit paradigm and theory in relation to the topic. We have already worked our way through our paradigms, but what about the theory within that paradigm? The answer will be guided by the level of social work practice we are studying, the people who will be in our study, and the problem our study addresses. So to decide on the theory we are using, we ask ourselves these questions:

1. What research question/focus/statement have I decided to study?

2. Which specific risk group is the focus of my study?

3. Which theories are generally used to analyze and understand the causes of risk for that group?

4. Is the level of social work practice I am studying individuals, families, groups, organizations, or communities?

5. Which theory is most relevant to that problem within that level of practice?

6. How do I understand and apply my theory or theories given the paradigm I have adopted?

Table I.3 is designed to guide us in a discussion and decision about the theory we are using based on the answers to these questions. It charts the most common risk groups, the generic theories that tend to be used to understand those risk groups, and the most common theories social workers use to guide interventions at each level of practice. The table is an aid to discussion and reflection, not a "cheat sheet" to pick a theory. It does not answer the question "What is my theory?" but rather suggests how we might discuss and reflect on that question.

Theories of intervention at the individual, family, group, organization level are mostly based on Turner's (2011) classification using two of his criteria: (1) that the theory is highly relevant to that level of intervention and (2) that the theory does not have a "minimal" rating on his assessment of the empirical basis for the theory. Instead it has a score of extensive (EX), strong (S), moderate (M) or emerging (EM). Theories of organization at the local, national and international level are based on Hasenfeld's (2010) discussion of complex human service organizations. Theories of communities at the local, national, and international level are based on Brueggemann's

(2006) discussion of macro social work practice. These classifications were also guided by Malcolm Payne's (2005) discussion of modern social work theory. As you can see, many of the theories can be used with several risk groups and at several levels of practice, so when selecting our theory we need to clearly make the case for how it underlies our approach to our research question/focus/statement.

Table I.3
Selecting our Theory

Common Target Risk Groups	Minority Ethnic/Racial Group Aging and Elderly Group Women/Girls GLBT Group Disabled Group Religious Group Geographical Groups (inner city, rural) Poverty/Working-class
Common Theories addressing the identity of these groups and the causes of risk for these groups	Theories of Class identity, neo Marxism Theories Ethnic/racial Identity; Theories of Aging biological and social Feminist Theory. Theories of sexual orientation, Theories of disability and accessibility Theories of spiritual identity Theories of geographical influences such as inner city and rural isolation
Generic Social Work Models of Practice for these groups	Empowerment Advocacy Anti Discrimination sensitivity
Practice Theories for Individual Level of Intervention	Behavior Theory (Ex) Client Centered Theory (S) Cognitive Theory (Ex) Communication Theory (M) Crisis Theory (Em) Ego Psychology (S) Existential Theory (Em) Hypnosis (Em) Life Model Theory (Em), Materialist Theory (S) Meditation Theory (M), Narrative Theory (Em), Neurolinguistic Theory (M), Problem Solving Theory (Em), Psychoanalytic Theory (Ex), Psychosocial Theory (Ex), Role Theory (M), Task Centered Theory (Ex), Trans Actional Analysis Theory (M),

Practice Theories for the family Level of Intervention	Behavior Theory (Ex) Cognitive Theory (Ex) Communication Theory (M) Life Model Theory (Em), Materialist Theory Narrative Theory (Em) Neurolinguistic Theory (M), Psychosocial Theory (Em), Role Theory (M) Systems Theory ((M), Task Centered Theory (Ex),
Practice Theories for the group Level of Intervention	Client Centered Theory (S) Cognitive Theory (Ex) Crisis Theory (Em) Life Model Theory (Em), Materialist Theory (S) Neurolinguistic Theory (M), Problem Solving Theory (Em), Psychosocial Theory (Ex), Role Theory (M) Systems Theory (Em), Task Centered Theory (Ex),
Practice Theories for the organizational Level of Intervention (both national and international)	The Rational Legal Model, The Human Relations School, Contingency Theory, Negotiated Order, Political Economy, Institutional Theory, Institutional-Logic Theory, Population-Ecology Theory, Niche Theory
Practice Theories for the Community Level of Intervention (both national and international)	Community Development Program Developer Community Organization Life Model Theory (Em), Materialist Theory (S) Neurolinguistic Theory (M), Psychosocial Theory (Ex), Social Policy Advocacy Social Movement Activist Social Work Planning Systems Theory (Em),

This ends our discussion of the Assessment and Engagement tasks and how they are carried out when we adopt the positivist paradigm. The major points of the chapter are summarized below with some associated learning assignments. Important cross cutting issues of ethics, politics, diversity, and technology, in relation to Positivism can be found in Chapter 5. Our next chapter considers Assessment and Engagement for the post positivist paradigm.

- Assessment and Engagement includes development of the problem question/focus/statement, development of the literature review, development of the theoretical orientation and understanding of the ethics, politics, and diversity issues associated with the research project

- For positivists, engagement of study participants at the beginning of the study tends to be limited to formal contracting and creating a relaxed atmosphere for data collection since further engagement between researcher and researched will threaten the objectivity required by the assumptions of positivism

- Positivist research is causal or correlational

- The assessment phase starts with a literature review, which is done at the beginning of the study and guides the study.

- Question and hypotheses are developed that include concepts/variables, operationalizaiton, dimensions, and the direction of relationships between variables before data gathering begins

- The literature review can be carried out electronically through university libraries and a "two card" referencing system organizes articles and books found in the literature search

- Developing a theoretical orientation involves consideration of 7 key questions.

- An ethical assessment of a project reviews moral, competency, and terminal values

- Sensitivity to politics and diversity needs to be a conscious mind set as we consider engaging study participants and review the literature.

Positivist Learning Assignments

1. Think of a research topic that you are interested in. In a class discussion, explore how as a positivist social work researcher you might resolve the dilemma of needing to adopt a distant stance to gather quantitative data and at the same time engage study participants at the start of the research project.
2. Think of a social work practice topic that you are interested in. Using tables I.1 and I.2 as examples;

    i. write down causal and correlational questions about that topic at the micro and macro levels of practice.

    ii. Give hypotheses for each question.

iii. Identify the concepts and variables.

iv. Identify the independent and dependent variables.

v. State how your questions address social work practice.

Get into pairs and then explain your questions and hypotheses to your partner.

Post positivism takes the positivist paradigm as its' starting point and, on the whole, accepts that worldview. It concurs that, indeed, an objective reality exists but suggests that the "immutable laws and mechanisms" driving that reality can never be fully comprehended. Quantitative measurement and hypothesis testing only offers a part of the picture; the rest must be discovered through open exploration. Post positivism's associated epistemology suggests that one can never step completely outside human experience to study it. However, since objectivity is the ideal, a good researcher must strive for objectivity by being aware of his or her biases, paying attention to the intellectual traditions of the field, and attending to the observations and judgments of key players through peer feedback. The post positivist takes an inductive exploratory approach to understanding an objective reality.

When we take the post positivist approach to our research project, as we saw in table 1.1, we begin with a problem focus and a more complete understanding of that problem focus evolves during the study. We are committed to gathering **qualitative data** (data in the form of words rather than numbers) in a **naturalistic setting** (the setting where people live out the focus of the research project), since we assume that this is the only way to capture the complexity of human experience. We start with an interest in a particular area and then gather information about it from literature, key players, observations, and personal experience so that we can narrow the focus. The generic question in all such research is "What is happening here?", and so our specific question is oriented toward process. For example, a study of gang life might start with questions such as "How does someone become aware of a gang?", "How does someone choose a gang, or does it choose them?", "What are the 'joining' rituals?", "When do social workers interface with gangs and how?" Considering such questions leads us to integrate the assessment and engagement process so that we develop sensitivity to the meaning of the data we are gathering and the capacity to distinguish the important data by comparing conclusions about our data with the literature and the conclusions of key informants. As post positivist researchers, we preserve a balance between the science of making sure we are following the rules of the research methodology and the art of being independently creative by periodically stepping back from the data to ask ourselves and other key informants "What is really going on here and am I seeing it all?"

We have three student studies to illustrate the post positivist approach to research that will be used throughout this book. One study (McNevin, 2011) explored the experiences of same sex parents, the second (Torres, 2007) explored the experiences of parolees, and the third (Young and Creacy, 1995) explored the perceptions of homeless children. These are:

McNevin, M (2011) *How Do Heteronormative Perspectives Affect Same-Sex Parents?* San Bernardino CA: School of Social Work, CSUSB

Torres, K (2007) *An Insight Into The Experience Of Parolees*. California State University, San Bernardino, CA: School of Social Work, CSUSB

Young, M.L. and Creacy, M. (1995) *Perceptions of Homeless Children*. San Bernardino CA; School of Social Work, CSUSB.

Developing the problem focus

At the beginning of a post positivist study, the first thing we will do is set up our research journals. Since post positivist research focuses on the process of gathering data as well as keeping a record of the data being collected we need to record, not only the data being gathered but also, our experiences and reflections during the research project.

Research journals are most often kept when we are gathering qualitative data. They contain a record of interactions with key gatekeepers at the research site, the data being gathered and any thoughts and reflections we might have on that data. They also include rationales for decisions we make about how to interpret the qualitative data. There are usually two research journals. The first is the *narrative account* of what is happening during the study from beginning to end. It includes descriptions of encounters and discussions during the Assessment, Engagement, and Planning stages of the study. It also includes data collected during the Implementation phase of the study in interviews and/or through observation, and any notes describing social artifacts and documents. It lists the source, time, and date of data collection and ideas about the interpretation of that data. In figure II.1 we have one page of an example journal from a student discussion evaluating a class on research methods using the content of this book. It is a transcript of part of the discussion. The second journal is more of a *reflective journal* and it records rationales for the research plan as well as sampling, data collection, and analysis decisions made as the study proceeds. It includes not only a clear articulation of the chosen approach to data collection but also an account of rationales for the problem focus that emerges from the study. In figure II.3 there is an example of a page from a reflective journal associated with the data in the narrative journal in figure II.2.

Figure II.1
Page from a Narrative Account Journal

Student 1:	Okay. This is (Student 1), and what I think that we've done, at least for me, in this course is to open up, at least my mind, to different ways of doing research, ways that we've never been exposed to before, and maybe that's why, initially, we were a little apprehensive about it, about being guinea pigs. But I think now that we've got an understanding—or now that I have an understanding of each of the different ones, I'm kinda happy that I have an option other than what was out there before.
Student 2:	My name is (Student 2). Traditionally, what I—when you think of research, think of qualitative and quantitative, and I really wasn't exposed to different paradigms. So, I know now that qualitative and quantitative are just characteristics of a—of these different paradigms. It's not exactly a paradigm. So, I learned the history of each of the different paradigms and got a—more understanding of research and how it came about.
Student 3:	This is (Student 3). I think going along this is the first time that I've ever seen research that's really practice oriented. Most research is—it seems really separate from actually practicing social work, and just in talking with my supervisor about the research idea that we wanna do, she was like, "Oh. So, that's like having a consultant." It's—it was something that was very much in line with what goes on in an agency day to day, which I think is different than traditional research. So, in that respect, I think that this course has done a good job of addressing the different options out there and in making research more applicable to what goes on in an agency setting.
Student 4:	This is (Student 4). What I got out of this course, in terms of the generalist model, is how to apply that within a research setting with each paradigm, which I found kind of interesting. The generalist model deals with the social issues _____ people and how to use that, so I kinda liked that. When I was writing my paper, it kind of _____ to be real for me, I guess, 'cause I didn't have a topic until the end. And it's not a permanent one, probably, 'cause—because of the _____, and I have to do something else. But even though this credit to get—or for my paper it kind of made more real, in terms of not just see in' it when you've got to explain it, but nice to put it in practice. So, it was—I liked that. I understood a little better.

Figure II.2
Page from a Reflective Journal

4-1 This is the first time I have taught a class using my book. I am concerned that the students will not understand it, or that I have not explained things well enough

4-12. after teaching for two weeks I can see that there is too much lecturing and not enough application. I need to develop some "hands on" assignments in class that apply the content

4-25 the exercises seemed to work but were very time consuming. I am worried that we will not get through all the content

5-5 We are getting ready for the midterm and the students are nervous. They want a study guide but I am trying to get them to read the book. I have referred them to the power point presentations and the book. They are now a little upset. I think I need to just walk through what we have done, even though they already have all the materials

5-20 well the midterm was a crisis moment for the students. They thought that it was too long. However, most did very well. I need to find a way to reassure them and reduce anxiety. This might not be possible since the class is on research methods.

6-1. we are now working on proposals. The students are really getting into the different approaches now that they are applying them to a topic that they are interested in and to a study that they will be carrying out next year.

6-5. I spoke too soon. The students are almost hysterical about their proposals. I am really stumped about how to reduce the anxiety. I have had one-on-one meetings with just about everybody and they seem OK when they leave my office but when we get together in class, the anxiety builds again.

6-10 minor break through, humor came to the rescue. One student started joking about her anxiety and the others chimed in, and the floodgates opened. We spent a lot of time processing what they were feeling and we seemed to move from anxiety to acceptance of the task at hand and their ability to do it.

6-14 had evaluation in class discussion today. Things were much more positive than I thought they would be. Of course, I know that the students are worried about their grades and so might be being careful, but they seemed to genuinely feel they had learned something important, now that it was almost over.

6-16 all proposals handed in: going to lock myself away to tackle grading and rethink class presentations.

So when we begin the post positivist study we start both journals. We describe what we are doing in the narrative journal and in the reflective journal we make entries about the issue we are interested in and possible approaches to that issue. This is how we begin the development of the problem focus. We state an area of interest, identify a study site, talk to a gatekeeper, make an observation, reflect on that information, and refine and focus the area of interest. We repeat this process at the beginning of the study and throughout the study so that we identify the components of the area of interest, describe them, and develop explanations for them.

Crabtree and Miller (1999) explain the development of the post positivist problem focus by categorizing qualitative research's aims, questions, and analysis objectives into identification, description, and explanation. Each of these categories, according to the authors, suggests associated questions. In Table II.4 these categories and ideas are applied to the Young and Creacy (1995) study of homeless children living in a temporary shelter and receiving services from MSW students over a period of nine months. The children were individually interviewed and invited to write or draw about their perceptions of their lives in group-sessions focused on building self-esteem. Eventually 30 homeless children were included in the study; however, because of the nature of the shelter, very few were part of the study for the whole nine months.

Table II.1 shows the aims, problem focus, and analysis objectives that emerged during the study. It starts by identifying the characteristics of the children and then moves on to descriptions of how they perceive their lives, their low self-esteem, and their ambivalence about being in a shelter with rules as opposed to being homeless without rules. Explanations emerge for socialwork interventions, including promoting self-actualization in the face of negative experiences. The guiding framework for developing this knowledge consisted of the identified aims, questions, and analysis objectives. The aim was to identify, describe and explain. Questions were developed to meet these aims, and the emergent analysis did indeed identify and name, give qualitative and normative descriptions, and give an interpretive explanation of appropriate social work practice with these children. Tutty et al (1996) convert the questions in Table II.1 into a process for developing our research aims, problem focus, and analysis objectives described in figure II.2.

Table II. 1
Study of Homeless Children

Aim	Problem Focus	Analysis Objective
Identification e.g. Who are the homeless children and what is their experience?	*What?* e.g. what are the dimensions of homeless ness for single parent, female headed families? *Who?* e.g. What are the characteristics of the children of such families? *What is the main focus?* e.g. What helps children survive homelessness and make a success of their lives?	*Identify and Name* e.g. 50% of homeless women are between the ages of 17 and 25 They have sporadic employment records. They have experienced family violence. The children are depressed, have behavioral problems, have no sense of privacy
Description e.g. what are homeless children's perceptions about their past and present life styles	What is going on here? What do we see? e.g. How are children experiencing homeless ness? What are the dimensions and variaitons of the concept? e.g. Which parts of the children's lives does homelessness affect (personal, social; school and leisure) and how? What meanings/practices occur in lived experiences? e.g. How do homeless children gain food and shelter, make friends or make progress at school? What is the value of the phenomenon? e.g. How can social workers	Qualitative and Normative Description e.g. Homeless children tend to have fragmented support networks. They see life, people, places and schools as temporary and out of their control. They have low self-esteem. If they live in a shelter, they consider themselves not homeless. The children experience ambivalence about the freedom of living on the streets versus the rules of

	learn more about such children so that they can promote success?	living in a shelter.
		    The children are preoccupied with getting money.
		    The children wish they had a stronger family and more friends
		    The children took a long time to trust the researchers and some of the older ones never did.

Explanation Generation
    e.g. What can we do to change children's perceptions about their future and promote a positive vision for their future?
	What is happening here? What patterns exist?
	    e.g. Are older children more pessimistic about their situation than younger children?
	    How do phenomena differ and relate to each other? How does it work?
	    How does moving from living in a car or on the streets to living in a temporary shelter impact children's ability to understand and cope with their situation?
	    How did something occur/happen?
	    How did the children get here? What do they need? How can they move forward with their lives?
		Interpretative Explanation Generation.
		    The children need to achieve self-actualization in the face of low self esteem and ambivalence about the shelter and their life experiences so far.

Figure II.3
Developing an Understanding of the Post Positivist Problem Focus

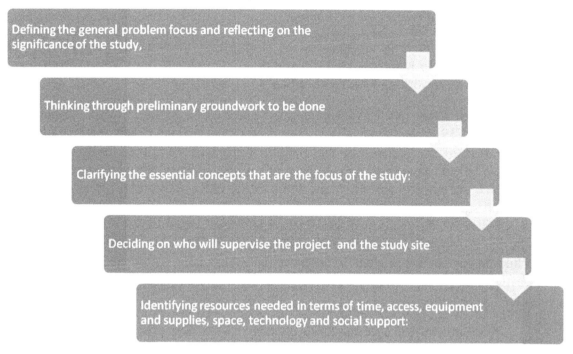

Defining the general problem focus and reflecting on the significance of the study,

Thinking through preliminary groundwork to be done

Clarifying the essential concepts that are the focus of the study:

Deciding on who will supervise the project and the study site

Identifying resources needed in terms of time, access, equipment and supplies, space, technology and social support:

When we *define the general problem focus* we reflect on our personal interest in the problem and the people who are affected by the problem. For example, Young and Creacy, (1995) carried out a study of homeless children because they were in a field placement setting in a homeless shelter and noticed an increase in families living at the shelter. They narrowed down the group to be studied by asking themselves, who are we studying?

Is it children?
Is it homeless children?
Is it homeless children in a particular shelter?
Is it the children of single parents?

They decided that it was the children of single parents living in one particular shelter and this led to another set of questions:

What do we know about homeless children at this shelter?
What does the literature say about the reasons for their homelessness and their experiences of homelessness?
What do we want to focus on in particular?

They decided that the focus of the study was the children's experiences of the homeless shelter and their wishes and dreams for the future. At this point they began to reflect on the significance of the study and asked themselves the "So what?" questions.

Why is this study important?
What contribution will it make to knowledge about social work practice?

What will social work practice gain from our study?

Why would we want to know about homeless children's perceptions of their physical, emotional and social well-being?

They answered these questions by noting that the study would give social workers insight into homeless children's realities that would improve sensitivity and competence when working with these children.

Thinking through the *preliminary groundwork* to be done in the Young and Creacy study (1995) included gaining permission from parents to talk the children and consideration of the feelings of the children regarding the intrusiveness of intense collaboration with the researchers on personal issue. Children were informed that they could leave the study at any time, and some of the older ones chose not to participate fully. The students knew that funding for homeless shelters is unstable, and so they were sensitive to the politics of the situation and were careful not to do anything that would put the shelter in a "bad light" and risk that funding. This was a diverse group of children and so the student researchers knew that they would need to constantly reviewed their sensitivity to the children and their mothers with both the shelter staff and their field instructors

Thinking through *the essential concepts* for a post positivist study includes asking questions such as:

What is our definition or articulation of the problem?
What is our conceptual map of the problem?
Can we articulate this to study sponsors, research sites and research supervisors?

Young and Creacy (1994) identified a series of circumstance that lead to single mothers' homelessness and characteristics of children's understanding of and response to their plight, and they used Maslow's hierarchy to identify homeless children's needs. They identified the essential concepts as children's perceptions of being homeless and how these perceptions affect their understanding of self and world.

When finding a *supervisor for the study*, it's a good idea to write a synopsis of the project to help the supervisor understand the chosen approach. It is also a good idea to think through what we need in a supervisor in terms of knowledge, knowledge, areas of our weakness that we need help with, level of independence we need, and just an overall comfort level with the supervisor. If possible we can negotiate an understanding with the supervisor regarding which parts of the study he or she will help with and how this help will be given. A similar process helps with *deciding on the study site*. A study synopsis of the study with clear descriptions of the extent of involvement will help key people at potential study sites make decisions about giving permission for the study. In the Young and Creacy (1994) study the site was a field placement but without such a contact clear descriptions of the project will facilitate entrée to the proposed research setting. Finally, we need to be realistic about the scale of the study given the *time and resources* we have. In this study the, the shelter provided the supplies needed for the groups and other students who were also completing research projects offered social support.

Our other example studies followed a similar process. The study of same sex parents (McNevin, 2011) examined how the assumptions behind heteronormativity and heterosexism affect same sex parents' relationship with their children and with representatives of institutions that are important in their children's lives such as teachers and physicians. These terms were defined and clarified and then transformed into questions that would make sense to study participants. The participants in the study were parents and the focus was both the parents' and children's experiences when disclosing that they were a family with same sex parents. The study site was not one agency but the community of churches who were willing to advertise her study. Engagement of the churches involved a number of letters to religious leaders and a number of meetings with church officials throughout the study. The study of parolees (Torres, 2007) addressed the prejudices experienced by convicted felons who had served their prison sentence and were now attempting to reintegrate into society. The particular characteristics of these parolees experiences were explored including, how they were raised, their family relationships, their experiences with gangs, their personal problems, experiences of services, coping strategies and life changes. The study site was the various group homes that the parolees lived in under the auspices of the California Department of Corrections and Rehabilitation. Engagement of the study site involved the engagement of one gatekeeper, who ran a counseling program for the parolees and was able to facilitate entrée to the various group homes.

So, with these examples, we have begun to develop an understanding of the development of the post positivist problem focus. We can see that this is not a clearly defined stage with a beginning and end stage but is an initial assessment of and engagement with an issue we are interested. There are several aspects to this process and we may well come back and revisit our problem focus as the study progresses. For now, however, we will move on to the development of the literature review.

Development of the Literature Review

To carry out the literature review for a post positivist project we will need to follow the procedures described in Chapter I. In addition, however, we need to consider the role of the literature review in post positivist research. At this initial stage the literature review informs our evolving "theoretical sensitivity." Strauss and Corbin (2008) use this term to describe the researcher's awareness and understanding of the meaning of the data. Since our interpretation of the data will be a mixture of the science of synthesis of information and the art of intuition, we need to consciously develop a mature understanding of the topic. Strategies for achieving this understanding include:

- Reviewing the literature

- Consulting with experts.

- Consulting with gatekeepers to study site

When reviewing the literature, we are looking for information that helps us build a theory. We are not using the literature to decide on our question and hypothesis; we are using the literature to help us answer questions we have asked about the emerging problem focus. We then consult with experts and gatekeepers to the research site and ask them about the answers to these questions. Given this process Strauss and Corbin (2008) suggest that the researcher need not read all the literature before the project starts but use reading as a stimulus for thinking about the topic throughout the project. This reading will influence data collection and interpretation of data. The literature can offer concepts we can compare to concepts emerging in data collection. It can help with formulating questions before and during the study. Thus the literature and data from experts and gatekeepers and later study participants at the study site have a parallel influence on the ongoing emergence of the problem focus.

Developing the Theoretical Orientation

The major goal of post positivist research is to develop an inductive understanding of the problem focus, so we do not begin the study with a theoretical orientation that guides our approach. However, part of the evolving development of the problem focus is to be aware of theories relevant to our area of interest that may later need to be included in our understanding of the problem focus. We should, therefore, follow the procedures identified in Chapter 1 to understand these theories but not to use them as the guiding framework for our study. In post positivist research, the naturalistic setting of the research site is always in equal partnership with previous theoretical knowledge when decisions are made about the perspective we are bringing to the study.

To sum up this chapter, post positivists need to consider the same tasks as positivists, however, the perspective and approach that they bring to the tasks is slightly different because of the paradigm, or worldview, that they have decided to adopt. As post positivists, because of our commitment to gathering qualitative data in naturalistic settings we must always be aware of the changes in the setting and our impact on the setting. This chapter ends with a summary of the key points of chapter II followed by learning assignments. Important cross cutting issues of ethics, politics, diversity and technology in relation to constructivism can be found in Chapter 5. We now can proceed to a discussion of Assessment and Engagement for Critical Theorists in chapter III

Summary of Chapter II

- Many of the issues raised in Chapter I 'Positivism' are relevant for post positivists

- Research Journals should be kept to keep a record of data gathering and reflections on data gathering

- Understanding the focus of the inquiry is an ongoing process throughout the study

- At the beginning of the study, clarity of thinking can be gained by outlining the research aim, the research questions and the analysis objectives

- Literature will be gathered throughout the study in response to data gathering

- The post positivist is open to adjustments in procedures as the study is implemented

- Engagements of the research site is a crucial research skill both at the beginning and throughout the study

- Ethical issues for post positivist research arise from prolonged engagement with study participants

Post Positivist Learning Assignments

1. Start keeping two journals on your research education. In one journal summaries what you are learning about research each week (your notes). In the second journal, write down your reactions to what you are learning. What are you enjoying? Which parts are difficult? How are your reactions changing as time goes by and you learn more?

2. In group discussion, share the insights from your journals and find out about other students insights.

3. Think of a research focus for an area of social work practice that interests you.

   a. What would be a potential site for that study and how would you gain entry to that site?

   b. Discuss these ideas with your partner and present them in a group discussion.

   c. Role-play the conversations you might have with key players at the research site. Note the approaches that make people feel comfortable with being engaged in a research project.

It is with this paradigm that we make a fundamental shift in our portrayal of the role of the researcher. As illustrated in figure III.1, the critical theory researcher agrees with the positivist that there is an objective reality, agrees with the post positivist that values mediate a researcher's understanding of that reality, but disagrees with both paradigms' view that the researcher is someone standing outside the research experience doing research *to* people rather than doing research *with* people. The critical theory paradigm assumes that we can never be free of our own values when observing the objective reality around us.

Figure III.1
Where critical theory differs from positivism and post positivism

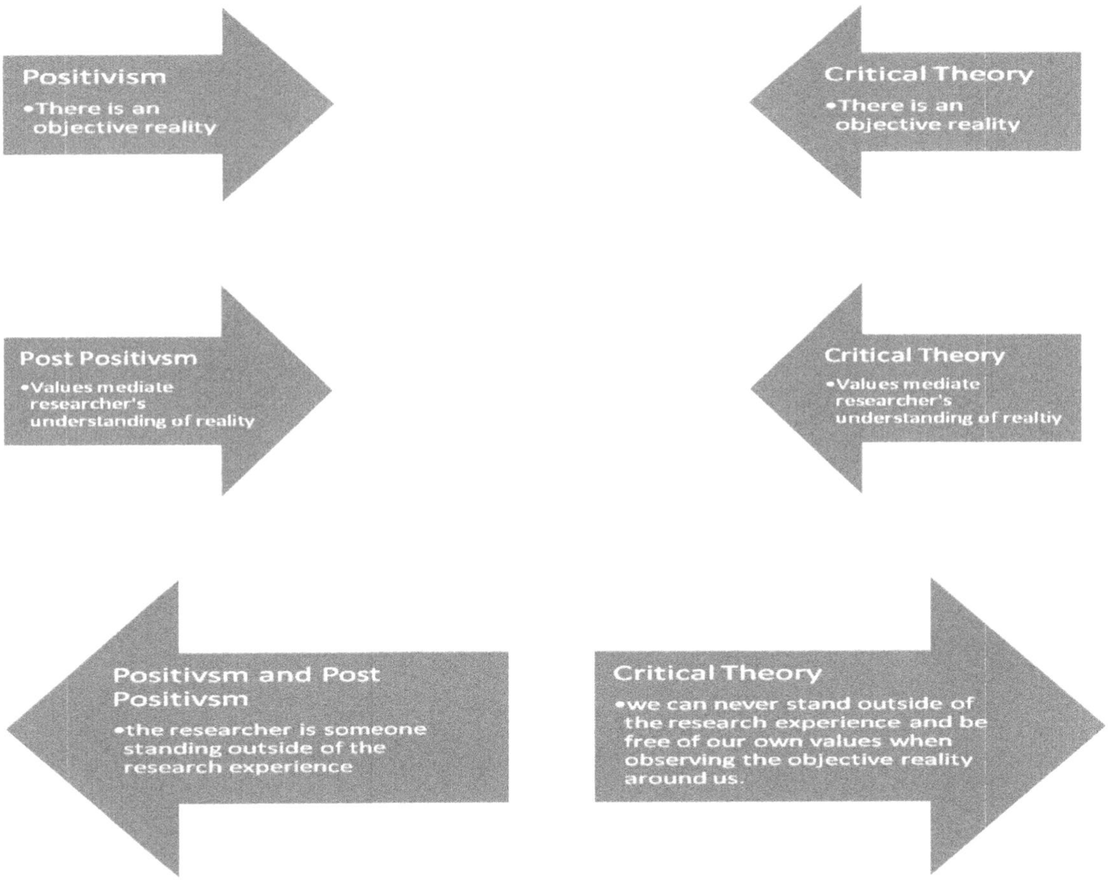

Unlike post positivism, critical theory demands that researchers embrace and promote their values when entering the research arena, rather than keeping them under control. The goal of the critical theory research project is to change the participants and their context through eliminating false consciousness and facilitating transformation. Kincheloe et al.(2011) define this approach as follows:

"We are defining a criticalist as a researcher or theorist who attempts to use her or his work as a form of social or cultural criticism and who accepts certain basic assumptions:

- *That all thought is fundamentally mediated by power relations that are social and historically constituted*

- *That facts can never be isolated from the domain of values or removed from some form of ideological inscription*

- *That the relationship between concept and object and between signifier and signified is never stable or fixed and is often mediated by the social relations of capitalist production and consumption*

- *That language is central to the formation of subjectivity (conscious and unconscious awareness)*

- *That certain groups in any society are privileged over others, and although the reasons for this privileging may vary widely, the oppression that characterizes contemporary societies is most forcefully reproduced when subordinates accept that social status as natural, necessary, or inevitable*

- *That oppression has many faces and that focusing on only one at the expense of others (e.g. class oppression vs. racism) often elides the interconnections among them*

- *That mainstream research practices are generally, although most often unwittingly, implicated in the reproduction of systems of class, race, and gender oppression (page 164)*

For a social worker committed to social action, this is an exciting alternative. It positions the researcher as both skeptical realist about people and their motivations, and convinced advocate for the downtrodden. This profile resonates with many people who have been attracted to social work. It can lead to research that is often controversial, may well threaten those who have power, and will certainly empower those who do not.

Brown and Stega (2005) assert that all modern research is "resistance" and they note that for too long, the illusion of neutrality has been fostered by using a positivist world view to frame the discussion of what constitutes true knowledge. They suggest that critical, indigenous, and anti-oppressive approaches to research that foster social justice need no longer be marginalized but can also be at the center of the debate. Two of the contributors to this book (Potts and Brown, 2005) offer three principles of anti-oppressive research,

1. Anti-oppressive research is social justice and resistance in process and in outcome. Carrying out this research is a commitment to personal reflection on one's own power relationships during the project and on one's personal commitment to taking action for change, during the project.

2. Anti-oppressive research recognizes that all knowledge is socially constructed and political. Thus this research is not a process of discovering knowledge but a partnership between researchers and researched to jointly create and re-discover knowledge

3. The anti-oppressive research process is all about power and relationships. There is an assumption that the researcher and the researched may well be starting a lifelong relationship where power and knowledge is shared.

So, we begin a critical theory study by identifying and describing our ideology. This ideology names the categories or classes of people who are oppressed by the power relationships identified in that ideology and who are therefore the focus of our research project. The core research question is,

"How is the oppression identified in the chosen ideology demonstrated in this class of people, and how can they and we be empowered to understand and address that oppression?"

If the ideology is Neo-Marxism, then the focus of the research is a subgroup of the poor. If the ideology is Feminism, then the focus is a subgroup of women. If it is racial inequity then the focus is members of particular racial or ethnic groups who are oppressed. Kincheloe et al (2011) note that "Critical research can be understood best in the context of the empowerment of individuals. Inquiry that aspires to the name "critical" must be connected to an attempt to confront the injustice of a particular society or public sphere within the society. Research becomes a transformative endeavor unembarrassed by the label "political" and unafraid to consummate a relationship with emancipatory consciousness. (page 164)." For example, social welfare is an institution that reflects many contradictory political functions. From a critical theory perspective it aims to help the poor, keep the poor content, develop a reserve army of labor, keep the poor poor, and support the continuation of capitalism. If we were to take a critical theory approach to studying social welfare, we would systematically inquire into the political functions and contradictions noted above by reviewing a history of those functions and contradictions, engaging in a teaching/learning exchange about this history with a group of poor people, and partnering with this group in developing empowering action strategies to address these contradictions. We have three student studies that will illustrate this approach throughout this book. The first is a study of eating disorders among high school students. The second is a study of folk healing in the Latino community, and the third is a study of transportation needs in an isolated, low income community. They are:

Christopulos, J. (1995) *Oppression through Obsession: A Feminist Theoretical Critique of Eating Disorders.* San Bernardino, CA: School of Social Work, CSUSB

Riech, J. R. (1994). *Psychotherapy Encounters Curanderismo: Implications for Clients Treated in the United States by Culturally Insensitive Social Workers.* San Bernardino: School of Social Work, CSUSB

Millet, K. R., and Otero, L. R. (2011) *The North Shore Public Transportation Dilemma: How Local Sociopolitical Ideologies, Ethnic Discrimination And Class Oppression Create Marginalization, And A Community's Quest For Social Justice.* San Bernardino, CA; School of Social Work, CSUSB.

Developing the Problem Statement

The first thing we do is start our **research journals** as described in Chapter II. In our reflective journal we describe the process by which we develop our ideological position and we record rationales for ideological statements, action strategies, and evaluation decisions. Indeed this journal will include reflections on each stage of the project, since there is so much potential for controversy and loss of clarity about the direction of the project. With the initial reflections as a starting point, we begin to engage the individuals, families, groups, organizations or communities that are the focus of the study. This means that we need to find study participants who are willing to take part in a process of consciousness-raising regarding the intent of the research. These participants might be the targets of the oppression, practitioners concerned about intervening to address the oppression, and/or a mixture of both interest groups. The characteristics of our research partners in developing the research focus will be that:

1. They are affected by the oppression being studied. They are either victims or practitioners who wish to intervene, but they are not disinterested observers;

2. They are willing and able to engage in a discussion of the oppression and empowerment being studied;

3. They are able to understand the ideas being presented and willing to engage in political discussions;

4. They have the time to take part in the discussions;

5. They are willing to commit to action strategies regarding empowerment that will be developed in these discussions; and

6. They are willing to change ideas as the discussion continues and information is shared.

The number of initial partners will depend on the focus of our study and our time and resources. Since, as critical theory researchers, we celebrate empowerment wherever it takes place, a small group is as acceptable to us as a large group. Finn and Jacobson (2008), when discussing social justice and social work practice, describe such partnering as "a socio-emotional, practical and political process of coming together with others to create a space of respect and hope, pose questions, and learn about one another." We begin with a commitment to engaging people in understanding their problems within a values context, which according to Stringer (2007), affirms "Democracy, Equality, Liberation and Life Enhancement" Finn and Jacobson (2008) describe such engagement as **teaching-learning;** an approach in which all parties both teach and learn. All parties share data, engage in a dialectical process of synthesizing data and experiences, explore taboo subjects such as discrimination, acknowledge that study participants are not alone in these experiences, offer emotional support that honors difficult emotions and experiences, encourage acceptance of responsibility, acknowledge expectations, facilitate problem solving, rehearse proposed action, and acknowledge the strength that comes from awareness of group identity. Thus as critical theory researchers, whether we are studying individuals, groups, organizations or communities, we promote the formation of groups that can engage in self-reflection, analysis, synthesis and the development of action strategies.

This teaching-learning process gathers data about participants' ideological awareness and information about how to initiate a process of consciousness-raising. Hope and Timmel (1999) when discussing "transformation" for community workers, offer a process for conducting a listening survey that identifies the generative themes for communities. We can use this approach when engaging individuals, groups or organization, as well as communities in the teaching learning process and Finn and Jacobson (2008) itemize the following characteristics of such a process:

- Questions to be asked include: What are participants worried about? happy about? sad about? angry about? fearful about? hopeful about?

- Interviewers are trained to pay attention to gender, race, age, and other dimensions of diversity.

- Researchers gather background statistical information on the participants and the issue that is the focus of inquiry.

- Interviews at this early stage of engagement are informal and unstructured.

- Researchers listen for themes addressing basic needs such as housing, food, shelter, safety, security, love, belonging, self respect, and personal growth.

- Interviewers make sure the six areas of life that concern people's well being are addressed:

  ○ Basic physical need

  ○ Relationship with people

  ○ Access to participation in decision-making processes and structures

  ○ Education and Socialization

  ○ Recreation

  ○ Beliefs and Values

- If the opportunity arises and permission is granted, researchers can observe as well as interview in formal and informal settings. However, data collected in this fashion is secondary to that being gathered in the teaching-learning process. Such observations are shared and reviewed by participants,

- Researchers inform people of the data being gathered, its purposes and uses.

- Researchers gather data on facts and feelings.

- Researchers have a colleague or research team with whom they can critically analyze the emerging themes in relation to the six areas of wellbeing.

- Researchers should make an initial assessment of the priority of each theme for those who are the focus of the study and share this assessment with participants.

To carry out such an intensive process, we need to establish ourselves as people who can be trusted to have participants' interests at heart. Stringer (2007) notes that the researcher will have little success if "perceived as a stranger prying into people's affairs for little apparent reason or as an authority attempting to impose an agenda" (page 47). This may well be an issue for critical theory researchers who do indeed have an ideological agenda. If our ideology does not resonate with those who are the focus of our inquiry, then the study cannot move forward. An important aspect of the listening exercise described above is to note non-response or non-concern about the six areas of wellbeing in relation to the researcher's chosen ideology. If this is the case, then the researcher may need to find a new research site or new participants for the study. An ideological position cannot be successfully, or ethically, imposed on study participants.

Stringer (2007) notes that researches engaged in such intense engagement with study participants need to **establish a role** and this has three elements: agenda (a clearly articulated ideological position), stance (openness to discussion and alternative ideas) and position (a commitment to empowerment). The critical theory researcher must explain his or her *agenda* by taking a *stance* that encourages exploration of ideas, rather than insists on the correctness of those ideas. For example, the label of feminist for many women has become a stigma rather than a simple description. Instead of challenging the feelings attached to the term, we can explore the perceived stigma using the listening procedures itemized above and appreciate how it links to a person's feeling of well-being. For the third element, *position*, Stinger notes three entities that anyone can make a claim to: physical space, social status, and symbolic territory. The researcher needs to be sensitive to who "owns" the space in which data gathering is taking place. A range of different informal and formal settings can make a statement that the researcher is not "owned" by any one person or group.

Examples of the partnerships described above can be found in Schulz et al.'s (2003) study that engaged women in community-based participatory research for health, and Rutman et al.'s (2005) study of youth transitioning out of care. Schultz et al. (2003) set up a partnership in the east side of Detroit that included community

57

health workers, representatives from community based organizations, health service providers and academics. Eventually, this steering committee surveyed the community over a nine-month period to discover community strengths, resources, and risk factors affecting community residents. According to the authors, "The emphasis was on the engagement of community partners in shaping the research questions, determining how those questions would be asked, and interpreting the results and integrating them into the action components of the partnership". (pages 298-9). Rutman et al (2005) formed an advisory committee that included the researchers, youth from care, community-based service providers, and government representatives. This group collaborated equally in developing data collection instruments, liaising with various interest groups, carrying out data gathering, developing and carrying out workshops, and developing and implementing action strategies.

The critical theory assessment and engagement process can seem a little overwhelming, but we have our three examples of student projects that illustrate how we can implement it in a scaled-down manner. In the study of eating disorders, Christopulos (1995) engaged a group of high school girls in the project by means of a presentation and discussion session on feminism and eating disorders as part of a high school activity. This was a pre-existing group who were already interested in the topic and the student researcher, with input from the group, developed the following problem statement:

> *This research project asked how obsession with weight and body image preoccupies women and adopted an ideology that suggests such obsession renders women powerless. The ideological position of this critical theory study is that eating disorders in women, brought on by the oppression of women and confusing messages delivered to women by society and the media, can be eliminated by re-socializing women's perspectives at the high-school level. Feminist critical theory suggests that indoctrinating women with the misconception that success is measured only by body size and the worthless pursuit for an unattainable "ideal" body is a method in which the patriarchy attempts to control women* (page 1)

In the study of students' awareness of the role of the Curanderismo in mental health healing for the Latino community, Riech (1994), met with local practitioners who were Curanderismos or Curanderismas and developed a video explaining these approaches, which he would later use as an educational aid with social work students. He developed the following problem statement:

> *This study addressed two questions. The first was, what is the social work student's current state of knowledge of and attitude toward folk healers, in particular, Curnaderos or Curanderas?. The second question was, how do these attitudes change after the social work student has been informed about the particular folk healer's approach and beliefs? Let us explore the following scenario; a Mexican child is escorted to your office by his mother with a complaint that the child is very anxious and has been exposed to the "evil eye". Many therapists would know how to deal with the anxiousness of the child, or at least know where to begin the exploration. But what about the evil*

eye? Do we give the mother a quick mental status exam, questioning her reasoning, call child protective services to protect the child, or do we refer the mother and child to a reputable Curandero or Curandera to cure the evil eye? Actually in this case the proper answer would be the latter, or if she or he were fluent in the folk treatment process, the therapist could perform a conjoint session to get rid of the evil eye. This would work if all parties involved were cooperative; if the child believed, and if the mother would agree to further treatment for the child. This is a basic social work practice in that it starts where the client is. Once the patient is grounded in reality, conventional therapy may begin (page 2-3)

In the study that empowered a remote desert community to advocate for public transportation, Millet and Otero (2011) organized a series of community events and meetings during macro social work practice courses and research courses, and together the community and researchers developed the following problem statement:

> *Public transportation is the most basic and common mode of commuting for minority and low-income individuals, families, and communities. Transportation serves as a gateway for individuals to move up the social mobility ladder in search of better jobs, basic education for children and pursuit of better careers for adult men and women living in poverty stricken areas (Brown, 2008). This research project asked key stakeholders and residents of North Shore about their perceptions of the absence of public transportation. The research project adopted a critical theory paradigm since it sought to expose the issues of the voiceless by exploring the systemic complexity of sociopolitical ideologies in society, and by revealing the ways in which current attitudes fail to acknowledge the effects of ethnic discrimination and class oppression. These effects were a lack of political education and inability to participate in the political change process that apparently originates from their invisible existence within the larger context of society. Education on the political process ultimately transformed the community from a powerless people to an empowered community that actively participated in the political change process.* (page 1-2)

As we can see, all three projects were able to engage study participants in a critical theory, political dialogue that resulted in an empowering problem statement and a call for collaborative action. Development of the problem statement does require a much more intense and perhaps emotional engagement than positivism and post positivism, however, it can often lead to an inspiring study. Of course an integral part of developing the problem statement is the development of the literature review and we will now discuss this.

Developing the Literature Review

As critical theory researchers we develop our literature review using the procedures described in, Chapter 1. However our literature review is a little more complex than other reviews. We actually develop two interwoven literature reviews: first, a review of the literature giving an analysis of the chosen ideological position, and second, a literature review of the specific research topic, which, of course, is interpreted through the chosen ideological worldview. Talsher (2003) suggests that we should analyze ideologies in three ways: diachronic, discursive, and conceptual.

- A *diachronic* analysis traces the thematic transformation as the ideology develops over time. For example, in her analysis of the ideology of the Green party in Germany Talsher notes the following stages of development: unity in diversity (1960s); ecology and politics (1970s and 80s); ecology versus the economy (1990); and multicultural democracy (since reunification of Germany).

- A *discursive* analysis tracks the ideology evolving from the integration of themes identified in the diachronic analysis In Talsher's example, the Green party developed "ecosocialism" with four pillars: ecological politics, social politics, grass roots democratic politics, and non-violent politics (page170). This was a risky expansion of the definition of politics into the domains of family and community that had not been entertained in Germany since the Nazi experience. Talsher states that this has now been reformed into "classical political liberalism," with a focus on the individual and the dignity of each human being rather than on the collective, and stresses the right to self-determination, justice and democracy.

- The *conceptual,* analysis gives a rationale for the ideological development described by the first two analyses and synthesizes the progression of thought over time, giving a historical and social context for such changes. For example, in their ideological analysis of Oscar Lewis's culture of poverty, Harvey and Reed (1996) begin with a review of the history or "career" of the concept and the misunderstandings of it. They give this review a historical context, noting the controversy over the Moynihan report (1965) on the African-American family and poverty in the sixties and the mood of the time, when many members of the New Left were competing to be perceived as the "most radical." They then review the career of Oscar Lewis and assess exactly what he was trying to say about poverty. They give a current understanding of the "culture of poverty" as a class analysis, suggesting that criticisms of the concept as racist have been unfair and misguided. They also suggest that with the rightward movement of political and social thought over the last thirty years, discussion of class has been undermined or at least ignored, and in its place we have interpretive studies of culture and subjectivity.

With these ideas in mind, we can carry out a similar analysis at the start of a social work critical theory study and address the following questions:

1. What is the history of this ideology?

    a. How has the ideology evolved over time? What are the themes?

b. What is the current ideology? What is its current name and definitions?

c. Why have these developments taken place?

d. Who are the key authors and spokespeople for this ideology?

2. Which power relations are identified by this ideology?

    a. Which group is considered powerful?

    b. Which group is to be empowered?

    c. What action is favored for empowerment?

3. When this ideology is used to understand the research topic what does it say about?

    i. The powerful

    ii. The oppressed

    iii. Action to empower

For example, in the study of eating disorders in young women, Christopulos (1995), the author developed the above problem statement while reviewing the literature on women's body image and eating disorders and the feminist "world view," addressing unity, diversity, personal power and responsibility. The study linked each of these principles to eating disorders by:

- Reviewing feminist writing on body image and eating disorders (e.g. Charles & Kerr, 1986; Chernin, K, 1981 and 1986; Mahowald, 1992) that reveal the patriarchal emphasis on competition rather than unity, and its impact on women who feel they have lost the "race" for beauty.

- Revealing the patriarchal lack of appreciation for each person's unique characteristics.

- Revealing an action orientation that addresses this patriarchy, acknowledging:

    ○ The value of a masculine appearance or body type in a patriarchal society.

    ○ The denial of nurturing for women, which is compensated for by eating.

    ○ The fact that being large breaks the rules regarding personal space women occupy. Large women are visible and they take up space!

○ The fact that medical reports stress, inaccurately, that being thin is healthy.

In the study of the empowerment of an isolated desert community through campaigning for public transportation, (Millet and Otero, 2011) an ideological position was again developed from the literature:

This literature review develops an analysis of the integration of neo-Marxist theory and theories of ethnic discrimination. It is then divided into four parts related to:

(1) poverty

(2) Maslow's Hierarchy of Needs

(3) the importance of transportation and its relationship to society and

(4) empowerment and social action.

A neo-Marxist's analysis of class oppression shows how the Mexican-American (first and second generation) immigrant and migrant worker population that resides in North Shore are socially, politically, and economically subordinate to other members in society who are in higher levels of the class hierarchy. The absence of power and the exclusion from participating in society leaves the residents of North Shore without agency, rendering them unable to present their needs for consideration. (pages6-7)

As critical theory researchers we carry out a traditional literature review as well as an ideological literature review. This leads to a statement about oppression and empowerment that is shared with study participants as the ideological position of the study is developed. The ideological analysis carried out during the assessment phase identifies societal assumptions regarding power and difference and is used to develop the focus of a research project aimed at empowerment, which leads us to a note on developing the theoretical orientation.

Developing the Theoretical Orientation

It will be helpful to us as critical theory researchers to review the procedures in Chapter I. However, it is clear, that during the development of the problem statement and the literature review we have put an emphasis on developing a theoretical orientation. We have investigated a critical theory that has led to an ideological position that it is the major focus of the study. This is usually sufficient theoretical development for a critical theory study. We do need to consider the ethical, political, and diversity implications of our critical theory orientation to our research project.

We have now completed our discussion of the Assessment and Engagement phase of a critical theory study. We have reviewed the core tasks and we have considered the unique questions that emerge when we take this approach that is so committed to political action and empowerment. A summary of the chapter followed by learning assignments completes this chapter. Important cross cutting issues of ethics, politics, diversity, and technology in relation to critical theory can be found in Chapter V. We now move on to Chapter IV and a discussion of the constructivist approach.

Summary of Chapter III

- The initial stages of a critical theory involve simultaneous assessment, engagement and planning

- Assessment includes reviewing the literature on the chosen ideology as well as the chosen research topic

- Ideology is analyzed in three ways: diachronic, discursive and conceptual.

- The Ideological position is developed through a combination of literature review and engagement of study participants at the chosen research site using a teaching-learning approach

- Engaging the research site also requires "establishing a role" through the agenda, stance and position

- Ethical issues for critical theory research arise from the political and activist involvement with study participants.

- Diversity issues surface at both the micro and macro levels of human organization.

Critical Theory Learning Assignments

1. Choose an ideology that identifies an oppressed group, a process of oppression, and those with power to oppress. Think of a group locally that is experiencing the consequences of that oppression. Together with your partner develop an action plan to address that oppression. Who would you need to talk to? What would you need to know?

It is with constructivism that we come to a completely different world view to the other three paradigms. The constructivist paradigm is the only one of the four that does not assume an objective reality but instead proposes that human experience can only be understood as a subjective reality. It recognizes that we all understand the world from our own points of view and supposes that nobody can stand outside the human experience to observe laws and regulatory mechanisms independent of situation and person. Thus the only way we can understand a human phenomenon is to completely and thoroughly understand the perceptions, or constructions, of those people who are engaged in that human phenomenon. Constructivists propose that researchers gathering new knowledge about the human experience must gather subjective data. To do this they collaborate with those involved in a particular human experience to create a valid authentic shared construction of the human experience being researched. Such a collaboration and construction is termed a **"hermeneutic dialectic"**. It is hermeneutic because it seeks out individual interpretations and it is a dialectic because individual interpretations are compared and contrasted and may well change during the hermeneutic dialectic.

The guiding principle of the constructivist subjective approach to research is that data is unique to its time and place. A researcher studying HIV-AIDS in California in August is assumed to be studying a different phenomenon to a researcher studying HIV-AIDS in Wisconsin in December. When we begin a constructivist study we consider our own understanding of the research topic. We then engage key players and sources who will also have a perspective on, or construction of, that topic. In this way we build a combined understanding of the topic in its context. As we move forward with the constructivist study we commit to using a rigorous subjectivist research methodology which provides data on the research topic that is "trustworthy". A number of authors (Guba, 1981: Lincoln and Guba 1985: Erlandson et al: 1993) offer criteria for evaluating whether constructions are trustworthy. They note that trustworthy constructions must have **credibility**, **transferability**, **dependability,** and **confirmability**:

> *Credibility* refers to the need for written constructions to be accurate description of study participants' perspectives. The researcher achieves this by means of: prolonged engagement with the research setting; ongoing analysis of and reflection on data in the form of written accounts of interviews and observations; compilation of constructions from key players with diverse points of view; reporting on artifacts, such as pictures and documents, that enrich understanding of the research context; peer debriefing during data collection; and checking with project participants that the written accounts of their constructions are accurate.

> *Transferability* refers to the accuracy with which the findings from one study can be applied to another setting. Since constructivist researchers do not assume there is a reality with demonstrable and immutable laws and

mechanisms, they must give the consumer of the research guidance for deciding whether the study findings are transferable to other settings. This guidance is offered by means of comprehensive descriptions of settings, participants and constructions.

Dependability and Confirmability are the validity of the data and the reliability of the interpretations of it. Put pragmatically, it addresses two questions: how was this data collected, and how was it interpreted? Was the collection of data exhaustive, and did the reasoning behind developing constructions reflect accurately the evidence provided by study participants? To address these questions, the constructivist researcher documents all processes of data collection and steps of data analysis used to build constructions **in research journals (see chapter II)**. These journals are subjected to external audit, and the auditing trail from initial conceptualization of the study through accounts of interviews and observations to the final agreed joint constructions is reviewed by, and justified to, an outside research specialist or faculty advisor.

Three examples of student projects illustrate the constructivist approach. Two are M.S.W. student projects and one is a doctoral student's dissertation. The first is a study of services to people living with HIV-AIDS, the second is a study of services to homeless children carried out by two different students in successive years, and the third is a study of the role of spirituality in delivering child welfare services to African-American families. They are:

Becker, J. E. (1994) *A Constructivist study of the social and educational needs of homeless children.* San Bernardino, CA: School of Social Work CSUSB

Kelly, G. (1995). *A Constructivist Second Year Study of the Social and Educational Needs of Homeless Children.* San Bernardino, CA: School of Social Work, CSUSB.

Brown, L.E. (2011) Spirituality's Role in the Interaction Between Child Welfare and Black Families. San Bernardino: Department of Social Work and Social Ecology, Loma Linda University.

Hogan, P. (1995) *A Constructivist study of Social Work's Involvement with HIV-AIDS.* San Bernardino, CA: School of Social Work, CSUSB,

Developing the Problem Statement

We begin out constructivist study by setting up our **research journals as** described Chapter II. The first entries in our reflective journal are thoughts on why the topic is interesting and relevant to learning about social work practice. Next are reflections on the selection of the research site, possible key players, and ideas about what is likely to happen and what the likely findings might be. This helps with developing a constructivist perspective since it acknowledges our subjective understanding of the topic. It also helps us develop empathy for study participants and how they will experience data collection as they take part in the constructivist process.

According to Erlandson et al. (1993), our constructivist **problem statement** should be broad enough to include central issues and narrow enough to serve as a data collection guide. According to Lincoln and Guba (1985), we could be studying a problem, evaluating an evaluand, or studying a policy option. A **problem** is defined as a "state of affairs resulting from the interaction of two or more factors...that yields (1)...a conceptual problem; (2)...an action problem; or (3) an undesirable consequence (a value problem) (page 226). An **evaluand** is a program, organization, performance, material or facility to be evaluated. A **policy option** is a proposed or existing policy "the utility of which is to be determined" (page 227).

A problem for example, might be HIV-AIDS in a particular community. We might plan to ask a general question such as, "What is this community's experience of social work services for people living with HIV-AIDS?" We would then explicate "what?" and "where?" questions, which are exploratory; "how?" and "why?" questions, which are explanatory; and action questions to address interventions with the issue. In this example such questions might be,

- What services are available in this community for people living with HIV-AIDS?

- Where and in what agencies are these services housed?

- How do these services meet the needs of people living with HIV-AIDS?

- Why were these services developed rather than other possible services?

- What action needs to be taken to address the concerns of people living with HIV-AIDS?

This may well lead to other studies that evaluate specific HIV-AIDS programs and policies. Like any other researcher, as constructivist researchers we begin with our own expertise on the subject to be researched. We also review the literature on the research focus using procedures described in Chapter I. However, we consider our expertise and the literature to be two of many possible constructions of the topic to be researched and these constructions have equal value with those collected from gatekeepers and participants in the study

Once we have narrowed down our problem statement we can then look for a research site. Erlandson (1993) suggests a number of strategies for selecting and engaging a research site. These include:

- Personal contact;

- Surveys of similar sites, for example, social service agencies with the required client group, or geographical communities with high incidents of the problem be studied; and

- Professional referrals.

In making the selection we need to be sure that we will be able to gain access to the site and all likely key players with pertinent constructions regarding the research statement. We might find a familiar site by contacting our field placement site or another site where we have volunteered or know some of the agency leaders. In other situations where we might be new to the site, it is essential that we build rapport and trust with the gate keepers to the site. These gatekeepers could be not only the institutional heads of the agencies or officials of the community but also the opinion leaders and trusted members of the agencies or community. When initially contacting the site, we need to be alert to indicators of who the formal and informal key gatekeepers are and how to engage their interest in the project.

Constructivist projects require intensive interaction with participants, sometimes, over a long period of time. We enter the site not as a data gatherer who will report back our findings at the end of the study, but as facilitators who will assist participants in reporting and interpreting their own data. Not only this, a successful constructivist study leads to action by the study participants that addresses the issues raised during data collection. This commitment to action calls for an equal partnership between the researcher and the study participants. We can take a leaf out of the book of micro practitioners when engaging in this partnership. Namely, we need to: "start where the client is" and respect his or her perceptions of the proposed project; use listening and attending skills to draw out descriptions of the participants experiences, issues and concerns with the project; develop effective questioning skills using open and closed ended questions appropriately; and reflect back not only our understanding of the content of the exchange with the participant but also our understanding of their feelings about that content (Evans et al, 2010).

We also need to make sure that the gatekeepers of the research site are aware of the inherent requirements of constructivist research. Such research demands time and energy and requires a more intensive commitment than traditional research. Lincoln and Guba (1989) itemize these demands by describing the following conditions for conducting constructivist research:

All participants must make a commitment to work from a position of integrity. Participants agree to genuinely try to tell the truth and be honest. If participants knowingly give misinformation, the various feedback sharing opportunities built in to the paradigm's methodology are likely to discover and challenge such data.

All participants must have minimal competence to communicate verbally and in written form. Thus young children, those who are severely developmentally delayed, and those who are severely mentally ill cannot participate in a constructivist study.

All participants must have a willingness to share power. If the leadership or high-status representatives of a particular program either sponsor or simply participate in a constructivist study, they need to be aware that their perceptions of the program will be seen as constructions that are equal to all other participants' constructions. Their views will not be more or less important than anyone else's.

All participants must have a willingness to reconsider their perspectives. During the constructivist data collection process, participants' constructions are shared and discussed. Each participant, on hearing another person's construction of the topic, may hear a perspective that challenges his or her own construction. In the face of such challenges, participants understand that they need to be open to changing their ideas if persuaded by another point of view.

All participants must have a willingness to reconsider their value positions. For most of us, this is a tougher commitment to make. Our value positions have guided our lives. However, the constructivist orientation includes a relativist assumption regarding values. That is, values are dictated by life experience and social context and are not an objective, never-changing set of rules. Participants in a constructivist study need to be able to accept this position, at least in relation to the topic that is the focus of the research project.

All participants must have a willingness to make the time and energy commitment needed in constructivist research. Accurately recording every study participant's complete construction of a research topic is time-consuming. The initial interview will be lengthy, and the follow-up between researcher and study participant to gain agreement on validity are additional conscientious commitments.

One example of the constructivist approach developing the problem statement is illustrated by the researcher who carried the study of HIV/AIDS (Hogan, 1995). She was a social work student with ten year's experience in the HIV/AIDS arena and, as she noted in her acknowledgements, had a family member who had died of AIDS. In her professional and personal experience of HIV/AIDS, she had noted a reticence among social workers to intervene with HIV/AIDS clients. She decided to look more deeply into her perception. A review of the literature at that time confirmed that, although there had been social work pioneers fighting discrimination against people living with HIV-AIDS, the social work profession had been slow to respond to this client population's need for services. At the same time she identified a research site, a place she lived in and was familiar with: the Coachella Valley in Southern California, a desert community 100 miles east of Los Angeles. At the beginning of her report on the study, she gives this research statement:

"What are the factors that may inhibit and facilitate social work practice in the HIV/AIDS arena in Coachella Valley? The study was conducted in the Coachella Valley, a region of eastern Riverside County in Southern California. There is a disproportionately high incidence and prevalence of HIV/AIDS in this area. According to Congressman Sonny Bono the Coachella Valley has a rate of incidence of diagnosed AIDS nearly equal to areas such as San Francisco and New York……The

objective is to gain an awareness of thoughts, beliefs and feelings of social workers and other key professionals working in agencies and organizations serving HIV/AIDS affected communities in the Coachella Valley……to facilitate action and policies that will increase and enhance a social work response (to the needs of people living with HIV-AIDS) in all arenas of social work practice". (Hogan; pages 11-14)

Having developed her focus, she next identified a circle of stakeholder groups associated with services for people living with HIV-AIDS in this geographical area relying on a preliminary survey and her own knowledge of the region. Agencies that specifically served such clients as well as those serving the general population, who most likely also served HIV-AIDS clients, were initially included. In addition, faculty representatives from the local M.S.W. programs were invited to participate. Thus the initial stakeholder groups in the circle of key informants included:

1. AIDS-specific agencies

2. Medical Clinics

3. County Substance Abuse Programs

4. Charitable Organizations

5. Universities' social work departments

6. The County Department of Social Services

7. Hospice Agencies

8. Local Hospitals

9. Persons Living with HIV/AIDS

10. Professional Social Workers

11. The Researcher

12. The Literature on Social Work practice with HIV/AIDS

Our second example of a constructivist study addresses the educational needs of homeless children. This study was carried out over two years by successive students living in the same geographical area as our HIV-AIDS study, the Coachella Valley (Becker, 1994; Kelly, 1995). One student developed the study and conducted the first round of interviews, while another student picked up where the first had left off and continued it into a second year of data gathering. Both students had experience working with homeless children. The initial research focus was as follows:

Coachella Valley is comprised of several desert resort cities (Palm Spring and the like) located in the southern tip of California…Income levels within the valley vary from the extreme poverty of migrant farm workers to those whose economic status exceeds the highest national level. Although once a retirement community…the valley has experienced a demographic shift resulting in the growth of families. Estimates of the number of homeless families within the valley (show) one shelter reporting 110% increase in demand for shelter space...It is, therefore, the purpose of this research to explore the educational as well as social needs of homeless children within the Coachella Valley. And it is hoped that through a greater understanding of the needs of these children, existing services may be strengthened, or new services developed, which may forestall, or even eliminate, future negative consequences" (Becker; pages 4-5)

The first student researcher (Becker) used her knowledge and the advice of other professionals to select the initial stakeholder groups in the circle of key informants. These included:

1. Homeless Shelters

2. Counseling Centers

3. Riverside County Department of Social Services

4. Area Hospitals

5. Local Head Start Program

6. Literature

7. Local School Districts

8. Local Department of Children's Services

However, as data collection continued and agencies were contacted, the initial circle was reduced to the listing below, because either the agency had little contact with homeless children or it did not have a representative willing to take part in the study:

1. Homeless Shelters

2. Homeless Families

3. School Districts

4. Public Health Department

5. Literature

6. Researcher's Own Construction

Our third example of a constructivist study is a doctoral dissertation on the role of spirituality in working with African-American families in the child welfare system (Brown, 2012). The researcher had over thirty years' experience as a social worker in the child welfare system and was aware of the importance of religion and spirituality to African-American families. However, she observed that, when working with

African-American families in the child welfare system, social workers rarely discussed spirituality with clients. She thought this may well be one of the reasons for the over-representation of African-American families in her region of the child welfare system. Her problem statement was,

> *The disparate and disproportionate involvement of African American families in the child welfare system continues to lead to negative outcomes for African American children, their families and communities. Culturally competent practices may facilitate better engagement of African American families in the assessment and case planning processes and ultimately to improved outcomes for these children. The role of spirituality/religion as a significant strength in African American communities deserves to be explored as a resource to improving practice, and to increasing engagement and the effectiveness of services.*

> *In the public child welfare arena the acknowledgement of spirituality/religion is almost completely ignored both in the child welfare research and practice literature. It is believed that cultural competence cannot be achieved when working with African American families, without the acknowledgement and inclusion of spirituality/religion. It is further suggested that the recognition of spirituality/religion as a strength and resource in the assessment, planning and service provision phases of the child welfare process is both culturally competent practice and most effective in engaging and assisting African American parents. (page 7)*

The two circles of key stakeholders included in the study were:

1. Child Welfare Staff;

    i.   Administrative,

    ii. Line workers, and

2. African-American parents who had been in the child welfare system in the past

Here we have three examples of the integrated process of developing the constructivist problem statement that are both action and values problems. Each student developed a statement based on her own perceptions, data, and the literature and then identified the circle of key informants who would be able to contribute to the building of a joint construction of that problem statement. In these examples, each student was personally aware of a problem to be researched and lived in the region chosen for the research study. They were familiar with the service-structures and knew some of the key players in the initial circle of informants. Initial approaches were made to key players who were all very busy people. There was an interest in the research topics, but the researchers needed to be persistent to actually gain access and carry out engagement of key players. The fact that they were known to most of the key players, or were referred by somebody they knew, helped with access. Having considered development of the problem statement we are now ready to consider the development of the literature review.

Developing the Literature Review

The constructivist researcher carries out the literature review in the same way as any other researcher as describe in Chapter I. However, the constructivist researcher sees the literature as one of many possible "constructions" of the research focus. The literature does not drive the development of the research focus; it influences the development of the focus in partnership with study participants and the researcher. It contributes to the joint construction of the problem focus that emerges from the study. This is illustrated in the study of the role of spirituality in child welfare practice with African-American families (Brown, 2011). When she outlines the hermeneutic dialectic circle for the study, she creates the diagram in Figure 2.12, demonstrating an equal partnership between the literature, study participants, and the researcher.

Figure IV.1 – An example of the Role of Literature in a Constructivist Study

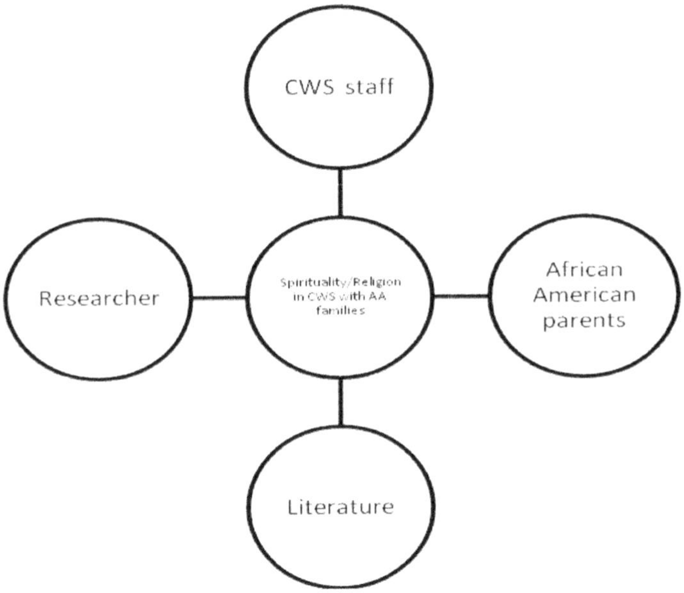

Here we see that the researcher has included the literature in the circle of key informants as having as equal influence on the problem focus as other members of the circle of key informants. This is the only additional issue that needs to be considered when developing the literature review for a constructivist study. The procedures describe in chapter I for positivist studies work just as well for this kind of study.

Developing the Theoretical Orientation

As with the literature review, theories are seen as possible constructions of the research focus. It would be useful to review the discussion of developing the theoretical orientation in Chapter I. However, these theories would simply be added to the circle of key informants and shared with other key informants for comment and reflection. The constructivist, subjective, approach assumes that the project will not be guided by a particular theoretical orientation but will include theoretical orientations noted by participants in the development of the shared construction. Having considered the core constructivist tasks in the Assessment and Engagement phase of the study, we are now ready to reflect on the contextual issues of ethics, politics and diversity.

To sum up this chapter, we have discussed the unique constructivist worldview, the development of the problem statement, literature review, and theoretical orientation. We have seen some overlap with approaches used in other paradigms but we have also seen the unique subjective orientation that constructivists bring to carrying out research. Important cross cutting issues of ethics, politics, diversity, and technology in relation to the constructivist approach can be found in Chapter V

Summary of Chapter IV

- Initial engagement of research sites needs to be thoughtful, well planned and persistent

- Each constructivist study is considered unique to its time and place

- The quality of a constructivist study is measured by its credibility, transferability, dependability and confirmability

- The literature is considered to be one construction of the research statement.

- Constructivist studies ask exploratory, explanatory and action questions

- A constructivist study demands an intensive commitment of time and energy

- Constructivist studies focus on problems, evaluands or policy options.

- Ethical issues in constructivist research arise from the open engagement of study participants.

Constructivist Learning Assignment

1. Think of a research topic that you are interested in and a site where you might study that topic. Who are the key players in relation to this topic at that site? How would you engage those key players so that you could find out about their perspectives on your topic?

Before moving on to Part 2 and making the plan for our study, we need to consider cross cutting issues associated with Assessment and Engagement. These include ethics, politics, diversity, and technology. These remind us to be aware of the dignity of participants in our study and sensitive to the context of our study.

Ethical Issues

Because of the power differential between the researcher and the study participant in positivist research, in the past, there was a potential to ignore the rights of study participants in the name of science. There are a number of, now famous, abuses of the research process (the Milgram study of obedience 1963, 1965, 1974 (You Tube video); the Humphrey's study of male homosexuals, 1975 (You Tube video); and the Zimbardo et al. study of prison behavior, 1974 (You Tube video). Now we must anticipate harm that might be done by the study, review the impact of any deception of participants, guarantee anonymity or confidentiality and acknowledge the possible distorting influence of our commitment to the study sponsor. Even with these protections, there can be unintended unethical treatment of study participants. All research projects sponsored by universities must undergo a **Human Subjects Review** process managed by an **Institutional Review Board** (IRB) where a university committee assesses the research project's potential for harm using federal guidelines. Practice agencies also tend to have research review committees.

As ethical social workers, regardless of the review process, we will want to consider the morality of our research project. When Greenbank (2003) discussed morality in relation to research, he talked about personal values systems. He cited Rokeach (1973) who developed the concept of instrumental values. There are three kinds of instrumental values: moral, competency and terminal. Each of these is guided by a different approach to answering the question; what is the ethical thing to do?

- *Moral values*: decisions that are made based on moral values are guided by principles that tell us the 'right' thing to do. We may have a value that calls us to respect diversity. Thus we decide that is wrong to use sexist or racist approaches to carrying out research.

- *Competency values*: decisions that are based on competency values are guided by principles that tell us the most effective way to do something. By keeping up with current knowledge on best social work practice, we make sure that we intervene in the most effective way possible with our clients. By being knowledgeable about research methods, we make sure that we build authentic knowledge.

- *Terminal values (two kinds):*

  o *Personal values*: decisions that are based on personal values are guided by what a person hopes to achieve for himself or herself. If someone strives to be a skilled community worker, then this aspiration will guide approaches to social work practice. Of course there is a negative aspect to personal values. If a person is, for example, striving for power at any cost, then decisions will be guided by this ambition.

  o *Societal values*: decisions that are based on societal values are guided by how a person wishes society to operate. A socialist vision calls for sharing and community gain, an entrepreneurial vision calls for individual competitive effort.

All of these values come into play when we are considering the ethics of our research project. Sometimes they lead to answers to ethical problems that contradict each other. We have guidelines for basic research practice but quite often, such guidelines are only a starting point and we are left with difficult decisions to make. For example,

1. Is it ethical to withhold interventions, which are showing effectiveness during a research project, until the end of the study?

2. Conversely, is it ethical to stop the study and start offering the intervention to all appropriate clients before completing the study?

In this dilemma, the moral imperative suggests answering both "yes" and "no" to both questions; the *competency* principle suggests we follow correct research methodology and finish the study; *terminal* values lead us to reflect on our personal and societal visions, do we want to be seen as impetuous researchers who ended the study prematurely or are we so sure that the intervention is effective and that society will benefit from premature termination of the study? There are no easy answers to these questions but it is important that we are mindful of the implications of our ethical reasoning when deciding what to do.

So we need to make a conscious formal consideration of whether our study is ethical. If we believe that study participants' knowledge about the study will threaten the scientific approach to the proof of causality then the necessity for deceptions and the potential for harm must be reviewed and assessed (*terminal value*). For example, if we wish to prove that parent education training is more effective in reducing families' incidents of child abuse than an alternative intervention such as family therapy, it will be important for the families in the study to be unaware of our hypothesis regarding the enhanced efficacy of the parenting program. We also need to decide whether the harm and deception resulting from withholding a program that we believe is more effective in protecting children is balanced by the families' access to family therapy and the need to know which of these interventions is thought to protect children most effectively.

As social work researchers we must also consider the potential harm arising from coercion of special populations such as mandated clients or clients who may well feel that their services will be threatened if they do not agree to be in the study (*moral value*). One strategy for reducing harm is offered by Wethington (2003) who gives examples of two studies where she spent a year pre-testing telephone interview protocols specifically to discover whether they caused harm to participants. She asked a small sample of study participants to engage in the process and then give specific feedback on the experience of being interviewed about sensitive topics on the phone. She then adjusted the training of interviewers accordingly so that when the large-scale study was carried out, harm was minimized.

In addition to doing no harm and not coercing study participants, we also need to address study participants' privacy anonymity and confidentiality. Are we intruding into the study participant's privacy by observing their behaviors in a parenting class? Is the study important enough to warrant this? Anonymity is the protection of a person's identity while confidentiality is the protection of that person's information. We must develop procedures for such protections before data collection begins. The solution to many of these ethical concerns, for positivists, is to lay out the risks and benefits in an informed consent form and gain a signature on that form from study participants at the beginning of the study. In addition, often, a debriefing at the end of the study is porovided. The informed consent will describe the study, how it will be carried out, any potential risks, any guarantees, who the researcher is, and the auspices of the project. However, this is not always as straightforward as it appears. Many researchers will admit that the more information you put into an informed consent, the less likely it is that a participant will sign it. Participants do not help design the positivist project. Ultimately, they can either trust that the researcher will treat them ethically or refuse to participate in the study. Many disenfranchised groups have reacted negatively to this situation and now demand more collaborative approaches to research such as the alternatives described in this book.

As post positivists we face all the ethical issues discussed above in relation to the positivist approach. Like any other researcher, we must undergo a human subjects' review and develop procedures for informed consent, debriefing and any ethical issues associated with the research project. However, since there is an engagement with study participants when the initial research focus is developed, there is more opportunity for consideration of and response to any ethical concerns that participants may mention during the initial stages of the project. Post positivist research requires an intense social involvement for both the participants and the researchers. We need to thoroughly think through the informed consent procedures. If we plan to gather data using interviews, the interviewee needs to be informed at the beginning about the subject of the interview and the length of time the interview is likely to take. We always have face to face contact with study participants in this form of research, and thus there is a potential to betray any promised anonymity and confidentiality. We need to take extra care to make sure that respondents' names are not made public and that either the data they give is separated from their name or, if data needs to be linked to its source that the list of names connected to data is kept in a secure place.

If the mode of data collection is going to be observation, we need to give those being observed the opportunity to think through the implications of close watching for them. In a formal work setting, what risks are those being observed taking regarding supervisory reaction to observations made by researchers? If the researcher/observer masques his or her role in some way, how is voluntary informed consent gained, how is the right to voluntary withdrawal from the study protected, and what are the procedures for debriefing participants? Many of these ethical issues make observation, especially if it involves deception, an undesirable data collection mode for post positivists. Indeed Angrosino and Rosenberg (2011) note that there is currently a widespread ethical suspicion of observational research. Others (Adler & Adler, 1994) have suggested that it's most fruitful use is as an integrated technique combined with interviewing. In this context, it can enrich researchers' understandings of participants' statements during interviews. However it is used, the ethical treatment of study participants must be addressed. So at the Assessment and Engagement stage of a post positivist research project, as well as addressing all the ethical issues faced by positivists, post positivist really need to consider the implications of intense involvement with gatekeepers and study participants.

As an aside, often this IRB submission is a difficult stage if we are using the post positivist, (or critical theory or constructivist paradigms) because we often need to gather data from the research site during the Engagement stage but we don't yet have permission to do so. One way to address this dilemma is to be clear about our Engagement activities so that we can explain that the contact we have with the study site during Engagement is developing the ground work for the study not gathering data that will be reported in the final study report. A clear description of such an Engagement phase is given in figure V.4 by Millet and Otero (2011) in the final report on their study addressing public transportation in a small, desert, community. These are the kinds of activities that would be described in a proposal applying for Human Subjects Approval from an IRB for a study like this.

Figure V.1
An Important Human Subjects Approval Issue Example of Description of Engagement

---

Engagement Phases

Introduction

Each engagement phase was incredibly emotionally and physically taxing and required thorough preparation and strategic planning. Items such as food, condiments, drinks, games, clip-boards, tables, pens, informational copies, fliers, sign-in sheets, large easel pad etc., had to be acquired, accounted for, and taken to each event as specified. Furthermore, the appropriate contacts were made to store owners at Reyes Market and administrative coordinator of (DACE) in order to make reservations for the engagement and community meeting events at the North Shore Yacht Club. Fliers were designed and mailed to the appropriate community spaces. All written communication was provided in English and Spanish. Community members were informed about the events via phone. One hundred and thirty community members were contacted on several occasions. Preparation was a complex and timely process that depended upon multi-tasking, teamwork and additional outside help from cohort, friends, other cause supporters and family members as describe below. (details of this Engagement are in Attachment A)

The ethical issues for critical theory research relate to the impact of teaching/learning about oppressions and action for empowerment on study participants. The harm that we might do by taking an ideological position and acting on it needs to be thoroughly reviewed in relation to the vulnerability of the oppressed group that is the focus of the study. For example, our example study of eating disorders in adolescent female highs school students took a feminist position on the causes of those eating disorders and intervened in the school setting to educate a group of adolescent girls about the feminist position on eating disorders and body image. The researcher needed to firstly make it clear that it was okay to challenge and debate these positions and secondly, reassure students that success in high school was not influenced by their acceptance, or non-acceptance, of these ideas. In any critical theory study we must consider the potential harm associated with taking action to challenges power over an oppressed group. For example, a study that confronts differential services to racial groups has the potential to antagonize service providers so that they withdraw from an underserved neighborhood so that the unintended impact of the action is that the services, although inadequate, completely disappear.

As critical theory researchers we are of course bound by the traditional human subjects' mandates of doing no harm, avoiding deception, assuring privacy and confidentiality and formally gaining informed consent as described for the positivist and post positivist approaches. However, an additional constraint is the importance of informing participants about the ideological orientation of the study and the intent to empower. Since the study has a political agenda that may be contradictory to participants' own ideologies or experiences, we must engage opposing opinions and clearly explain the rationale for the ideological orientation and intent of the study. Study participants must be informed about the activity that they are getting involved in, including the potential for coercion by others who disagree. The teaching-learning dialogue is seen as the key to keeping all participants informed and negotiating conflict.

An additional ethical issue for some critical theorists is the commitment that many make to a lifelong relationship with participants in the research project (Brown and Stega, 2005). Those that take this position are implying that the boundary between social work practitioner and client should be erased if genuine empowerment is to take place. This contradicts much of the practice wisdom about such relationships, not to mention parts of the NASW code of ethics, specifically part 1.06 (Conflict of Interest), part (b), which states that *"Social workers should not take unfair advantage of any professional relationship or exploit others to further their personal, religious, political, or business interests"* and part (c), which states that *"Social workers should not engage in dual or multiple relationships with clients or former clients in which there is a risk of exploitation or potential harm to the client. In instances when dual or multiple relationships are unavoidable, social workers should take steps to protect clients and are responsible for setting clear, appropriate, and culturally sensitive boundaries."* The potential exists for the social work researcher, using the more "committed" critical theory approach to become unclear about the personal boundary between a social work practitioner who is carrying out research as part of practice and the participants in the study who are looking to the researcher for professional services. We must identify and maintain clear boundaries throughout the period of the study.

As with all the other approaches to research, constructivist research is subject to human subjects review processes assuring that participants are not harmed and that privacy, confidentiality and anonymity are protected as discussed above for the other approaches. This is a challenge given the open nature of the constructivist approach to research. The ever changing focus of the study, the desire to build accurate constructions for each respondent, the goal of sharing those constructions, and the openness of the process intensifies and broadens informed consent. Protection of privacy and confidentiality becomes an intensive process of constant renegotiation throughout the study as the focus emerges and evolves. Anonymity is difficult to guarantee in constructivist research. Even if a name is removed from the construction, an individual's point of view may be a known one and its author easily identified by other key players in the research arena. The only solution to this is to make sure that study participants are aware of the risk. The goal of the constructivist researcher is to empower, educate, and connect participants (Erlandson et al.; 1993), and a failure to openly confront the issues would weaken the methodology of the study and threaten the validity of the data collected for the constructions. Thus we openly share the anonymity and confidentiality dilemma with participants so that they can make a decision about the terms of their participation.

If a stakeholder decides not to participate and another person cannot be found who plays a similar stakeholder role then that construction is missing from the final joint construction. We would note this when reporting the final construction and the stakeholder group would be informed that a particular perspective has not yet been included in the process of building the joint construction. Also, a participant who is comfortable sharing data at the beginning of a study may be put in a politically or professionally embarrassing situation by some of the issues that surface during data collection as the focus of the study emerges and changes. The researcher would need to discuss with this participant whether to present any of his or her data. It is difficult to anticipate exactly what the ethical issues will be as the study continues but adjustments and accommodations will need to be made throughout the process. This was particularly evident in the HIV-AIDS study example (Hogan, 1995). Many participants asked for anonymity and most participants were uncomfortable with a prolonged engagement with the study. This was a sad but valid comment on the HIV-AIDS situation in that region at that time. Anonymity was perceived as necessary and this need limited the study.

The principles of sensitivity and integrity that guide constructivist research are required for collection of valid and reliable data that guarantees trustworthy constructions. These principles determine appropriate solutions to ethical dilemmas regarding harm to participants. With such a fluid process, unanticipated situations that may harm the participant and/or researcher may surface. Acknowledging these and changing the study so that protection from harm is achieved will not weaken or even threaten a constructivist study. Such accommodations are all part of the process of building the joint construction and accurately reporting subjective understandings. Deceiving participants would not be a strategy that constructivist researchers would use, since such deception would threaten the process and product of constructivist research. If participants should find out that, for example, that a researcher was really studying HIV-AIDS but was pretending to study substance abuse or sexually transmitted diseases in general, the process by which participants engaged in the project would be compromised. Indeed the accuracy of the subjective data and the likelihood that the action stage is implemented would be compromised if participants were not clear on the focus and intent of the study. By sharing, confronting, reflecting and changing perspectives, the constructivist process is believed to offer a comprehensive approach to protecting those who engage in these studies. This overall philosophy will certainly facilitated addressing ethical issues

Political Issues

We can understand the politics of our research project when we ask ourselves a series of macro questions.

1)   Who decides appropriate arenas and topics for research?

In the research world some topics become the "hot" topics while others go away. In the sixties, poverty was a hot topic. Now we may see a study of income maintenance or the effectiveness of TANF but we rarely see studies on the causes of poverty and its amelioration. HIV-AIDS is a hot topic but it tends to be studied in the USA rather than Africa where per capita incidents are higher. Since child welfare is a major employer of social workers, in the social work arena, we tend to see a lot of research on child abuse and neglect but not so much on aging, even with the infusion of Hartford Foundation money.

2)   How are such choices made?

Well, as deep throat said in the movie, *"All the President's Men"*, "Follow the money". If there is money, either government or private, for a research topic, then it will be studied. Private funding usually comes from foundations with a particular mission while public funding is linked to political decisions about important topics. When, Ronald Reagan's funeral was all over the television, members of his family were making a plea for the funding of stem cell research to find a cure for Alzheimer's. When the O.J. Simpson case was our national, nay international, obsession, research into spouse abuse was advocated. After any high school shooting, studies of adolescent gun violence are called for. Government decisions about research are influenced by public opinion that favors certain topics and public criticism of other topics. While HIV-AIDS was seen as a "gay" disease, in the early eighties, limited funding was made available for research but once it was seen as a threat to us all it became an expanded, acceptable and fundable research arena.

3)   Who defines social constructs?

Employment is a good example of this. In the nineteen sixties the unemployment rate was calculated by simply adding up the number of people who did not have job. It was the total work force minus those who had a job. However, when these numbers crept up definitions of both the workforce and unemployment began to be massaged so that numbers of unemployed decreased. The workforce was redefined as those employed in non-military positions. The unemployed were redefined as "those actively seeking employment". The requirements for being officially unemployed were, therefore, tightened and rates declined. A different political problem surfaces when struggling with a definition of child abuse. The only data we have enumerating rates of child abuse, is numbers of reports of child abuse. However some reports are substantiated and others are not. If we use substantiated reports of child abuse we notice a correlation with poverty. In fact checking the correlation of child abuse rates with rates of poverty is often the method researchers use to determine the validity of the data on substantiated rates of child abuse. However, the poor are more likely to be reported for child abuse since they tend to experience more public scrutiny from social workers and other health and human service officials than other classes of society. In addition being poor can sometimes look like child neglect. As a result, the poor are labeled as child abusers while middle and upper class families, not subject to the same scrutiny, are not.

4)   *What data is available and how was it collected and organized?*

The census bureau has collected demographic data on the US for about 200 years. However collecting valid and reliable data on ethnicity has only been addressed in the last 10 to 15 years. Until quite recently, data on the Latino ethnic group was collected by noting those with a Spanish last name. These could have been members of any ethnic group who had married someone with a Spanish last name. Also, we have only recently acknowledged the need for a category of identification for those of mixed ethnicity or race. When gathering data from social service agencies, the case records, which are usually the source of agency data often contain data that has been collected for the purposes of auditing services rather than evaluating outcomes. Thus a client service might have been checked off in the file but the length of service and its content may well not be there. The auditor wants to know if the service was delivered, the researcher wants to know how much of the service was delivered and what kind of service was delivered. It is the auditor to whom social services agencies must pay much more attention.

5)   *Who sponsors and funds the research and for what reasons?*

This is a major issue with program evaluation. Generally the agency funds its own evaluation. Outcome evaluations address program effectiveness. However, an agency may well have difficulty paying money to be told that it is ineffective. The pressure on the positivist researchers is, therefore, to cushion the blow or perhaps modify the findings. Often a process (formative) process evaluation is preferred to an outcome (summative) evaluation since the findings from a formative evaluation are less threatening to agencies and offer suggestions for more efficient functioning.

6)   *Who will know about the research findings?*

What will be done with the research findings? This brings us to the question of exploitation of research participants and research sites. In the past, most positivists have reported research findings to the academic community in academic journals. They may have written a report for the funder and they may promise access to findings to respondents but the reality is that study participants have to take the initiative to find out about the study. Positivists do not, generally, see a return to the research site to engage study participants in a discussion of study findings as a stage of the research process.

So, when we consider our project, we will want to ask ourselves these questions and think about how we will address the political issues that emerge from answers to these questions. If we are familiar with the site we will need to limit the influence of colleagues on the interpretation of findings while maintaining their commitment to the study. If we are using data that the agency collects, we need to reflect on how that data was collected and whether it changes our interpretation of the research question. If we accept limitations on reporting findings, we need to review the impact on the usefulness of the study. Often there is little we can do about the politics of the research project but we should make sure that we are at least aware of the issues and try to address them.

Moving on to post positivism we remind ourselves that the purpose of this approach is to develop the problem focus in a naturalistic setting. So it does not have the same political issues as positivism. We should be aware of the issues discussed above. However, the political issues for post positivists relate more to a worldview that is a combination of assumptions about the researcher being more powerful than the respondent and an intense social engagement between researchers and study participants that implies a partnership. The post positivist can consult with participants but he or she keeps the power to decide which data shall be collected and how data will be used. Post positivists attempt to curb the influence of their values on the research project and maintain the stance that the researcher, if careful, will not affect the research setting. Thus, for the post positivist, study participants are a source of data. They are not collaborators in the project. For example in the Young and Creacy (1994) study, it needed to be made clear that the artwork and poems that were being produced in sessions on building children's self esteem were being used as data to discuss the hopes and aspirations of the children and would be reported in a research report to an academic setting. This was a decision made by the researchers and the university, not by the study participants. The developing relationship between the researcher and study participants at the research site can often disguise this political reality and so all parties to the study may need to be reminded from time to time during the study.

Of course, everything about critical theory research is political: the choice of ideology, the teaching-learning process, and the action to promote empowerment. In fact the explicit political agenda of critical theory research is one of its strengths. It openly defines power relationships in the research setting, takes action to address them and then reports back to the community on the impact of the action. Meanwhile the relationship between the researcher and the researched is an action partnership. Thus the political issues that are associated with this approach are not the differential power relationship between us and our study participants but, more likely, the potential for conflict and emotional responses to the actual study. The political issues highlighted by this approach are likely to generate emotional responses to injustice and the success or failure of action for empowerment. We will need to think through a responsible plan for these experiences in partnership with study participants. For example, in our example study of eating disorders in teenage girls, (Christopulos, 1995) the high school students in the study needed to be aware of, and ready to discuss, the impact of adopting feminist interpretations of issues on both their friends and teachers. Would they be seen as "trouble makers"? Would they be laughed at by their teenage friends for articulating a political stance? How could they prepare for this? In the transportation study (Millet and Otero, 2011), community members needed to be ready for the impact of becoming more "high profile" on their immigrations status. The researchers did not ask about this status but did warn community members to be aware of the impact of taking action, should they be undocumented.

The politics of a constructivist study are negotiated before the study starts. Study sponsors commit to the constructivist process that requires, sharing of power, honesty and an intense commitment. If these conditions cannot be agreed to then the study cannot commence. The constructivist commitment to developing true partnerships with study participants and explaining the process and product of the research during initial negotiations with the site is a powerful strategy. It practically eliminates the possibility of colluding with study sponsors to produce favorable findings since the concept of favorable or unfavorable findings does not make sense. In the constructivist context there is an assumption that the shared constructions will identify both areas of agreement and areas of disagreement between stakeholders, and a plan for action to improve the situation. Even if stakeholders tend to agree that a particular program or issue is being handled badly, the commitment of the stakeholders is to building a joint construction of solutions and action strategies for progress rather than as assessment of failure or success. At the end of the study an agenda for action that addresses collaboratively the areas of agreement and disagreement emerges. If it becomes impossible to do this because of the politics of the research setting, this outcome is reported and explained.

Diversity Issues

Like any other social work practitioner, as social work researcher we must deliver services that acknowledge and engage the diverse characteristics and contexts of study participants, who are our clients, at both the micro and macro levels of human organization. During the engagement and assessment phases of the project we develop the question and identify the unit of analysis, the unit of observation, the people who will participate in the study, and the research setting. These can be individuals, families, groups, organizations or communities. The unique characteristics of these human beings in various settings who are "sources of data" should be immediately considered. What is their history? What are their demographic characteristics? What are their cultural norms? What is their history with being involved in research projects? How will their unique identities be acknowledged, honored, and respected during the research project? What is their history with members of the researcher's socio-economic group?

Farmer and Bess (2010) note that relying on past literature and hypothesis testing models may lead us to focus on the "problems" of minority groups (often in relation to the dominant group) rather than focusing on strengths and resiliencies". (page 580). When talking about research with lesbians and gay men, Martin and Knox (2000) discuss problem development and the role of established theories in promoting misinformation. They note that, until recently, theories of sexuality had an implicit assumption that heterosexuality was normal while homosexuality was either abnormal or just did not exist. We can screen the literature for erroneous assumptions about diversity by asking the questions in figure V.2, adapted from questions on the elements of thought from the Foundation for Critical Thinking (Paul & Elder, 2004), about each reading that is used to develop the research focus facilitates this review. The answers to these questions will help raise our consciousness about the diversity issues associated with our project as we develop our research question(s) and hypothesis(es) complete our literature review, and develop our theoretical orientation.

Figure V.2
Criteria for Reviewing a Reading's Assumptions about Diversity

1. What was the purpose of the reading, does this purpose include a discussion of diversity (gender, ethnicity, age, sexual orientation, income levels, education levels, and so on)?
2. What evidence was used to develop the reading's purpose, did that evidence include acknowledgement of diverse groups and did it make implicit assumptions about diverse groups?
3. What inferences were made using that evidence, were these inferences appropriately or inappropriately extended to diverse groups?
4. What are the concepts and/or variables, in the reading and how are they defined, was the data collection instrument used to operationalize these variables tested on diverse groups?
5. What assumptions are being made in those definitions and what do those assumptions say about diverse groups: anything?
6. If this reading is accepted as valid knowledge, what are the implications for members of diverse groups?
7. What point of view has been taken in this reading, are there other possible points of view on this topic that tend to be held by members of diverse groups?
8. Overall, what does this reading assume or demonstrate regarding diversity?

When we begin to engage the gatekeepers to our research site and start to consider further likely engagement with study participants we will need to reflect on another set of diversity issues. We will need to understand the following differences between the researcher and the researched:

- *Differences in appearance*: not only dress but the more significant differences of gender, ethnicity, age, etc. What are the differences between researchers and researched and how will they be recognized, discussed, understood, and addressed so that the research project can be effectively carried out from the beginning conceptualization stages to the final reporting stage; from engagement to termination and follow up?

- *Differences in perceived power* over the situation: male versus female, minority versus majority ethnic identity, and vulnerable client versus researcher with status. Can a partnership be formed between the researcher and the researched by acknowledging and reflecting on these differentials? What arrangements of mutual benefit can be brokered?

- *Differences in assumptions and norms* about the topic being researched and the actual implementation of research: For example, there will be differences in assumption about what a happy child looks like, or what a healthy functioning family looks like, or the extent of involvement in groups and communities, or organizational norms and cultures. How are these being identified and integrated into the study processes?

- *Differences in norms about appropriate behavior*: How will researcher and researched recognize and honor each other's code of behavior both formal and informal? What strategies will be used to explore and understand these assumptions? For some, the formal and transitory engagement of filling out a survey to give personal information will be offensive and ineffective in the end. Feminist researchers have repeatedly stressed women's reticence to give any meaningful data in such situations. On the other hand, for some, the intense engagement of observation and in-depth interviews is intrusive. How will the researcher become knowledgeable about these assumptions and accommodate them?

- *Differences in perspective*: Is the researcher looking at things as an outsider looking inward or an insider looking outward? How will this affect the exchanges between the researcher and the researched and what can be done about these effects?

- *Differences in language, or vocabulary within a language*. If language is the difference, how will interpreters be used? If vocabulary (research terms versus informal language; or informal street talk versus formal language) is the issue, who's language will be used and who will be accommodated?

- *Differences in History*: what is the immigration experience of the researcher's ethnic group compared to that of the study participants? What is each group's historical experience in the country they now live in? Will this history have an impact on data gathering?

Evans et al (2011) give some useful advice about differences when they summarized their experience with "the micro-counseling approach", which has been used throughout the world with over 500,000 professionals. They note that they have learned through wide use of their model and cultural feedback (page 15) that attending and listening have the following cultural differences.

- *Eye Contact:* The direct European North American pattern of eye contact is considered intrusive and rude in some cultures. Many Native Americans, Latinos/Latinas, and people from other countries prefer less eye contact. For some cultures a reverse pattern is considered appropriate. You should gaze at the person while talking and avoid eye contact when listening.

- *Body Language and Space:* The shaking of the head for "yes" or "no" varies across different cultures. For many, an arms-length is a comfortable distance between people. However some, such as those of recent Arab descent, may be comfortable with a closer 6 to 12 inches separating people engaged in conversation and others (such as Australian aborigines) may need a distance.

- *Verbal Following*: Being direct about listening and reflecting back what you hear may not be appropriate for Chinese Canadian or Japanese American participants in a study.

- *Listening First, then Acting*: For some groups, action is needed early to develop trust. For example, in a critical theory study it may be necessary to take some action during the ideological analysis stage. This could be as simple as contacting key informants suggested by the group. The point is to show that the researchers are capable of doing more than just gathering data.

At the Assessment and Engagement stage of positivist research there are a number of diversity issues to be aware of relating to stereotypes embedded in the literature and differences between researchers and study participants. We need to develop awareness of these issues when developing our research projects and make sure that we address them.

The post positivist researcher needs to be aware of the same diversity issues that were discussed above for positivists. The intense involvement with study participants demands a commitment to sensitivity and competence in addressing the diversity issues that are identified there. Explicit training in the history and current manifestations of differences for specific sub populations are essential elements of the post positivist's preparation if we are to engage study participants to the extent that is required by this approach to research.

Diversity issues discussed above also apply to the critical theory researcher. In addition the critical theorist needs to be aware of issues related to the macro level of human organization, Chavez et al (2008) refer to action research with communities as Community Based Research (CBR) and in this context they note three kinds of racism:

- institutionalized racism, which is exhibited through differential access to services such as quality education and health care as well as to information and power;

- personally mediated racism, which is exhibited through discrimination and prejudice; and

- internalized racism, which is exhibited through peoples' belief in negative messages about their own race or ethnicity.

CBR, reliant as it is on community collaboration, addresses these forms of racism through:

1. being aware of the class and ethnic makeup of the research team;

2. being aware of the potential to stereotype community members as "insiders" with deficits that need to be addressed by the researcher as an "outsider" who has privilege and knowledge; and

3. making it possible for researchers of color to acknowledge their own experiences with racism and being in the role of outsider or insider.

When discussing "white privilege" Chavez et al. (2008) quote Omni (2000) who states, "Whites tend to locate racism in color consciousness and find its absence in color blindness. In so doing, they see the affirmation of difference and racial identity among racially defined minority students as racist. Black students, by contract, see racism as a system of power, and correspondingly argue that they cannot be racist because they lack power". (page 99). With this perspective in mind, these authors' recommendations regarding carrying out CBR include the following: (paraphrased from pages 101-102),

- Practice cultural humility and be aware of your personal cultural lens;

- Acknowledge the diversity within racial and ethnic groups. Expand data collection to include questions on ancestry, migration history, and language. Be attentive to the increasing heterogeneity of racial/ethnic groups and rethink the nature and types of research questions asked;

- Acknowledge that race is a social construct, not a biologic determinant, and model race as a contextual variable in multivariate analysis;

- Address the present-day existence and impacts of racism not only as variables to measure but also as lived experiences within the research process as the study is carried out;

- Emphasize the "intersectionality" (e.g. Black women versus Black men or poor Latino women versus wealthy Latino women) of race, gender, age and class to examine how the resultant different categories engage with racism and with each other;

- Use the research process and findings to mobilize and advocate for change to reduce disparities and enhance race relations;

- Listen, listen, listen. Pay close attention and try to recognize both hidden (discourse by those without power when they are not in the presence of those with power) and public transcripts (the official discourse that happens in the presence of those with power); speak out about white privilege and racism;

- Accept that outsiders cannot fully understand community and interpersonal dynamics. Do not, however, let this stop you from taking part; and

- Recognize that privilege, especially white privilege, is continually operating to some degree and creating situations of power imbalance. Such an understanding is crucial in honest, ongoing communication that builds trust and respect. Build true multicultural working relationships, in partnership mode, develop guidelines for research data collection, analysis, publication, and dissemination of research findings.

It is clear that we must train ourselves in both the micro diversity issues discussed above and macro diversity issues discussed here, which will inevitably surface in a critical theory study.

Given the openness of the constructivist process, issues of diversity, can be acknowledge throughout the study. It is important to review the discussion of diversity above, however, so that we develop sensitivity and cultural competence. One interesting diversity issue for constructivists is the use of interpreters. How will this affect data gathering? The presence of the interpreter is assumed to affect the construction being offered. The constructivist researcher, when contracting with an interpreter would need to know something of that interpreter's experience and perspective regarding the research focus. Monolingual Spanish speaking participants were not included in our example HIV-AIDS study. However, the region in which that study was carried out is at least 30% Hispanic. The student researcher did not have the resources to hire a Spanish/English interpreter. If she had then she would have assumed that interpreter had feelings and partial knowledge about the topic. She would have explored the interpreter's construction and paid attention to its possible influence on the interpretation process. With written surveys we use "back translation" to test if questions mean the same thing in different languages. This is a process where we write the questions in one language, say English, and then translate them to another language, say Spanish, and then translate the Spanish version back to English and compare this with the original questions. This may well be the approach the constructivist takes with developing a construction using interpreters. The interpreter's translation of an interview would be translated back to the study participants language. The participant would review the construction and make any changes. This would then be translated back to English and the process would continue until the participant was satisfied with the translation. Overall, diversity issues are addressed in the open collaborative way that the constructivist approach requires. Awareness and sensitivity must of course be developed and then any diversity issues need to be addressed collaboratively with study participants.

Technology Issues

Before we finish and move on to Part 2 and how we will plan to carry out our research project, it would be useful to briefly consider the role of technology in Assessment and Engagement. We have already seen how the internet makes our literature search faster and more efficient. However, we can also consider how technology might also enhance Engagement activities. Apart from using phones for initial contact arrangements, this is the stage where human contact is crucial. We need to build a foundation of trust and commitment to the project with research site gatekeepers and study participants. Gatekeepers and participants, though, are busy people and will not have time for protracted meetings. Thus, once initial personal comfort has been established phone and email contact can assist development of the relationship. A further possibility for ongoing efficient communication is the use of communication software allowing people to converse and see each other while sitting at their computers at a distance from each other. As engagement proceeds, such virtual human contact can be integrated with face-to-face meetings with individuals and groups. Also, social networking sites can be set up for ongoing communication between our study participants and us. Fawcett et al. (2003) note that the U.S. Department of Health and Human Services supports ongoing list servs for those working on disability, aging, and long term care. Also, the U.S. Administration on Aging has an on line guide with guidelines for engaging undeserved or underrepresented groups at http://www.aoa.gov/prof/adddiv/cultural/addiv_cult.asp

After initial engagement, both critical theorists and constructivists need to develop a more intense engagement that includes a commitment to a partnership based on a set of values and commitment to action. Fawcett et al (2003) discuss the use of Internet tools when developing this intense relationship with community groups. These authors have developed an online resource for community change (Fawcett et al: 2000) that can be found at http://ctb.ku.edu With reference to understanding community context and collaborative planning, these authors offer six core competencies. These are creating and maintaining coalitions, assessing community needs and resources, analyzing community-identified problems and goals, developing a framework or model for change, developing strategic action plans, and building leadership. Creating and maintaining coalitions, parallels the engagement phase of research discussed in this book. Such coalitions are built at both the micro and macro levels of human interaction. These authors cite web site containing resource information that can be downloaded by researchers or community members looking for help with group discussions of community problems such as http://www.communityhlth.org/communityhlth/index.jsp and http://www.ncl.org) These resource are not a substitute for engagement skills but they can enhance and inform the engagement process.

This concludes our discussion of the Assessment and Engagement stage of the research process for our four paradigms. We have reviewed four different approaches to beginning our research project and seen how these four different worldviews lead us to alternative perspectives on the role of Engagement in research and how to ask research questions. We have also reviewed important cross-cutting issues. We can now move on to Part 2 and how we make a plan for implementation of our research project.

Adler, P.A. & Adler, P. (1994). "Observational Techniques" In (Eds.) Denzin, N.K. and Lincoln, Y.S. *Handbook of Qualitative Research.* Thousand Oaks, CA: Sage

Angrosino, M and Rosenberg, J. (2011) "Observations on Observation" in (Eds.) Denzin, N.K. and Lincoln, Y.S. *The SAGE Handbook of Qualitative Research.* Thousand Oaks, CA: Sage

Becker, J. E. (1994) *A Constructivist study of the social and educational needs of homeless children.* San Bernardino, CA: School of Social Work CSUSB

Berg, B.L. (2008). *Qualitative Research Methods for the Social Sciences.* Boston: Allyn Bacon.

Brown, L.B. & Strega, S. (2005) *Research as resistance.* Canadian Scholars' Press: Toronto.

Brown, L.E. (2011) Spirituality's Role in the Interaction Between Child Welfare and Black Families. San Bernardino: Department of Social Work and Social Ecology, Loma Linda University.

Brueggemann, W. G. (2006). *The practice of macro social work.* (3rd Edition) Belmont, CA: Thomson.

Chavez. V., Duran, B., Baker, Q.E., Avila, M., Wallerstein, N. (2008) The dance of race and privilege in community based participatory research. In Minkler, M & Wallerstein, N. (Eds.) *Community based participatory research.* San Francisco: Jossey-Bass.

Christopulos, J. (1995) Oppression through Obsession: A Feminist Theoretical Critique of Eating Disorders. San Bernardino, CA: School of Social Work, CSUSB

Crabtree, B.F., Miller, W.L. (1999). *Doing Qualitative Research.* Thousand Oaks, CA: Sage

Evans, D. R., Hearn, M.T., Uhlemann, M.R., Ivey, A.E. (2010) *Essential Interviewing: A Programmed Approach to Effective Communication.* Belmont, CA: Brooks Cole-Thomson Learning

Erlandson, D. A., Harris, E. L., Skipper, B. L., & Allen, S. D. (1993). *Doing naturalistic inquiry.* Thousand Oaks, CA: Sage.

Farquhar, S. & Wing, S. (2003) Methodological and ethical considerations in community-driven environmental justice research. In M. Minkler & M. Wallerstein (Eds.) *Community-based participatory research for health.* Pages 221241. San Francisco: Josey-Bass.

Fawcett, S. B., Schultz, J.A., Carson, V. L., Renault, V.A., Francisco, B.T. (2003). Using internet tools to build capacity for community based participatory research and other efforts to promote community health and development. In M. Minkler & M. Wallerstein (Eds.) *Community-based participatory research for health*. Pages 155-178. San Francisco: Josey-Bass.

Finn, J.L. and Jacobson, M. (2008). *Just Practice: A Social Justice Approach to Social Work*. Peosta, Iowa: eddie bowers publishing.

Guba, E. G. (1981). Criteria for assessing the trustworthiness of naturalistic inquiries. *Educational Communicatiojn and technology Journal, 29*, 75-92

Harvey, D.L. & Reed, M.H. (1996) "The culture of poverty: an ideological analysis. In *Sociological Perspectives*. 465, Vol 39, No 4 pages 1-20.

Hazenfeld, Y (2010) *Human services as complex organizations*. Thousand Oaks: Sage

Hogan, P. (1995) *A Constructivist study of Social Work's Involvement with HIV-AIDS*. San Bernardino, CA: School of Social Work, CSUSB,

Hope, A. & Timmel, S. (1999). *Training for Transformation: A Handbook for Community Workers*. London, UK: Intermediate Technology (ITDG Publishing)

Kelly, G. (1995). *A Constructivist Second Year Study of the Social and Educational Needs of Homeless Children*. San Bernardino, CA: School of Social Work, CSUSB.

Kincheloe, J.L., McLaren, P., & Steinberg, S. R. (2011) Critical Pedagogy and Qualitative Research. In *The Sage Handbook of Qualitative Research*. [pages 163-177) Thousand Oaks, CA: Sage.

Lincoln, Y. S., & Guba, E. G. (1985). *Naturalistic inquiry*. Newbury Park, CA: Sage

Martin, I. M. and Knox, J. (2000) Methodological and Ethical issues in research on lesbians and gay men. In *Social Work Research* 24 (1) pp. 51-59.

McNevin, M (2011) *How Do Heteronormative Perspectives Affect Same-Sex Parents?* San Bernardino, CA; School of Social Work, CSUSB, M.S.W. student research project

Millet, K. R., and Otero, L. R. (2011) The North Shore Public Transportation Dilemma: How Local Sociopolitical Ideologies, Ethnic Discrimination And Class Oppression Create Marginalization, And A Community's Quest For Social Justice. San Bernardino, CA; School of Social Work, CSUSB.

Moynihan, D. P (1965) The Negro Family: The Case For National Action. Office of Policy Planning and Research, United States Department of Labor, March 1965

Neuman, W.L. and Kreuger, L.W. (2003) *Social Work Research Methods: Qualitative and Quantitative Applications.* Boson: Allyn and Bacon.

Paul, R & Elder, L. (2004) *The miniature guide to critical thinking: concepts and tools.* Dillon Beach, CA: Foundation for Critical Thinking.

Payne, M (2005) *Modern Social Work* Theory Chicago: Lyceum

Potts, K., & Brown, L. (2005) Becoming an anti oppressive researcher. In, Brown and Strega (Eds.) *Research as Resistance.* Canadian Scholars' Press: Toronto.

Riech, J. R. (1994). Psychotherapy Encounters Curanderismo: Implications for Clients Treated in the United States by Culturally Insensitive Social Workers. San Bernardino: School of Social Work, CSUSB

Ruttman, D., Hubberstey, C., Barlow, A., & Brown, E (2005). Supporting young peoples' transitions from care: reflections on doing participatory action research with youth from care. In, Brown and Strega (Eds.) *Research as Resistance.* Pages 153-180Canadian Scholars' Press: Toronto.

Schulz, A., Israel, B.A., Parker, E., Lockett, M., Hill, Y., Wills, R. (2003) Engaging women in community based participatory research for health. In Minkler, M. & Wallerstein, N. (Eds.) *Community based participatory research for health.* San Francisco: Jossey-Bass

Strauss, A & Corbin, J. (2008) *Basics of Qualitative Research.* Thousand Oaks, CA: Sage (3rd Edition.

Stringer, E.T. (2007). *Action Research.* Thousand Oaks, CA: Sage.

Talsher, G. (2003. "A threefold ideological analysis of Die Grunen: from ecologized socialism to political liberalism?" In *Journal of Political ideologies* 8(2) pages 157-184

Torres, K (2007) *An Insight Into The Experience Of Parolees.* California State University, San Bernardino, CA: School of Social Work, CSUSB

Turner, F. (2011) *Social Work Treatment: interlocking theoretical approaches.* (Fifth Edition). Oxford: Oxford University Press

Tutty, L. M., Rothery, M.A. Grinnell, Jr. R.M. (1996). *Qualitative Research for Social Workers.* Boston: Allyn and Bacon

Wethington, E. (2003). "Research protocols grounded in ethics". In *Human Ecology.* December.

Young, M.L. and Creacy, M. (1995) *Perceptions of Homeless Children.* San Bernardino CA: School of Social Work, CSUSB, M.S.W. student research project.

Engagement Phases in Millet, K. R., and Otero, L. R. (2011)

Engagement Phase One

Engagement phase one was implemented on April 28, 2010. On this date the researchers and five fellow California State University of San Bernardino (CSUSB) cohort members participated in a community resource fair located at the Mecca Family and Farm worker Resource Center in the town of Mecca. This culturally traditional day called Dia del Nino, or Day of the Child, reveres the importance of health and education of children. The researchers participated by having an interactive booth with games for children and provided adult community members with information regarding the local transportation dilemma. This permitted the researchers to establish a presence in the community as well as provide a platform by which community members were able to divulge information about the existence of a problem in relation to transportation and how the problem affected them personally. Community members were also given information about the possible research topic and the need for community participation to successfully resolve the problem. The researchers also solicited community member contact information such as telephone numbers and email addresses for future community participation at events.

Engagement Phase Two

The second engagement phase consisted of a community barbeque located at Reyes Market in North Shore on July 10, 2010. The market is the only market located within the unincorporated town limits and is considered to be a communal space frequented by most of North Shore community members. The owner of Reyes Market was approached before hand and made aware of the research topic. He provided additional information about community dynamics such as prevalent community leaders and prior attempts to resolve the transportation issue. He also established himself as a valuable ally and granted the researchers permission to hold community events at his local as well as post advertisement posters for all events at the store. This event was once again implemented to establish researcher presence and to continue to build rapport with community members as well as gather more community support and contact information. The event consisted of music from a live disc jockey (researcher number two) accompanied by hot dogs, popcorn, and water. Propaganda and fliers for the following community event (engagement phase three) was also given to all community members. The event was motivationally invigorating yet physically taxing as barbeque event was held in 110 degree sweltering heat. The community was very receptive to the researchers and the need for a public transportation system was confirmed through various conversations held with community members. Seventy-three community members provided their contact information.

Engagement Phase Three

The third engagement phase consisted of a community meeting at the North Shore Yacht Club on July 31, 2010. Community members that provided their contact information at previous outreach events were contacted and asked to attend a community gathering to discuss the lack of a public transportation system in their community. Twenty-five community members attended the event. Topics discussed included the need for community solidarity in the form of participation and dedication, the importance of perseverance, a brief outline of the *policy change process, and information about the SunLine Transit Agency such as their mission statement, the importance of public transportation and the identification of key stakeholders.*

Engagement Phase Four

During the fourth engagement phase the researchers and a fellow CSUSB cohort member attended a food bank event held at the North Shore Yacht Club on October 29, 2010. A community member that participated at the July 31st meeting reported that many community members frequent the food bank and that it would provide an ideal platform to inform several community members about the research project. At this event the researchers spoke with all community members in attendance, provided research topic information and solicited additional community contact information for participation at upcoming community events. Sixty-one community members provided contact information.

Engagement Phase Five

The fifth engagement phase was a second community meeting held at the North Shore Yacht Club on November 20, 2010. All community members that provided contact information at all prior events were contacted and asked to attend the community meeting. The teaching-learning phase was enhanced at this meeting as the researchers recapitulated the SunLine Transit Agency informational packet and policy change flow chart (Appendix C). Forty community members attended the meeting.(pages 56-60)

Part 2

Planning

Design and Sampling

Contents

> Part 2 discusses Planning in relation to positivism, post positivism, critical theory and constructivism. Each paradigm is discussed in a separate chapter and important cross cutting themes are discussed in the final chapter:
>
> Chapter I: Positivism
> Chapter II: Post Positivism
> Chapter III: Critical Theory
> Chapter IV: Constructivism
> Chapter V: Important Cross Cutting Issues
>
> **However, there is some overlap between the paradigm. Where an overlap is noted, there are links to the shared information.**

Planning focuses on the overall study design and sampling for each of our paradigms. As outlined in Table 2.1. The planning stage of our research project is when we begin to think about how we are going to carry out our study. It is a good time to start writing a proposal for our study. If we are using the positivist paradigm, writing the proposal is a logical task, since all planning is done before data gathering begins. However, if we are using one of the other three paradigms, our plan can change as we carry out our study and writing a proposal becomes a little less straight forward. For this reason we include an alternative structure for the proposal in Attachment A. This alternative structure is organized around the steps of the social work practice research model and facilitates a discussion of possible changes for each of these steps.

Table 2.1:
Design and Sampling Strategies for Each Paradigm

	Overall Design	Sampling
Positivism	Explanatory (Causal) Descriptive (Correlational)	Random Assignment Random Sampling
Post Positivism	Basic Applied Summative Evaluation Formative Evaluation	Purposive Sampling (15 alternatives)
Critical Theory	Teaching/Learning Process Action Plan	Representatives of Oppressed and Power Groups
Constructivism	Hermeneutic Dialectic Circle Action Plan	Maximum Variation, Purposive Sampling

97

In a plan, or design, for positivist research, we identify the question, hypothesis, research design, data collection strategy, and data analysis procedures before the study begins because these are guided by previous literature on our chosen research question. Any changes made during implementation of the study are seen as weakening the validity of the research findings and, well, just bad research practice. There are two kinds of positivist designs, **explanatory designs** that address causality and **descriptive designs** that address correlation

Explanatory designs are rooted in the discipline of psychology while descriptive design spring from the traditions of sociology. The explanatory or **experimental design** evolved from psychology's early history as a discipline that needed to prove that it was not just a philosophy or branch of metaphysics. Herbert Spencer (1902) when discussing *the principles of psychology* noted that psychologists study the reasons for the connections between stimuli from the external world and the responses of humans to those stimuli. Ernest Mach (1959) when talking about *the analysis of the sensations* linked this definition to the physical sciences and their related experimental research methodologies. This linking later fitted neatly with the evolution of behaviorism in the United States with its focus on the study of stimulus and response (Skinner, 1953; Watson, 1963).

The descriptive design aims to generate findings that can be generalized to a wider population than the sample included in the research project. It is a response to Emile Durkheim (1938), who, when laying out *the rules of sociological method*, stated that a scientific treatment is a treatment that demands such generalization. He further stated that for sociologists, causality is addressed through the comparative method and that "the method of concomitant variations or *correlation*" is *the* method of sociology. Although other thinkers such as J.S. Mill challenged these positions (Manic as, 1988) they are still apparent in the rationales offered today for the legitimacy of the survey design.

The **explanatory** design is the most robust positivist design and it follows procedures that meet the criteria for proving causality. It is also called a **causal** or **classical experimental**, design. This design addresses threats to **internal validity, i.e.** threats to the proof that the independent variable did indeed cause the change in the dependent variable. It:

- identifies independent and dependent variables;

- requires **random assignment** of research subjects to experimental and control groups where research subjects have an equal chance of being in either group so that both groups are the same; and

- describes procedures for manipulation of the dependent variable(s), and requires development of pre and post test instruments and time frames.

Descriptive or correlational designs, in contrast, address **correlational** relationships between independent and dependent variables, usually through large-scale surveys. Samples are preferably random, i.e. they are representative of the population being studied, but theses samples are not manipulated into control and experimental groups. They are surveyed using valid and reliable data collection instruments developed in advance of data collection. Descriptive designs do not address threats to internal validity, but they are considered to have stronger external validity, which means that the findings for such studies are generalizable to the population of interest. So to sum up, explanatory designs have strong internal validity while descriptive designs have strong external validity.

Explanatory Designs

An explanatory or classical experimental design aims to prove that the independent variable(s) caused changes to the dependent variable(s), and that no alternative explanations for changes in the dependent variable can be identified. In our examples of explanatory studies, introduced in Part 1, we want to prove that the two different employment training programs were the *cause* of differing employment experiences for TANF recipients in those programs, and we want to prove that the type of mental health clinic *caused* changes in the uptake of mental health services. To do this we need to set up a research design that allows us to exclude all alternative explanations for the relationship we observe between our independent variables and dependent variables. We measure changes in the dependent variable during the study and we prove that the independent variable caused those change because we have controlled for alternative explanations for these changes. Alternative explanations for those changes in the dependent variable are called "**threats to internal validity**."

Threats to internal validity are generally grouped under the following headings:

1. *History:* The **History** threat to internal validity happens when events that take place outside of the study, while the study is implemented, cause changes in the dependent variable. In our sample micro practice study, this event might be the opening of a new industrial plant in the neighborhood where TANF recipients were living that hired all TANF recipients regardless of training. In our example macro practice study, this might be a media campaign informing people about the range of services that local mental health departments offer that caused people to use more mental health services.

2. *Maturation:* The **Maturation**threat to internal validity happens whenchanges in the dependent variable are caused by the passage of time. In our micro practice study, this might be that TANF recipients, over time, simply had a better understanding of how to get and keep a job because time had passed and they simply literally had a more mature approach to the workplace. In our macro practice study, potential clients of mental health services might seek services because they have lived with their mental illness for longer.

3. *Testing:* The **Testing** threat to internal validity happens when the changes in the dependent variable are caused by participants being pretested on items that measure the dependent variable and are, therefore, made aware of potential changes they could make. In our micro practice study, being assessed for employability by employment specialists might have caused TANF recipients to pursue job search strategies that they were not aware of before being asked about them in the pretest interview. In our macro practice study, collecting aggregate statistics on service use in two counties might have led administrators to target their services more effectively.

4. *Instrumentation:* The **Instrumentation** threat to internal validity happens when changes in the dependent variable are caused by changes in the test instrument between the pretest and the posttest. In our micro practice study, TANF participants may receive a thorough employability assessment at the beginning of the study but may just receive a telephone call checking on their employment status at the end of the study. The two different ways of testing may cause changes in results. In our macro practice example, there might have been changes in the efficiency with which statistics on uptake of mental health services were collected between the pretest and posttest that caused changes in measurement of such service used.

5. *Statistical Regression:* The **Statistical Regression** threat to internal validity happens when changes in the dependent variable are caused by natural changes in the extremely high or extremely low ends of any distribution of numbers. Group scores, for example on income, cluster around the average score. That is why it is the average score. If participants in a study have extremely high or extremely low scores on a dependent variable, as a group, they will change their scores simply because they are outliers. In our micro practice study, we probably have participants with extremely low scores on poverty and employability. Their mean scores are likely to improve, if only slightly, because, as a group, they are far away from the averages core. In our macro practice study, the group of people with extremely low scores on use of mental health services is likely to increase its use of services *because* it is at the extreme low end of usage.

6. *Selection Bias:* The **Selection Bias** threat to internal validity happens when changes in the dependent variable are caused by the characteristics of participants in the study. In our micro practice example it may be that people who are more motivated to get a job chose the program that immediately places participants in employment, while those who were not as motivated chose to go to employment training. In our macro practice study, potential mental health clients in one of the counties may have had cultural or religious beliefs promoting a cultural norm that frowns upon the use of mental health services.

7. *Experimental Mortality:* The **Experimental Mortality** threat to internal validity happens when changes in the dependent variable are caused by participants dropping out of the study before it is completed. In our micro

practice study, TANF recipients who tend to be transitory populations living in marginal housing may be forced to move to another area. One of the counties in our macro practice study may experience a reduction in service use because people are leaving the county to live in a neighboring county with improved and more convenient services.

8. *The Effect of the Study:* The **effect of the study** threat to internal validity happens when changes in the dependent variable are caused by participation in the study. TANF participants in each of the training programs may learn employment tips from each other, so that the training being received by the two groups of participants starts to merge. Groups might begin a rivalry with each other once they discover they are being compared. The researcher might start to affect TANF recipients by subtly communicating the expectation that one group is going to be more employable than anther. In the macro practice study, these kinds of effects would be less likely because of the use of aggregate statistics and reduced personal contact between study participants and researchers.

The strength of an explanatory design is assessed by how well it controls for the threats to internal validity described above. We can best understand how the design allows us to control for threats to internal validity by reviewing a number of example designs as noted in table I.1

Table I.1
Positivists Research Designs

Design	Sample Question that would be answered	Threats to Internal Validity
One One Group Post Test Only X O	1. Are recipients of TANF employment training employed after the end of the training? 2. Are recipients of no training only TANF employment placement services employed at the end of the program? **(Two separate micro practice studies)** 1. What is the rate of mental health service use in the county with neighborhood clinics? 2. What is the rate of mental health service use in the county with a centralized clinic? **(Two separate macro practice studies)**	History Maturation Testing Instrumentation Statistical-Regression Selection Bias Experimental Mortality The effects of the study.
Two One group pretest posttest O X O	*The above questions as well as,* 1. What is the difference in employment for recipients of TANF employment training between the start of the program and the end of the program? 2. What is the difference in employment for recipients of no training only TANF employment placement services between the start of the program and the end of the program? **(Two separate micro practice studies)**	History Maturation Testing Instrumentation Statistical-Regression Selection Bias Experimental Mortality The effects of the study.

	1. What is the rate of mental health service use in counties with neighborhood clinics? 2. What is the rate of mental health service use in the counties with a centralized clinic? **(Two separate macro practice studies)**	
Three Two non Equivalent Groups, Pretest Posttest. O . X O O X O	*The above questions as well as,* 1. What is the difference in employment between TANF recipients who receive TANF employment training and TANF recipients who received TANF employment placement services only? 2. What is the difference in uptake of mental health services between counties with neighborhood mental health clinics and those with a centralized mental health clinic?	History Maturation Testing Instrumentation Statistical-Regression Selection Bias Experimental Mortality The effects of the study.
Four Two equivalent groups, pretest posttest (classic experimental design) R O X O R O X O	*The above questions as well as,* 1. What is the differential effectiveness on TANF clients of two approaches to employment training where one group receives training and the other receives no training and is simply placed immediately into a job? 2. What is the difference in uptake of mental health services between counties with neighborhood mental health clinics and those with a central mental health clinic?	Testing Instrumentation
Five Two equivalent groups, posttest only R X O R X O	1. Did the difference in employment programs cause[1] the differences observed in employment for TANF recipients who received theses services? 2. Did the difference in the structure of mental health service delivery cause the difference in service uptake observed?	

This table shows how we can develop a design that controls for all threats to internal validity. There are some practical problems with this design for our macro practice study that we will address in a moment. For the purposes of understanding the implications of each of these designs, however, let us walk our way through each of them.

In design one we simply measure employment in our micro practice study and uptake of services in our macro practice study after the independent variables have been implemented. We know the amount of the dependent variable at the end of the study but we do not know what caused that amount of employment or uptake of services. In design two, we measure employment and uptake of services both before and after the independent variable was implemented. At the end of the study we know

---

[1] Note: Causality is being assigned here because of the ruling out of threats to internal validity, the problem with assuming causality as a result of one study that rejects the null hypothesis is discussed below under data analysis

the difference in employment and uptake of services but, again, we do not know what caused that difference.

In design three we introduce comparison groups. One group **(the experimental group)** experiences the independent variable while the other group **(the control group)** does not. However, we have done nothing to check if the characteristics of these groups are similar. Thus we have, in the micro practice study, one group of TANF recipients receiving employment training and another receiving employment services only. We measure employment both before and after each group participates in its different programs. At the end of the program we can compare the employment rates of the two groups but we do not know what caused those differences. It may have been differences between the groups. The same with our macro practice study, we can compare the two counties' uptake of mental health services but we do not know what caused those differences.

In designs four and five we **randomly assign** study participants to each of the two comparison groups so we need to take a brief detour into a discussion of **random assignment** and what it means. To ensure that the researcher does not influence the composition of the two comparison groups to favor one of the employment programs or service delivery systems and make it appear to be more effective than it is, we need a systematic process for assigning study participants to the two comparison groups. Also, to be able to use statistically procedures based on probability theory to analyze our data discussed in Part 4, we need to know the probability of each study participant's being assigned to each of the two groups.

Random assignment is a process during which all study participants have an equal chance of being assigned to either the experimental group or the control group. The researcher can, for example, give all TANF recipients a number before the employment services begin and then place all those with an even number in the employment-training program and all those with an odd number into the employment services group. Or the researcher can use a table of random numbers, each of which has an equal chance of being included at any point in the table. You can generate a table of random number and see exactly what one looks like by going to a web site such as http://www.randomizer.org/form.htm.

The use of **random assignment** increases the likelihood that the two comparison groups in the study will be similar. Then we can rule out most of the threats to internal validity because, if any of those threats had been the cause of the change in the dependent variable, they would have had the same effect on each of our comparison groups. Thus the only explanation for differences between our two groups on the posttest of the dependent variable is the impact of the independent variable. To be really sure, though, we need to consider design five. In this design we have our two equivalent groups, but we do not pretest them so we can rule out the two remaining threats to internal validity, testing and instrumentation. If we need to know the difference between the pretest and the posttest, we can combined designs three and four and randomly assign participants to four comparison groups, two of which are pretested and two of which are not. This is known as a "**Solomon four-group design**."

These randomized designs work for our micro practice example, but you have probably been wondering about our macro practice example. We can't exactly randomly assign mental health clients to two different counties and uproot them for the duration of our study. But remember, this is a macro practice study; we are targeting service structure not individuals. The ideal way to carry out this study is to identify all counties within a given area, say a state. Then we would randomly assign each to implement either a centralized or local system of mental health clinics. Finally, we would measure service uptake in each of the groups of county service delivery systems. This method is as impractical as moving people out of their homes for the purposes of a research project. Each county has its own history, culture and resources for mental health services.

Thus, in this case we will need to do something called **matching**. This is not as statistically robust as random assignment, but it is the next best thing. As macro practitioners we will identify characteristics of counties we think are particularly appropriate for studying the delivery of mental health services. These might include counties' rates of chronic schizophrenia, dual diagnosed clients with both a mental illness and a substance abuse problem, and/or distribution of ethnic groups and sexes within a county. We will then make sure that counties with similar rates on these characteristics are matched: one with a centralized system of mental health services, and the other with a neighborhood system of mental health services. We then have our two comparison groups.

So far we have talked about comparison groups that are either equivalent or non equivalent. As you can probably see, getting two equivalent groups is not an easy matter. However, rather than give up on having a more robust design, we can approximate proof of causality with **a time series design.** With this design we can have one group or two groups, depending on the research question, and rather than do one pre test and one post test, we can start by repeating the pretest several times to get a baseline and then introduce the independent variable and, finally, repeat several post tests.

In our micro practice study we could have one group of TANF recipients for each of the employment strategies being used. We could assess their employment every week for six months before the programs begin, then introduce the employment strategies, and then assesses their employment for six months afterwards. We could then compare the trends in employment for the two groups and assume that– if there were a change in the employment trend after the employment strategy was implemented– the employment strategy had something to do with causing that trend. We cannot absolutely state the probability because we do not have random assignment, but we _can_ rule out those employment strategies as effective programs if nothing changes in the employment data in the six months after the intervention.

With this overview of explanatory designs, we can begin to decide whether this approach will answer the questions we developed in the Assessment and Engagement phase of our study. We've seen there are some practical issues to address when implementing a causal study, and we've suggested some remedies. However, if it is becoming clear that the explanatory design will not answer our question, then the alternative positivist design is the **descriptive or correlational** design.

Descriptive/Correlational Designs

You might have noticed that many of the designs outlined in the discussion above could address correlation. A social work researcher could go ahead and set up the above designs and prove a correlation between the independent variable and the dependent variable. However, with the strategies for selecting study participants associated with those designs, such a correlation would be true only for the actual study that showed the correlation and could not be generalized beyond the unique setting of the study. Indeed this is a problem with explanatory designs; their **internal validity** is strong, but their **external validity**– the ability to generalize to the total population of interest– is weak.

There are two ways we can generalize findings from a sample to a total population of interest. The first is to keep replicating a study until we arrive at a finding that is true in all relevant situations. The second way is to find a shortcut around such time-intensive repetition and identify a rationale for generalizing the findings of one study to a larger group of people: enter **probability theory,** which is the basis for making assumptions for predicting the likelihood that something will happen, combined with the characteristics of **sampling distributions**. The characteristics of sampling distributions are discussed here while probability theory is explained in more detail in Part 4 when we discuss the analysis of quantitative data.

Sampling Theory

Both Frankel (1983) and Rubin and Babbie (2011) show clearly how we can select various samples of people from a larger population of people and justify the assumption that what is true for the sample is true for the total population from which it was selected. We can make this assumptionusing the classical *theory of inference*. This theory suggests that one sample is a sample of 1 from the many possible samples. The larger this one sample, the more likely that its characteristics approximate the characteristics of the **population** from which it was selected, since it is more likely to be drawn from the samples clustered around the mean of samples.

Here is an example adapted from Frankel (2010) need permission where, to make the arithmetic more understandable, we will be considering samples of 2. Let us return to the example macro practice correlational study in table I.1 in Part 1. The research question is: how do the contrasting supervisory styles in two departments of children's services affect staff retention rates for social workers? Imagine that we are interested in six departments of children's services. Their hypothetical average staff retention rates for the last year are shown below in table I.2

Table I.2
Hypothetical retention rate of social workers in children's services departments

County Departments of Children's Services	Staff Retention Rate
1. A County in California	20%
2. A County in New York	40%
3. A County in Florida	70%
4. A County in Washington State	30%
5. A County in Wisconsin	60%
6. A County in Texas	50%

Mean = 45% and SD=17

The mean (average) retention rate for this **population** of six county departments of children's services is 45%. Now suppose we consider all the possible random samples of 2 that we can draw from this **population** of 6 children's services. There are 15 possibilities, shown in Table I.3.

Table I.3
Fifteen Possible Samples of 2 drawn from a population of 6

Column 1 Sample Number	Column 2 The two counties selected into the sample	Column 3 Staff Retention rates for the two counties	Column 4 The mean staff retention rates for the two counties	Column 5 Standard Deviation (square root of total of differences between scores and mean squared, divided by sample size)
1	1 and 2	20% and 40%	30%	15 squared = 225
2	1 and 3	20% and 70%	45%	0 squared = 0
3	1 and 4	20% and 30%	25%	20 squared = 400
4	1 and 5	20% and 60%	40%	5 squared = 25
5	1 and 6	20% and 50%	35%	10 squared = 100
6	2 and 3	40% and 70%	55%	10 squared = 100
7	2 and 4	40% and 30%	35%	10 squared =100
8	2 and 5	40% and 60%	50%	5 squared = 25
9	2 and 6	40% and 50%	45%	0 squared = 0
10	3 and 4	70% and 30%	50%	5 squared = 25
11	3 and 5	70% and 60%	65%	20 squared = 400
12	3 and 6	70% and 50%	60%	15 squared = 225
13	4 and 5	30% and 60%	45%	0 squared = 0
14	4 and 6	30% and 50%	40%	5 squared = 25
15	5 and 6	60% and 50%	55%	10 squared = 100

$$SD = \sqrt{(1750/15)} = 11$$

The distribution of means of hypothetical social work staff retention rates in the fourth column has some interesting properties. The mean of these means is 45, which is the same as the mean for the total population of 6 children's services agencies listed in table I.2. Also, if you look at the distribution of the means, 45% occurs 3 times and is the most frequently occurring mean. In addition, the values of the other means in column 4 range from 25 to 65, while the values of the actual staff retention rates for the six agencies range from 20 to 70. Thus the sample means in table I.3 tend to cluster around the actual mean more closely than in the original population of interest in table I.2. These means are plotted out in figure I.1 and they form a *bell shaped curve* (roughly)

Figure I.1
Distribution of Mean Retention Rates

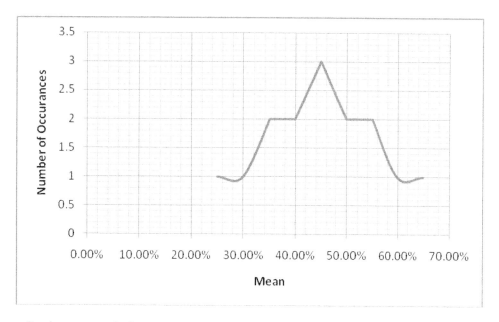

Such a curve is known as a **normal distribution** and shows visually how far each mean deviates from the overall mean. Usually the deviations of scores from their mean are transformed into a standardized statistic known as a **standard deviation (S.D.)**, which is the average deviation of all scores from their mean. You can see these in column 5 of table I.3. In any normal curve the following **confidence levels** can be assumed:

- 68% of the area falling under the curve of that distribution falls between plus and minus **1** standard deviation from the mean;

- 95% of the area falling under the curve of that distribution falls between plus and minus **2**standard deviations from the mean; and

- 99.9% of the area falling under the curve of that distribution falls between plus and minus **3** standard deviations from the mean.

We can see proof of these **confidence levels** in figure I.2.

Figure I.2.
Distribution of Retention Rates with Standard Deviations Marked

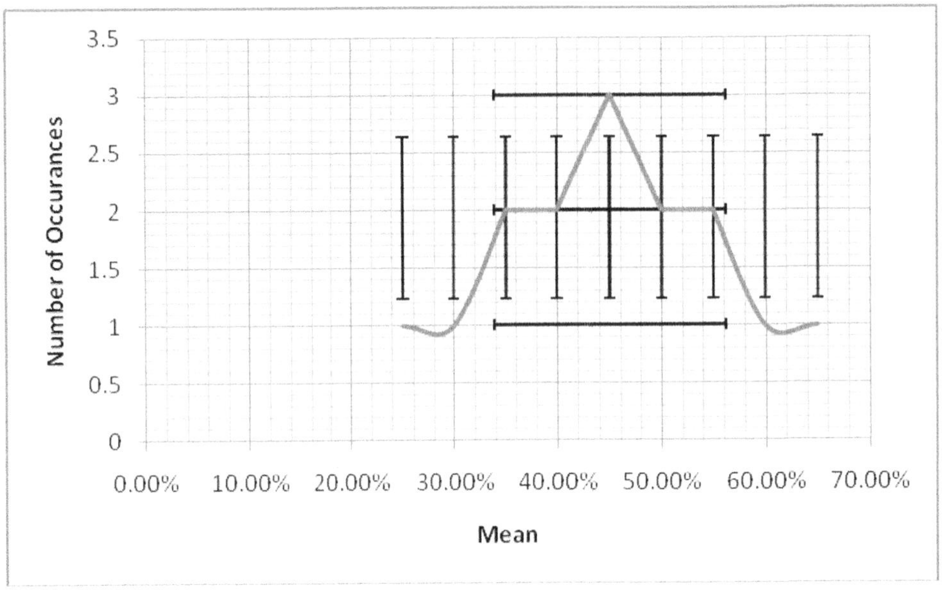

These properties of means drawn from samples as discussed above are known as the **Central Limit Theorem (CLT),** which states that the distribution of sample means tends towards a normal distribution. We can use the principles of this theorem to estimate how close the mean scores we calculate in our sample are to the true mean score in the population from which the sample was drawn. We do this by calculatingthe **standard error(S.E.).** When we calculate a standard error, we take into account the sample size in relation to the population size. According to Frankel (2010), it is calculated by the formula,

S.E. of Mean = √ [(1 – n/N) S (squared)/n]

Where n = the sample size, N = the size of the population of interest, and S squared divided by n is the **variance,** which is the sum of the squares of the difference between scores and the means divided by the sample size. So to return to our study of retention rates, imagine we are indeed studying staff retention rates for a population of six counties as listed above. We do not have the resources to study all the 6 counties, so we select one sample of two counties. The sample we choose happens to be sample 12, where the mean staff retention rate is 60% and we will use this as an estimate of the mean retention rate for all of the 6 counties, a number that is unknown to us because we only have data on one sample. So, we want to know how good an estimate this is, or how close the retention rate in our sample is to the average retention rate for all 6 counties. We find this by calculating the standard error for our sample. That is, we use the characteristics of our sample to calculate where that sample falls in the normal distribution of means for all samples. The calculation for this is,

√[(1-2/6)*200/2 = 8

A standard error of 8 tells us how large our confidence levels are. The mean score in our sample is 60% and so we can estimate that 68% of the retention scores in the population of interest fall one standard error above and below that mean, 95% of the population of interest falls 2 standard errors above and below that mean and 99.9% of the population falls 3 standard errors above and below that mean as illustrated in figure I.3

Figure I.3
Distribution of Staff Retention Rates with a mean of 60% and a
Standard Error of 8%

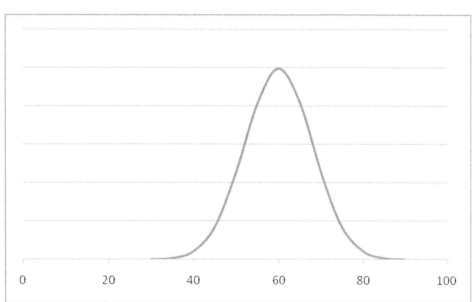

We can now use onesample to estimate the mean retention rate in all 6 counties using a **Bayesian** interpretation, which is a method of statistical inference that does not rest on the notion of repeated sampling. It reinterprets confidence levels as *credible intervals* that simply state the likelihood of a result. This method is possible because the likelihood function of a given statistic is assumed to be a random variable with a normal distribution of its own. So we can now state that there is a:

- 68% chance that the mean retention rate for all 6 counties is between 52% and 68%.

- 95% chance that the mean retention rate for all 6 counties is between 44% and 76%: and

- 99.9% chance that the mean retention rate is between 36% and 84%.

Because our sample size is small, the mean retention rate from our sample turns out to be a poor estimate of the mean retention rate for all 6 counties. According to Frankel, the CLT holds only if the sample is of a "reasonable size" (page 94). He suggests samples sizes of 30 or more. So, to generalize from a sample to a population of interest, we need a reasonable sample size. However, this is not the only thing we need; we also need a **random sample,** which leads us to a discussion of the implementation of sampling theory, i.e. sample design.

Sample Design

A **random sample** is a sample drawn from a population where all members of that population have an equal chance of being selected into the sample. This requirement allows us to generalize from a sample to a population. To understand the implications of the need for **random samples** we need to understand various sample designs and to understand these designs we need to review certain sampling terms, some of which we have already come across.

- **Element**– the unit about which the information is collected (individuals, families, groups, organizations or communities)

- **Population**– the total of all elements. For example if we are carrying out a study of individual social workers in the United States, the population is all social workers in the United States.

- **Study Population**– the total number of elements in the population from which the sample is selected. This is often different than the population because sometimes we don't know the total number in the population. So, to approximate the population we find a study population. For example we don't know exactly how many social workers there are in the United States. To approximate it we might get a list of all social workers who are members of the National Association of Social Workers (NASW). This would be our study population. However, note that moving from a hypothetical total population of social workers where randomization is assumed to a membership list where we cannot assume randomization. That is, we cannot assume that every social worker in the United States has an equal chance of being selected into the sample. This threatens the assumptions of probability and sampling theory that allow us to generalize from one sample to a population of interest. In this case we would be generalizing any study findings to members of NASW.

- **Sampling unit**– the same as an element in simple designs, but in a complex sampling design it can vary. It could be a selection of chapters of NASW at one stage and then a selection of individuals from those chapters at another stage.

- **Sampling frame**– the actual list of sampling elements or units from which a sample is selected. This may be the same as a study population but it could be different, the NASW membership list we use to select a sample from may be incomplete and only a partial listing of the membership of NASW.

- **Observation unit**– the source from which we collect data, which may or may not be the same as an element. For example the *element* might be the overall social work supervision style for a department of children's services, but the *observation unit* may be individual social workers within that department.

- **Variable**– the set of attributes of an element. For example, a social worker's supervision style can range from authoritarian to supportive.

- **Parameter**– a summary description (such as"mean") of a variable in the population. For example, the mean staff retention rate for all agencies in our population in the example above was 45%.

- **Statistic**– a summary description (such as "mean") of a variable in the sample. In our example county retention study above, the mean staff retention rate in the sample of 2 is 60%, that is a statistic

- **Sampling error**– the degree of error between a **statistic** and a **parameter.** In our example county retention study above, our mean staff retention rate is 60% in the sample, while in the population it is 45%.

- **Confidence level** and **confidence interval**– the limits within which we can assume our estimates of sampling error, and therefore of the parameter, are correct.

- **Credible intervals**– the percentage likelihood that a statistics is a parameter as used in the Bayesian interpretation.

Sample designs include:

- **Simple random sampling**: We give each element in the sampling frame a number and then use a table of random numbers to select the sample size required.

- **Systematic random sampling**: We give each element in the sampling frame a number and then make a structured selection in which we choose elements that are equally spaced apart, for example every tenth or fifth element in the list. If we need a sample of 100 from a sampling frame of 1,000, then we select every tenth element.

- **Stratified sampling**: We divide the sampling frame into groups and either randomly sample or systematically random sample each group. We might divide our sampling frame into three ethnic groups and then randomly sample elements within each group.

- **Multistage cluster sampling**: We might get a list of all Departments of Children's Services in the United States and stratify the list according to regions in the United States. Then within each region we would randomly select a sample of agencies and within each randomly select supervisors to find about their supervisory style.

To return to our examples of correlational studies, we have two study questions:

1. How does a family assessment tool assess families from three different ethnic groups (micro practice)?

2. How do contrasting supervisory styles in two different departments of children's services affect staff retention rates (macro practice)?

We are searching for answers to these questions by carrying out one study whose findings can be generalized to the populations of interest. In correlational, or survey research[2], the sample design is the key to our being able to do this. For each of our example studies we will need to select a random sample. Various alternative designs are shown in table I.4. First we operationalize the components of our sampling strategy and then we decide on the complexity of our design. We can choose to select a simple random sample, or insure representation of groups we are interested by choosing the more complex options.

Table I.4
Sampling Designs for Example Correlational Studies

Question	How does a family assessment tool assess families from three different ethnic groups (Hawaiian American, Japanese American, Anglo)?	How do the contrasting supervisory styles in two departments of children's services affect staff retention rates?
Concepts	Element= families Population= All members of three identified ethnic groups Study Population= All members of Catholic, Zen Buddhist and Anglican churches in Honolulu who have identified their ethnicity as one of the three in this study. Sampling unit=individuals Sampling frame=lists from churches where ethnicity is identified Observation unit=individuals who will report on families Variable = family functioning Parameter=scores on FAD in population of church members Statistic= scores on FAD in selected sample Sampling Error=difference between FAD scores in sample and in total list of church members	Element=Children's Services Departments Population= All Children's Services Departments in one region Study Population = All Children's Services Departments in one region Sampling Unit = All Children's Services Departments in one region Sampling frame = Listing of all Children's Services Departments from county websites. Variable = Staff Retention rates in each Department of Children's Services in one region Parameter = Percentage staff retention rate in each department of children's services in one region Statistic = Percentage staff retention rate in sample of departments of children's services. Sampling Error = Difference between percentage staff retention rates in all departments of children's services in one regions and the percentage staff retention

---

[2] Some authors suggest that causality is addressed in survey research by means of multivariate statistical analysis or through a time series design. However, the threats to internal validity with their roots in Hume's statement of causality cannot be ruled out using a survey design.

	Confidence level and Confidence interval=statement of sampling error in FAD scores Credible Level=Likelihood of FAD score in sample being correct.	rates in the sample of departments of children's services. Confidence level and Confidence interval = statement of sampling error in percentage staff retention rates Credible Level = Likelihood of sample retention rate being correct.
Simple Random Sample	Selection of 300 church members with identified ethnicities from list of church members using a table of random numbers. (See discussion and table below)	Selection of 20 agencies from list using a table of random numbers. (See discussion and table below)
Systematic Random Sample	Select cases at regular intervals from the list until a sample of 300 is selected.	Select cases at regular intervals from the list until a sample of 20 agencies is selected.
Stratified Sample	Divide list of church members into three ethnic groups. Randomly or systematically select a sample of 100 from each of the three divisions of the list.	Divided Departments of Children's Services into two groups, those with above average retention rates and those with below average retention rates. Randomly or systematically select a sample of 10 agencies from each division.
Multistage cluster sampling	Develop a list of all churches in Hawaii. Divide into regions where the densest populations of Hawaiian-Americans, Japanese-Americans and Anglos are found. Give all the churches in each region a number and randomly select five churches. Select a sample of 100 church members fore each of these churches for a total sample of 1,500 [(5*100)*3]	Develop a list of all Departments of Children's Services in the United States. Stratify the list according to regions in the United States. Then within each region divide departments into those with above average staff retention rates and those with below average staff retention rates. Select a sample of 10 agencies in each division for each region. Randomly select a sample of 10 supervisors within each agency for a sample total of 200. [20*10] for each region.

For question one, simple random sampling would not guarantee that we had the sufficient sample size for each ethnic group, neither would systematic random sampling. The stratified sample would give us the division into three ethnic groups that we need but we would not be addressing the issue of the random selection of the churches that are the source of our list. The multistage cluster sample does address all our needs but may well not be practical. Thus we see the balance that must be achieved between theoretical requirements of the question and the practical feasibility of achieving the desired sample. The multistage, cluster sample meets our theoretical needs. However, to implement it we would have to make some pragmatic decisions. One solution would be to divide the island of Oahu into three regions, find one church in each region that clearly serves the designated ethnic group, and then select our stratified sample from the three churches.

For question two, the simple and systematic random samples will not guarantee that we have a range of agencies with a range of staff retention rates. The stratified random sample will give us the range of agencies that we need but does not address the regional differences in the United States. The Multistage cluster sample

113

will give us the theoretically correct sample but may require excessive resources. If resources are limited then this same sample design could be used in just one region. Just as a reminder, though, once we move away from using the simple random sample, then the assumptions of normal distributions associated with probability theory and sampling theory may no longer hold true.

Once we resolve these issues and select our sample design, we will need to consider the size of our sample. Land and Zheng (2010) give guidelines for **statistical power analysis** that will determine the appropriate sample size before the study begins. They note that statistical power is determined bysix parameters;

1. **Power:** the probability of concluding that there is a relationship between explanatory variables *(independent variables)* and outcome variables*(dependent variables)* when there is no such relationship. A level of 0.80 is conventionally considered adequate;

2. **Effect size:** A measure of how much impact independent variables will have on dependent variables, 0.2 is considered low, 0.5 is considered medium, and 0.8 is considered large. Before the study is carried out we should use criteria for the sample size that assume a low effect size, and then if we eventually get a medium or high effect when the study is completed, our findings are even stronger. However, sometimes we need to raise the effect size because the size of the required sample becomes too large. This is explained in more detail below.

3. **Statistical significance level**: the criterion used to decide if the statistical analysis carried out shows a significant relationship between independent and dependent variables. A level of 0.5 is conventionally considered adequate.

4. **Sample size:** which is determined by the 3 parameters above.

5. **Degrees of Freedom of Independent Variable:** which is calculated by subtracting 1 from the levels of the independent variable. For example if we have the independent variable, supervision, with 5 different styles (or levels) as shown in Part 1 Table I.2, the degrees of freedom is 5-1=4

6. **Degrees of Freedom of Error;** which is found by using a pre prepared table which can be found in Marsden and Right (2010) on page 208 and matching the desired effect size (column "d') with the degrees of freedom across the top. The formula for deciding sample size is,

Degrees of freedom+degrees of freedom of error+1

So, with our supervision study as our example,

- we assume a power level of 0.08,

- we assume an effect size of 0.2.

- we assume a statistical significance level of 0.5,

- we know our degrees of freedom is 4, and

- table 3.6 tells us that our degrees of freedom of error is 1165 and so our sample size is:

$$4+1165+1=1170$$

This is quite a large sample. However, as we can see on table 3.6, if we raise the effect size to 0.51, then our sample size is reduced to

$$4+189+1=194$$

If this is looking too much like higher level math, there is another more pragmatic route that we can take to deciding on our sample size. Sudman (1983) collected data on average sample sizes. It turns out that national studies of people and households tend to have samples of 1000-1500 for a few subgroups and 2500 for many subgroups; regional studies have 200-500 and 1000 respectively. For samples of institutions the numbers for national studies are 200 to 500 and 1000 plus; and for regional studies 50 to 200 and 500 plus. Weinberg (1983) tells us that sample size must be adjusted to the task, time, cost of data collection and budget. Cochran (1954) reviewed the theoretical implications of using one particular statistic, the CHI square with small samples and developed the following rule "If no more than 20% of the cells have expectations (values) less than 5 then a single expectation (value) near 1 is allowable in computing chi square".

Given this data and advice, our example correlational studies would require the samples shown in table I.5 and I.6. For the micro study we have a sample of 300 and for the macro study we have a sample of 20.

Table I.5
Sample size for micro practice correlational question:
How does a family assessment tool assess families from three different ethnic groups?

	Hawaiian American		Japanese American		Anglo	
FAD Score	Below Norm	Above Norm	Below Norm	Above Norm	Below Norm	Above Norm
	50	50	50	50	50	50

Table I.6
Sample size for macro practice correlational question: How do contrasting supervisory styles in two different departments of children's services affect staff retention rates?

	Departments with high staff retention rates	Departments with low staff retention rates
Autocratic Supervision style	5	5
Facilitative Supervision style	5	5

To sum up, since the aim of correlational studies is to generalize findings from one sample to a larger population of interest, sample design incorporating probability theory and sampling theory is the key to developing a rigorous study. This facilitates calculation of the standard error between the sample and the population of interest. There are a number of strategies for selecting random sampling and the most appropriate sample will depend upon the research question.

Before we finish our discussion of positivism, we should note two forms of explanatory and correlational designs that tend to be most useful for social work practice researchers: program evaluation and single subject designs. Program evaluation contributes to macro practice research while single subject designs contribute to micro practice research.

Program Evaluation

A program evaluation is simply a research project that addresses a particular kind of macro practice research question. It can be explanatory or descriptive. Positivist program evaluations are divided into summative (outcome) and formative (process) evaluations. Outcome evaluations ask and answer the question, does the program work? Process evaluations ask and answer the question, how does this program work? Both of these types of evaluations use the designs identified in the discussions above. Weiss and Jacobs (1988), when discussing strategies for evaluating family programs, suggest that the program evaluation to be carried out depends on the developmental stage of the program to be evaluated. They identify five levels of evaluation that can be carried out as a program matures. Some are summative and others are formative.

Level 1: This is simply a needs assessment before the program is implemented documenting characteristics of proposed program, cost of program, community support for program and statistics describing the population to be served. This is essentially a "One group post test only" design. The group is the community and the posttest is the data on the community need for the program and the identification of services that will meet those needs.

Level 2: This is a formative study documenting the program's use, and its penetration into the target population. This kind of evaluation gathers data that justifies current expenditures and makes the case for any requests for increases in funding. This is essentially a version of a one-group pretest posttest design. The independent variable is the program and the extent of service to the target community is the dependent variable. The pretest was the needs assessment carried out in the level one evaluation. The posttest is the documentation of the community use of services

Level 3: This is a formative study of the program reviewing the mission and goals of the program, the characteristics of clients who receive services and which services they are using. This is to check whether the original mission and program should be revised now that the staff has experience with the actual implementation of the program. This is essentially a version of a one-group posttest design where the group is the program and the posttest is service use.

Level 4: With this level we move to summative outcomes. This is an outcome evaluation of success with individual clients. Data is collected on client need at the intake phase and then again at the end of the delivery of services. This is a one-group pretest posttest where the pretest is the client assessment at intake and the posttest is client assessment at termination of services.

Level 5: This is the final level and the one where the ultimate question is addressed, what it the program's impact? Generally it is a two-group comparison study of the effectiveness of the program. One group receives services and the other does not. Members of each group are pretested and post tested on progress with the problem being addressed. This is essentially the two group non-equivalent groups pretest posttest or, if possible, the classic experimental design. These authors suggest that this kind of evaluation should only be carried out when the program is up and running and the other tiers of evaluation have been completed.

Single Subject Evaluations

The single subject evaluation is a form of micro practice research project. It can be descriptive or explanatory. Rubin and Babbie (2011) describe a range of designs that basically suggest that the practitioner should collect baseline information on the target problem, which is the dependent variable, and then intervene while continuing to track scores on the dependent variable. The designs where only one client is being tracked are descriptive while the designs where two or more clients, who receive the intervention at different times, are being tracked and compared address causality since they offer evidence for ruling out alternative explanations for the changes in the dependent variable.

For example, we might be intervening with a client with anxiety; we may decide to use one of the many online anxiety tests such as the anxiety screen test at http://psychcentral.com/quizzes/anxiety.htm On this test you can score from 0 to 38 and up. The higher your score the more anxiety you are experiencing (don't try this at home). So we might decide to get a baseline score on this test with a client who is exhibiting anxiety. This baseline may be at the upper end of the scores. We would then decide to intervene and have perhaps weekly sessions with this client. We would then track scores on this test and, if our intervention is effective, scores would go down. If we had 2 or 3 clients with anxiety we might track each client's score on this test and, if scores went down for each client when we intervened, we would have data that suggests that our interventions are effective at the micro practice level. If score are not going in the "healthy" direction, we would then have data that suggests we need to reconsider our interventions.

In this chapter we have reviewed positivist study design and sampling procedures. We have reviewed the rationales and issues associated with various design and sampling strategies. We have also discussed two applications of these designs, program evaluation and single subject studies. Important cross cutting issues beyond those considered in Part 1 relate to diversity and technology need link and are discussed in Chapter V. Below is a summary of this chapter and positivist learning assignments. We can now move on to consider the Planning stage for post positivist research projects.

Summary of Chapter I
_____

- There are two kinds if positivist designs, explanatory (causal) and descriptive (correlational)

- The classical experimental design is the favored explanatory design because it controls for all threats to internal validity

- When implementing the classical experimental designs, practical issues may lead us to make modifications such as matching and time series designs.

- Descriptive (correlational) studies require the selection of random samples for strong external validity.

- The rationale for being able to generalize from one sample to the population of interest is developed from both the classical central limit theorem (CLT) and Bayesian theories of inference

- The key to being able to make such assumptions is the selection of a random sample because this allows the assumptions of the central limit theorem to be made regarding the prediction of a population mean from a sample mean using the standard error.

- There are a range of strategies for collecting random sampling that include simple random sampling, systematic random sampling, stratified random sampling, and multistage cluster sampling,

- Two commonly used adaptations of causal and correlational studies are program evaluations addressing macro practice questions and single subject designs addressing micro practice questions.

- The ethical, political, and diversity issues that need to be addressed in the Planning stage are similar to those addressed in the Assessment and Engagement stage

Positivist Learning Assignments
_____

1. Think of a research topic that interests you. Briefly describe a causal and a correlational design that would address that an aspect of that topic.

   a. Which level of social work practice are you researching, micro or macro?

   b. Identify any threats to internal validity in your causal design.

   c. Are there any practical problems with implementing this design?

d. How will you guarantee external validity in your correlational design? Is this feasible?

e. How will you select your sample and why will you use that particular sampling strategy?

2. Working in small groups, take one of the groups member's topics and discuss whether the designs do indeed answer causal and correlational questions about social work practice and discuss how easy or hard it would be to set up this design. Also, answer the "so what" question. How important are the answers to these questions to social work practice knowledge? Give reasons for your conclusions? Would your practice be improved if you knew the answer to these questions?

When planning data collection procedures for our post positivist research project we develop strategies that will uncover as many meanings as possible. Our plan includes sequences of interviews and/or observations and/or document review that comprehensively discover data addressing the research focus. In a study of gang life, for example, we may decide that participant observation is the most appropriate starting point for emersion in the topic. This might be intertwined with interviews with professionals who intervene with gangs, including law enforcement officials and various human service professionals. In time, in-depth conversations with family members and other members of the neighborhood might be our sampling and data collection strategy. Such intensive experiences will of course, require periods away from the gang experience for reflection and input from other experts. Thus the key to the planning phase is immersion in the topic to be studied, reflection on the most appropriate ways to gather data, and continual reappraisal in collaboration with other trusted experts.

Patton's (2002) division of research foci into four purposes on a continuum from theory to actioncan help us clarify and solidify our approach to our post positivist study. He suggests that research can be basic, applied, a formative program evaluation, a summative program evaluation, or action research[3]. Basic research is grounded theory development, as described by Strauss and Corbin (1990, 1998) that requires lengthy intensive fieldwork. Applied research takes the findings of basic research and applies them to real-world problems. Applied researchers are trying to understand how to intervene with and solve a problem in contrast to basic researchers who are trying to understand why that problem happened in the first place. Evaluation research assesses both the operations and the impact of the solutions to problems that have been implemented through policies and programs based on the results of basic and applied research. Action research aims to solve a specific problem within a program, organization, or community. The inductive, exploratory nature of post positivist research offers fresh approaches to each of these kinds of research. If we return to our example study of homeless children we can illustrate hypothetical post positivist approaches to each of these research modes as shown in table II.1adapted from Patton (2002) page 224.

---

[3] Action in this paradigm is not the same as action in critical theory and constructivist research where the action is seen as integral to implementing the research project.

Table II.1
Types of Research and their associated methodologies

Type of Research	Purpose	Question	Data Collection Strategies	Impact of Findings
Basic	To discover knowledge, to discover the truth	What are the variations in food and shelter experienced by family units in poverty and how do those variations affect the family unit? (this could be a local, national or international study)	A Combination of interviews, field observations, literature reviews and review of documents with a purposefully selected sample of families in poverty	An in-depth statement about variations in food and shelter for the sampled range of families in poverty.
Applied	Understand the nature and sources of human and societal problems	How can we intervene with family units in poverty to reduce homelessness among children? (this could be a local, national or international study)	A Combination of interviews, field observations, literature reviews and review of documents with a purposefully selected sample of families and children living in poverty, as well as human service practitioners who intervene with homeless children.	An in-depth statement about the needs of the sampled range of families and children in poverty, and services to address these needs.
Summative Evaluation	To determine effectiveness of interventions with a societal problem	What is the impact of this shelter program on homelessness among children in its service area?	A Combination of interviews, field observations, literature reviews and review of documents with a purposefully selected sample of shelter personnel, clients and other key informants identified by data gathering and analysis	An in-depth statement about what is and is not working in a specified shelter program.
Formative Evaluation	To improve the performance of interventions with a societal	How does this shelter program deliver services (qualifications of employees and volunteers, content of	A Combination of interviews, field observations, literature reviews and review of documents with a purposefully	An in-depth statement about the quality of services in a specified shelter.

	problem	services, timelines of services, focus of outreach, budgetary constraints, etc)	selected sample of shelter personnel	
Action Research	To Solve Problems in a program, organization, or community	What should we do to fix the problem with high school children at the shelter playing truant from school	A Combination of interviews, field observations, literature reviews and review of documents with a purposefully selected sample of shelter high school children, family members, school personnel and shelter personnel	Statement of and implementation of an action plan to address the problem of truancy

The type of research, purpose and the research question identified in the table above are fairly self-explanatory. They identify stages of a process: understanding an issue, identifying interventions with that issue, evaluating the impact of the intervention and maintaining the quality of that intervention, and taking action to address specific problems that have been identified. Having decided on a research purpose, we can develop the plan for implementing the study in terms of **units of analysis** and **purposive sampling**.

Units of Analysis

In post positivist research, ultimately, the unit of analysis is the whole entity being researched. However, while the study is being carried out, we identify various units of analysis. In our example homeless study, the unit of analysis was the children themselves. In table II.1, the unit of analysis varies between families, children, and human service practitioners. In our hypothetical example of basic research families in poverty are the unit of analysis and data is reported using families as the organizing entity. In our example of applied research, both families and children are the units of analysis. We may well hold an interview with the family but we can report data from the family as a group and specifically highlight the data from children as a sub category of data, since we are primarily aiming to make a statement about children in general but are acknowledging the children's family context. In our example of summative evaluation, the shelter program is the unit of analysis and a holistic approach is taken to gathering data on that program from shelter personnel, clients, and other appropriate key informants. For our summative evaluation example, the same holds true.

Thus the goal here is not to enumerate and compare findings for a class of people so that tested generalizable statements can be made. The goal is to make an in-depth statement about a particular research issue that enriches our understanding and offers general theoretical statements about the phenomenon. Indeed for post positivist researchers units of analysis go beyond human units and can be particular kinds of events, times in the day, week, month or season of the year for a particular program. Patton (2002) suggests that, "The key issue in selecting and making decisions about the appropriate unit of analysis is to decide what it is you want to be able to say something about at the end of the study" (page 229). In social work practice research, is it individuals, families, groups, organizations or communities or all of the above? For example, in our student study of homeless children, our unit of analysis was the children. The researchers, not only wanted to describe children's experiences of homelessness but they also wanted to offer social work practitioners some guidance on how to intervene with such children. Thus the level of practice being studies was micro practice interventions with individuals.

Purposive Sampling

Having decided on the type of research and the unit of analysis we now need to decide on a method of sampling. Who will be in the study? As a reminder, as post positivists, we accept the notion of an objective reality where the mechanics and patterns of human behavior can be identified, but we do not try to understand these mechanics through the testing of preconceived hypotheses about those patterns with representative samples. We see our research as discovering objective reality in a naturalistic setting and verifying reality through rigorous qualitative analysis. Thus the most appropriate approach to sampling is not random sampling but "purposive" sampling where we look for study participants who will give the most complete data about the study focus. To further illustrate, as Patton (2002) says for example, "if the purpose of an evaluation is to increase the effectiveness of a program in reaching lower-socioeconomic groups, one may learn a great deal more by focusing in depth on understanding the needs, interests, and incentives of a small number of carefully selected poor families than by gathering standardized information from a large, statistically representative sample of the whole program." (page 230).

Patton (2002) and Strauss and Corbin (2008) talk about purposive sampling in different ways. Patton talks about various strategies to gather purposive samples of people whereas Strauss and Corbin discuss sampling in terms of "representativeness of concepts and how concepts vary dimensionally" (page 144). They discuss sampling of the data that is being collected. This sampling of the data leads to the development of an understanding of the data and reveals the necessary direction for further data gathering. This is where we see the integration of data gathering and data analysis. For the purposes of clarity, Patton's approach to sampling will be discussed here. Strauss and Corbin's approach to sampling will be discussed in relation to qualitative data analysis in Part 4

Patton's approach to sampling identifies a group of people who have particular experience of a social phenomenon and a range of strategies for selecting a purposeful sample from that group of people. His approach assumes that one sample is selected according to the stated purpose of the study. He offers 15 possible purposeful sampling strategies.

1. **Extreme or deviant case sampling** suggests that if we already know the range of experience of a particular social phenomenon, and we have time and resource limitations, in-depth understanding of the extremes of that range of experience will give us insight into its' manifestations and appropriate interventions. For example in the homeless children studies identified in table II.1: for the basic research project, we would select samples of poor families who have permanent housing and those who live on the streets; for the applied research project, we would select samples of those who have experienced chronic homelessness and those who have experienced acute episodes of homelessness; and for the summative and formative evaluations, we would select samples of successful and unsuccessful client cases.

2. **Sampling Intensity** uses the same logic as extreme case sampling but chooses to identify cases that are good examples of the phenomena being studied and offer rich information on its manifestation. Extreme cases might be dismissed as distortions of the reality but less extreme, information rich cases can offer in-depth understanding. In the example studies: for the basic research question we would select samples of homeless families that have experienced neither chronic nor acute homelessness but nonetheless have had an intense experience of homelessness; for the applied question, we would select samples of families and practitioners that have experience with various aspects of homelessness; and for the summative and formative evaluations, we would select practitioners and clients who have had in-depth contact with the program.

3. **Maximum Variation Sampling** identifies the diversity of experiences with a social phenomenon and gives in depth descriptions of unique cases as well as any important shared patterns that are common to diverse cases. In all our example studies we would sample families and case records from various ethnic groups as well as perhaps cases from various age groups of parents, geographical areas, and any other pertinent dimensions of diversity.

4. **Homogeneous Sampling** uses the opposite logic of maximum variation sampling and identifies a sub group for in depth study. This could be, in our examples: for the basic research question all homeless families at one particular income level; for the applied study, all homeless families that received one particular intervention such as a work training program; and for our summative and formative evaluations, all cases that have been in the program for more than a year.

5. **Typical Case Sampling**. Is used to describe an issue or program to those who are not familiar with it. Data from this sample gives a profile of regular or routine experiences of the program or issue. In our example studies in table 3.9: for the basic research question, it would be all families who have experienced homelessness for the average time period; for the

applied research question, it could be all families and practitioners who have experience of the typical homeless program providing shelter and work assistance; and for the summative and formative evaluations it could be all client cases that stay in the program for the average length of time.

6. **Critical Case Sampling** is used to select people or cases who tend to be "markers" of the key events included in the phenomenon being studied. In our example program evaluation studies in table II.1, if we are evaluating whether an after school program in the shelter will assist homeless children, we might select children who are doing particularly badly at school into the sample. Our rationale for this sample would be to test whether the program works for those most in need of it. This is a useful approach if resources are limited and the study must be completed in a short period of time.

7. **Snowball or chain sampling** is a way of understanding and utilizing the networks between key people in relation to the study focus. In our example studies in table 3.9, members of homeless families or practitioners who work with the homeless would be invited to participate in the study. After they had been interviewed they would be invited to identify other people they knew who are experiencing homelessness or who are practitioners who work with the homeless population.

8. **Criterion Sampling** is sampling based on a particular characteristic of the population that can be potentially included in the study. It is generally useful in formative evaluations. For example, if a homeless shelter had an employment program for parents that lasted 6 weeks then all participants who were not employed at the end of six weeks would be included in the study sample so that service delivery to tougher cases could be improved.

9. **Theory-based or operational construct sampling** is the kind of sampling that Strauss and Corbin (2008) rely on. We gather data that illustrates a particular concept or theory that is emerging in the data. We sample events, time periods, or people for their potential to exhibit the concept or theory. In our example study on homeless children from chapter 2 (Young and Creach, 1995), the theory that lack of education combined with family and friends who are substance abusers leads to single parent homeless families might be emerging from the data. If they had time and resources, these student researchers might then choose to spend some time sampling participants in substance abuse programs to further explore this pattern.

10. **Confirming and Disconfirming Cases** is much like the "standing back" strategy that Strauss and Corbin (2008) describe. If we are developing a theory, we should also be looking for data or cases that not only confirm the theory but also those that contradict that theory.

11. **Stratified Purposeful Sampling** is a combination of extreme case sampling and typical case sampling. In our sample studies in table 3.9: for

125

the basic research question, the sample could be a selection of families who have experienced chronic, acute, and episodic periods of homelessness; in our applied research study, it could be a sample of practitioners from various kinds of homelessness programs; and for the summative and formative program evaluations it could be a sampling of clients with, perhaps, below average and above average characteristics of poverty and homelessness.

12. **Opportunistic or Emergent Sampling** is simply deciding to sample a particular person, event or document because something important seems to be happening. It is an on-the-spot decision to gather data that might be important

13. **Purposeful Random Sampling**: The post positivist researcher may well decided to gather a small random sample, not with the goal of generalizing findings to a larger population but more with the intention of systematizing data. Patton (2002) describes an agency that would regularly report case histories to the legislature to illustrate the need for funding. They would report say 10 cases out of a client group of 300. To give the presentation more credibility, they systematized the selection of the cases, not to make generalizations about their clients but to reduce suspicion about biases when selecting cases for presentation.

14. **Sampling politically important cases** is blatantly using the politics of the situation to decide on a sample. For example, if the chair of the legislative committee that funds homeless shelters sees a study of a shelter in his or her district, the issue may gain more attention.

15. **Convenience Sampling** is a common strategy in qualitative sampling and the least desirable. It has no rationale and no clear function. As Patton (2002) says "it is neither purposeful not strategic" (page 242). Other strategies described here meet more rigorous standards and are as easy and inexpensive as this approach.

The underlying rationale for choosing any of these approaches to sampling will depend on the type of research we are carrying out, the purpose of our research, the questions we are asking and the resources available. We may use a combination of these sampling strategies in the same study depending on the concepts and theories that are emerging from the data. The size of the sample will be driven by data collection. One rule is to stop when we seem to have reached a saturation point and any additional data being gathered is becoming redundant. However in truth there are no rules regarding sample size for post positivist research. The sample can be one, a case study, or several hundred if resources and time allow. The quality of the sample is judged on whether it has the potential to provide data that addresses the purpose of the research. In the study of homeless children (Young and Creacy, 1995), the sample was all children housed in one particular temporary shelter over a nine-month period. This accumulated to a total of 30 children who lived in the shelter for various periods of time during the course of the study. This sample was a criterion-based sample since the focus of the study was children's experience of homelessness in one shelter over a period of time.

To sum up this discussion of planning for a post positivist study, at the planning stage we need to decide on the aim of the research, the unit of analysis and the strategy (ies) for selecting the sample of participants. This is all driven by our original research focus. Important cross cutting issues of ethics, politics, diversity, and technology are the same as those discussed in Part 1. Additional technology issues can be found in Chapter V. We can now move on to a discussion of planning for our first action paradigm, critical theory

Summary of Chapter II

- Post positivist research can be basic, applied, a formative evaluation or a summative evaluation.

- The unit of analysis needs to be clear: individuals, families, groups, organizations or communities

- Various strategies for purposive sampling are available, the choice of strategy depends on the study question and purpose

- The ethical, political, and diversity issues that need to be addressed in the Planning stage are similar to those addressed in the Assessment and Engagement stage

Post Positivist Learning Assignments

1. Think of a social work practice research issue that you are interested. Formulate a post positivist question about that issue. Decide if your research question is basic, applied, or an evaluation. Identify,

   a. your unit of analysis

   b. your sampling strategy

   c. your method of collecting data

The plan for implementing a critical theory study emerges as the study progresses. As discussed in Part 1, the critical theorist starts be developing an ideological position that is guided, not only by the ideological and research topic literature review but also by data gathered through engagement of the community. Our research plan includes strategies for:

- identifying participants and engaging those participants in the teaching-learning process;

- recording and analyzing data that describes oppression and empowerment;

- expanding the circle of research participants, if necessary;

- jointly developing action strategies for empowerment;

- taking action; and evaluating, celebrating and reflecting on action.

We see this as a circular process of understanding, connecting, empowering, taking action, reflecting, understanding, connecting, empowering….and so on. Stringer (2007), when discussing action research, suggests that the researcher needs to be carrying out three major activities, "**Look**", "**Think**", and "**Act**". The critical theory action researcher makes plans to carry out these three activities while integrating the teaching-learning process throughout.

Looking Using Teaching-Learning

During the Assessment and Engagement stage we will have identified a number of emerging themes. These relate to participants' concerns regarding the topic of inquiry and the power relationships affecting these concerns. They guide further decisions about who should be interviewed and observed. For example, Riech in 1994, carried out a student study of "Curanderismo", a Mexican folk healing art. After being initially engaged in an M.S.W. program, he noted that textbooks and journals tended not to address ethnic approaches to micro practice with individuals, families and groups. In particular the practice of Curanderismo was rarely mentioned. Students, field placement instructors, and social work practice educators were not conversant with Curanderismo and did not have an appreciation of its value. This student researcher was also aware of concerns among Mexican clients that a Curandero, a practitioner of Curanderismo, could not easily be found when seeking mental health services. After discussing this issue with various students, and Mexican-American clients and friends, certain generative themes emerged:

- The Curandero tends to be dismissed as a charlatan or "quack"

- Definitions of mental health and mental illness are mostly derived from the dominant Anglo culture

- Interventions, such as "limpia" ceremonies that bring mystical messages are dismissed as subjective interpretations rather than objective occurrences

- Mexican or Mexican-American clients of mental health agencies who have traditional Mexican values and prefer traditional approaches to the treatment of illness, experience a sense of marginality

- Minority clients in general experience difficulty in receiving adequate mental health services

- There are class as well as ethnic differences between middle class white therapists and working class traditional Mexican clients

- The Latino culture does not make the same distinction between physical and emotional health that the dominant Anglo culture makes.

- Social work students need to be empowered to confront and challenge the Anglo culture's definitions of appropriate mental health interventions found in M.S.W. curricula.

This researcher through a process of informal interviews gathered these themes from students, Curanderos, Mexican friends and colleagues, faculty members and a review of the literature. Another illustration of this process is offered by the study of eating disorders introduced in Chapter 2 (Christopulos, 1995). In that study, emergent themes identified after talking to adolescent girls and reviewing the literature included:

- Mixed messages to women about the importance of the perfect body: diet, weight, and body image.

- The prevalence of eating disorders, 5% to 10% of adolescent females suffer from Anorexia Nervosa and 30% to 60% of adolescent girls suffer from Bulimia

- The prevalent conclusion that the media equates female beauty with being very thin

- Knowledge that Feminist Principles suggest:

    ○ Women should join together rather than compete with each other

    ○ We should respect individual difference

    ○ Each individual has the right and responsibility to be and become her or his unique self

- Issues Regarding Eating disorders

    ○ Men are the valued gender in society, thus the more masculine you look the greater your chance of success and respect. Thus being thin is powerful and having curves and breasts reduces power. Many women are almost in denial about having curves and breasts

- ○ Women are taught to deny themselves pleasure and take care of others

- ○ Being large and curvy and feeding herself means that a women is breaking the rules of personal power that suggest that power lies with thin women who look like men.

- ○ "Science" allows misconceptions about the healthiness of being thin to prevail

- The potential to re-socialized young women about these issues and perceptions

In their study aimed at bringing public transportation to an isolated, low income community in an isolated community in Southern California, Millet and Otero (2011) noted that

- The Coachella Valley continues to rapidly expand in societal developments. This region of Eastern Riverside County is not different from other areas that demonstrate similar characteristics of simultaneous semi-urban and rural developmental evolution within the confines of its geographic limits.

- However, this area is unique in its historical background, cultural diversity, political atmosphere, extreme spectrum of economical disparity, and abundance of available natural resources along with the procurement, production, consumption and allocation of said resources.

- For example, in the 1950's the Salton Sea area and the North Shore community were considered a desert oasis and desired vacation destination. The Salton Sea however proved to be an ecological disaster and as the rising salinity of the water increased, the influx of tourism decreased and the North Shore community faded into a virtual desert ghost town.

- It ceased to exist in the eyes of affluent Anglos, political figures, and community planners. The North Shore community has continued to maintain a marginalized existence and the unincorporated town's political matters are addressed and subjected to review under the legal statutes of its neighboring town, Mecca.

- Due to this, no information is offered in regards to the North Shore area. The census does not recognize its existence and the inhabitants are counted along with Mecca residents.

- Therefore, services are not adequately appropriated. The study will provided information about a virtually undocumented region and people.

- This study attempts to explain, as well as provide, invaluable insight of the sociopolitical attitudes and behaviors that essentially govern the implementation of policy and therefore, the allocation of infrastructural resources such as public transportation.

- The research also delves into the cultural dynamics of the North Shore community. It also gives an oppositional view into how this community thinks they are perceived and why.

- The data collected by both quantitative and qualitative means can provide policy makers, social workers, service providers and social work practice with a method of reaching and identify services urgently needed by rural populations like the North Shore community.

- The study along with the critical theory paradigm, suggests that social action is alive as well as sociopolitical ideology which continue to impact the well being of the vulnerable, oppressed and those living in poverty.

Our example student studies developed ideological positions, engaged study participants in a teaching-learning process to develop those positions, and thus identified emergent themes. These themes guided further selection of research participants, decisions about further data to be collected, and ideas for action strategies.

Thinking and Understanding

Stringer (2007) suggests various strategies for interpreting or thinking about what the data collected in the looking stage means. One of these is "Concept Mapping" and another is "Problem Analysis". In concept mapping, a diagram of the connections between generative themes is developed while in problem analysis a table of antecedents and consequences is developed. The conceptual map for the Curanderismo study is show in table III.1.

Table III.1
Conceptual Map for study of Curanderismo

	Mental Health Interventions Framed by Majority Culture	Mental Health Interventions Framed by Folk Healing
Mental Health Clients with Traditional, Culture of Origin Values	*Option 1* Culturally Inappropriate Interventions (Usually Happens)	*Option 2* Culturally Appropriate Intervention (Rarely Happens)
Mental Health Clients with Anglo Values	*Option 3* Culturally Appropriate Intervention (Usually Happens)	*Option 4* Culturally Inappropriate Intervention (Never Happens)

131

This map reveals four options. Option 1 is the situation where the Mexican client with traditional values is confronted with mental health services that are based only on Anglo values and customs. Option 2 is the situation where the traditional Mexican client can find mental health services that incorporate traditional Mexican folk healing. Option 3 is the most common situation where Anglo clients receive services based on Anglo values and customs. Option 4, is not likely to happen but it is theoretically possible, it is the situation where an Anglo client can only find Mental Health services offering traditional folk healing. The map suggested that action was needed to address Options 1 and 2.

In the Christopulos study of eating disorders a table of antecedents and consequences was developed from the literature and from talking to teenage girls. It is laid out in figure III.1 which shows two possible approaches to understanding the female body. One approach rests on feminist values that suggest all women are unique and valued and if women cooperate rather than compete they will understand their own strengths and know that the proposition that only one body type is attractive is wrong. If a woman accepts this approach, the study's ideological position suggests that she has more opportunity for learning about a healthy approach to eating and care of her body. The other approach rests on patriarchal values and suggests that since men are perceived as powerful, women must compete with each other and be like men if they want to be powerful. This competition includes looking like a man and having a male shaped body. The ideological position of the study suggests that, in the quest to get this kind of body, a woman will develop eating disorders.

Figure III.1
Antecedents and Consequences of Attitudes to Female Body

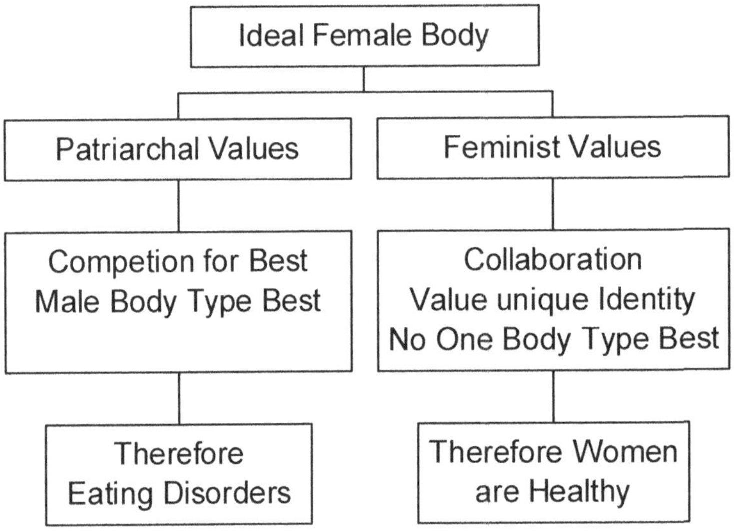

Millet and Otero (2011) also developed a conceptual map based on a sociopolitical analysis of human need as shown in table III.2.

Table III.2
Conceptual Map for study of Community Transportation Needs

	Owners of capital and power	Subordinate groups
Poverty	Unlived experience, lived by others	Lived experience
Ethnicity	Majority	Minority
Immigration	Acculturated to host society	Acculturated to society of origin or bicultural
Hierarchy of Needs	Deficiency needs met, growth needs met	Deficiency needs not met, growth needs not met

In this map, class is seen to divide people into powerful and subordinate groups. The subordinate group tends to experience poverty and include members of minority ethnic groups. In this study the subordinate group was an immigrant group experiencing an acculturative tension between the culture of origin and the host society and it was also a group whose deficiency and growth needs were not being met.

Organizing for Action

Having completed an ideological analysis and an interpretation of data gathered from both the literature and participants, as critical theory researchers, we now move on to a plan for action to address the empowerment issues we have identified. The action is developed and implemented in partnership with study participants. We share the results of the looking and thinking phases of the study and collaboratively: review the interpretations; make changes that respondents and the researchers deem appropriate and necessary; and then, develop action strategies to respond to these findings. This action planning takes place, ideally, at a meeting of participants but if this is not possible it can be carried out by a combination of meetings with individuals, emails, internet discussion boards, and internet meetings via streaming video. The goal for this process is for researchers and participants to agree with the ideological analysis and commit to action strategies.

Priorities are set with stated goals and objectives for action using the following questions adapted from Stringer (2007) (page 128-9):

- Why are we carrying out these activities?

  - In the Millet and Otero (2011) study of transportation the goal was to improve the capacity of a low income community to take part in civil society by providing public transportation that would allow community members to travel to work, shops, schools, entertainment, and any other activities

  - In the Reich (1994) study of Curanderismo, the goal was to improve the cultural competence of social work students by introducing them to native approaches to healing

133

- In the Christopulos (1995) study of eating disorders, the goal was to improve the lives of young women by educating them about the impact of inaccurate 'propaganda" about the ideal female body type on their health and self esteem.

- What activities are required?

    - In the Transportation study it was necessary to engage local politicians in a campaign that identified the need for public transportation and to confront the local transit authority with the community concern about the lack of service to their community.

    - In the Curanderismo study, if there had been time and resources, there could have been a plan to campaign for the introduction of folk healing into local social work education and training curricula. Specific objects might have been to develop a one-day workshop on folk healing and Curranderismo in a mental health setting or to develop an elective course on this topic in the local M.S.W. and B.S.W. programs.

    - In the eating disorders study specific objectives might have been: to start a self help group in the high school that was the site of the study and then network with other sigh schools to set up other such groups at these settings. There could have been a plan to develop local self help groups for adolescent girls focusing on body image, dieting, and eating disorders

- How are these activities to take place? What is the sequence of tasks?

    - In the transportation study, action plans were developed that involved community leaders and social work students in contacting local politicians and inviting them to meetings, circulating a petition asking for public transportation to community members, attending board meetings of the local transit authority, and a public demonstration that was reported on local media.

    - In the Curranderismo study, contacting the local universities, training contractors, NASW and other training providers would have been the first step followed by negotiation of curriculum development procedures

    - In the eating disorders study tasks would have included engaging the administration of the high school in the project, training facilitators, setting schedules, advertising the self help groups and generally networking with adolescent girls.

- Who is to carry out each task?

- In the transportation study, community leaders emerged who took responsibility for voicing the community concerns. The partnered with the study authors to organize meetings, a petition, and a demonstration that voiced the need for public transportation.

- In the Curranderismo study a task group of Curranderos, social work faculty, students, and potential clients would have been brought together to take on the organizational roles associated with developing a curriculum and steering it through a curriculum acceptance process.

- In the eating disorders study high school administrators, parents and other high school female students would have been recruited to campaign for, organize, and run the groups.

- Where will the action take place?

  - In the transportation study action took place at local community centers, already existing events such as community health fairs, the local transit authority's board meetings, and in the streets of the community.

  - In the Curranderismo study the action would have been implemented in a university setting.

  - In the eating disorders study, the action would be taking place in the high school setting.

- When will the action take place?

  - In the transportation study a series of events were scheduled over a 19 month period.

  - In the Curranderismo study, the timing of the annual curricula development processes would have dictated the action timelines.

  - In the eating disorders study, negotiation with high school administrators and scheduling of the school year would have dictated the timeline.

- What resources are needed and who will acquire them?

  - In the transportation study, social work students made donations to fund food for meetings and volunteered their cars to transport community members and students to meetings.

  - In the Curanderismo study, this would have been negotiated with training and education providers and would probably have led to applications for grant funding.

- In the eating disorders study, this would have been negotiated with high school administrators

- Should people who have not yet participated in the study be asked to help with the action?

  - In the transportation study, at first, the two student authors were the leaders of the project but as each meeting and event unfolded increased numbers of community leaders came forward to take leadership roles. The biggest issue was that this was a mostly Spanish speaking community. One of the study authors (Otero) was fluent in Spanish and was able to engage community members successfully. The other study author (Millet) had computer knowledge and was able to give technical assistance to some community members who were using the internet to move forward with the project. This brought more community members into the project and developed community capacity to include local politicians in the project.

  - In the Curanderismo study more Curanderos and social work academics would need to have been brought into the process to advocate for the curriculum change and manage the curriculum change process.

  - In the eating disorders study, those with expertise in building self help groups would have been needed as well as experts in group work to train the group facilitators

- Is the plan realistic?

  - In the transportation study, activities were developed that were within the capacity of the student authors with assistance from other social work students and community members. Even with this assistance, though, it was a demanding project that required considerable time and energy.

  - In both the other sample studies, the study participants and additional key players would have reviewed these plans for feasibility.

For the critical theory researcher, both the process and the outcome of the study are important. Throughout the development of the plan, we need to ensure that the project is empowering participants and that study participants feel that these activities will improve:

- pride and feeling of self worth;

- dignity and feeling of autonomy;

- sense of social identity (women are not doing "women's work);

- sense of control over what is happening to them;

- sense or responsibility; sense of unity;

- sense of comfort with the place where both the activity and the planning is taking place; and

- sense of connection to locations with which they have a historical, cultural or social tie.

Since much of the organizing and assignment of tasks will take place in task group settings, we must continually carry out a self-assessment, asking ourselves if the group processes we are using to develop action strategies are promoting the empowerment described above. Again we return to our practice colleagues for guidance on such self-assessment. While group work skills that interpret personal behavior or offer reflective responding to personal issues are not so important in this situation, building relationships through warmth, empathy and genuineness are crucial. As the task group facilitator we need to use listening skills and be able to summarize, clarify, and provide information (Kirst-Ashmen & Hull, 2009). Stringer lays out these skills under the following headings (page 133):

Relationships: promoting equality, handling conflicts, acceptance of group members, promoting cooperation, sensitive to diversity

Communication: understandable, truthful, open, sincere, socially and culturally appropriate, open to comment and change

Participation: everybody has a meaningful role, participants supported in role, have direct access to researchers.

Inclusion: all stakeholders included, all stakeholders' issues addressed, cooperation with other relevant entities, all relevant groups benefit from action.

Keeping participants committed to implementation, if they are not being paid or this is not part of their job, is a challenging process. Even with all the personal investment that has been described so far, volunteers over time develop other priorities or just run out of energy for a project. We need to have a plan to support participants as they move forward with implementation of action and face any obstacles. We need to keep in touch with participants via phone calls, emails and meetings. We need to reassure participants that they are doing well and help them reflect on and assess their progress or lack of progress. We need to keep people connected and share any information we may be discovering that will help with the action. We also need to facilitate a support network that is not focused on us as but allows each study participant to feel that he or she can get help from members of the group. All of this will help participants to stay committed to implementing the action plan as well as successful evaluation and celebration.

Millet and Otero (2011) give us a clear example of such processes by describing a series of meetings:

- The phases are as following:

    o 1) La Iglesia un Manatial del Desierto

    o 2) Catholic Charities Food Bank located in the North Shore Yacht Club community room;

    o 3) La Iglesia un Manatial en el Desierto; and

    o 4) North Shore Yacht Club community room.

- Phases two, three, and four were audio recorded for qualitative data gathering and analysis.

- The first phase of data collection was at La Iglesia un Manatial en el Desierto and sixty community members were in attendance. The event primarily focused on education the community members and organizing for action planning.

- The second phase was held at Catholic Charities Food Bank located in the North Shore Yacht Club community room. The demographic questionnaire was given to community members prior to the food distribution. Forty-six questionnaires were collected at this event.

- Phase three was at La Iglesia un Manatial del Desierto where twenty-six community members attended the meeting. This meeting was primarily used for further demographic data collection and action planning.

- The fourth data collection phase was at the North Shore Yacht Club. This meeting was attended by both community members and a senior Field Representative tothe Assembly Member of the 80th district, the Mayor of Coachella, the Vice-president of SunLine Transit Agency, and forty community members. Major topics addressed at this meeting were empowerment, additional plans for action, and support for the transportation needs of the North Shore Community.

After these students had met the deadline to submit their final report, they continued to work with this community and in a later eventover 70 residents from North Shore along with former MSW students, went to the SunLine Transit Agency located in Thousand Palms, CA to protest the lack of public transportation services in this community. The event persuaded the General Manager and the SunLine board to have a future meeting with the North Shore community about their transportation dilemma. The students continued working with the community by writing reports for the County Transportation Commission and building an ever stronger coalition. Finally in 2013 the SunLine bus service was expanded to the community of North Shore!

There is a nuance in the critical theory approach that we need to address. As critical theory researchers, we are the source of knowledge about the critical theory and ideology that is informing the study but we are also open to other ideas and committed to engaging in a dialogue with study participants so that a shared understanding of the ideological position is developed. We start in a "one-up" relationship with participants but move quickly to a partnership with participants. This raises issues regarding "informed" consent. Initially, participants may well give their informed consent to this approach to research but when they see and hear the interpretation of the critical theory and ideology as it relates to them, they may become uncomfortable and want to withdraw from the study. This kind of situation is discussed by Johensen and Norman (2004) in their article describing a conflict between researchers and the community in a community empowerment project in southern Norway. They note that there was,

> *"a lack of re-flectivity and learning in the RDC* (Regional Development Coalition), *and a rejection of the mandate of the program and the researchers' goal of radical change. The RDC became a part of or an instrument in the regional strategic power play. The researchers' activities were subsequently recognized not as reflective capacities, but as parts of a political process. (p. 230)*

These authors suggest that there is an inherent conflict between the role of practitioner and researcher in action research. They suggest that there is less potential for conflict when the project is simple and incremental rather than complex and radical where many stakeholders are involved. They suggest that the action researcher (in this book the critical theory researcher) in the complex radical situation needs to focus on understanding rather than success and deliberation rather than strategy. They also note that such a researcher is playing multiple roles: facilitator, observer and data collector, supplier of relevant knowledge, bridge builder between interested parties, and service provider during action. They believe that the critical theory researcher is frequently called on to be both outside the project looking in and understanding and inside the project looking out experiencing empowerment in the face of oppression.

In our example student studies, the Millet and Otero study of public transportation addressed these issues and successfully negotiated these multiple roles to truly collaborate with the community in developing an ideological analysis and taking action. The other two projects ended with an evaluation of the impact of an ideological analysis designed by the student researcher and so did not address the issues noted above. In these latter two studies, the students focused on empowering their study participants through presentations of ideology and data and did not move on to jointly develop actions plans to address the oppression identified in their educational presentation. If they had done this, participants may have disagreed with the critical theory approach and the issues noted above would have surfaced.

These issues are best addressed by negotiating strong partnerships in the looking, thinking and action phase using the following steps.

1. We begin with an ideological position. The study participants may have only a partial understanding of that ideological position but agree to find out more about it (otherwise the study ends right there, since the researcher cannot ethically or pragmatically impose a point of view on anyone). These understandings are clarified and negotiated in the initial informed consent process

2. We then impart our knowledge of the chosen ideology to participants in a teaching-learning process where participants respond and a dialogue is developed. Both researcher and participants teach and learn. At this stage we may add participants as themes emerge requiring new key informants. For example, in the Riech study of Curanderismo the researcher began by talking to social work students, and social work students were the targets of the action. However later, Curanderos, social work faculty members, Mexican clients, and other students were all added to the group of participants who gave input during the looking phase of the study.

3. We reformulate the ideological analysis through a synthesis of our knowledge and the data collected from respondents during the looking phase. This reformulation is shared with participants at the beginning of the action phase. The participants respond to the new ideological analysis, evaluate it, and decide if it applies to them. They also decide whether they are committed to taking action to address the oppression and empowerment included in the reformulated ideological analysis. The democracy of the critical theory approach, and the explicit acknowledgement that we are always engaged in some form of power relationship with each other, allows us to assume that any differences of interpretation are highly likely to be resolved. There is a fundamental truth being addressed here and a liberating process being experienced.

4. When we reach agreement, an action plan is developed that includes implementation, evaluation, reflection and celebration.

5. If we cannot reach agreement the partnership has not been successfully developed and we need to return to step one and repeat the process. If this is not successful we cannot continue and we begin a termination process that reviews where the spirit and process of the critical theory approach to problem solving was lost. This would include a reflection on whether a teaching-learning process had been honored. For example, did participants find the ideological approach irrelevant or threatening? Did researchers fail to address that point of view? Sometimes this discussion can lead to a revival of the partnership.

In the Millet and Otero study of transportation needs for a poorly resourced, low income community a strong community partnerships was successfully developed and researchers' and community participants' perceptions changed as they engaged each other and develop joint understandings of the ideological position of the community and the action plans that led to community action putting pressure on the local transit authority. In the Reich study, with more time and resources, a synthesis might have been reached where it was agreed that there are times when the Curanderismo approach is harmful given modern knowledge about mental health. Likewise, a synthesis for the eating disorders study might have been an agreement that, the inclusion of girls in more team sports, as a result of role modeling from college sports activities for women that have developed in response to the requirements of Title IX, has changed the body image favored by girls to a more muscular body type showing strength, not a thin type mimicking men.

Rutman et al (2005) in their study of youth transitioning out of care used a process of reflection and evaluation to develop a synthesis. During stage one of the study the project team carried out data collection and analysis. They then carried out an evaluation of stage one. They individually and collaboratively identified what worked well in stage one, the challenges faced in stage one, and strategies for doing things differently as they proceed to stage two action strategies. Schulz et al. (2003) similarly describe a process of building consensus in the context of differing individual visions for women's community health in Detroit. They noted that, "In 1999, Village Health Workers, and representatives from the steering committee gathered to determine priorities for the partnership for the next four years. Based on results from the community survey, descriptive data indicating the extent to which women living on Detroit's East Side reported a range of stressors, and partial correlations indicating the strength of the relationships between stressors and mental and physical health outcomes were incorporated into the dialogue… as all worked together in this process, an opportunity was provided for members of the partnership to act on their commitment to shared power and influence within the partnership itself". (pages 308 and 309))

There are also technological tools that can help us with critical theory research. Phones, emails and computer cams can assist efficiency. Also, Fawcett et al, offer some useful web based resources such as the Network for Good (http://www.networkforgood.org) that offers information and strategies for advocacy for community change. These authors' own web based Community Took Box (http://ctb.ku.edu) offers assistance with: building capacity for community change, learning and adjustments to be made during the process of community change, and evaluation and analysis of the contribution made by the intervention to community change.

To sum up, it is clear that for the critical theory researcher Planning is tightly intertwined with the Assessment and Engagement that was discussed in Part 1. With the foundation of Assessment and Engagement, in the Planning stage we are able to move forward with looking, thinking and acting. A teaching-learning approach that facilitates a partnership between the researcher and study participants is the core of these initial stages of the critical theory research project where the final product is action. This does not look like the research planning described in our discussions of positivism and post positivism. It is definitely not neutral and it definitely is an approach with an agenda that includes more than data gathering and analysis of findings. The critical theorist promotes changes in power relationships that empower the oppressed. This concludes our discussion of the Planning stage for critical theorists. The important cross cutting issues of ethics, politics, diversity, and technology are similar to those discussed in Part 1. However, there are some additional technology issues discussed in Chapter V. Below is a summary of this chapter and some critical theory learning assignments. We can now move on to a discussion of Planning for the constructivist researcher.

Summary of Chapter III

- The initial stages of a critical theory involve simultaneous assessment, engagement and planning

- Assessment includes reviewing the literature on the chosen ideology as well as the chosen research topic

- Ideology is analyzed in three ways: diachronic, discursive and conceptual.

- The Ideological position is developed through a combination of literature review and engagement of study participants at the chosen research site using a teaching-learning approach

- Engaging the research site also requires "establishing a role" through the agenda, stance and position

- The plan for critical theory research emerges as the study progresses. Phases of this kind of research are "looking" "thinking" "acting"

- Looking includes a teaching-learning dialogue with study participants guided by emerging ideological themes

- Thinking includes developing a concise statement of the ideological position using strategies such as concept mapping or problem analysis

- The ideological position is shared with the study participants and an action plan is collaboratively developed

- Throughout these stages it is important to pay attention to building and maintaining the researcher-participant partnerships

- The action phase includes planning, implementation, evaluation, and celebration.

- During the action phase the researcher is both gathering data and facilitating a task group. These two role require research and group work skills

Critical Theory Learning Assignments

1. Choose an ideology that identifies an oppressed group, a process of oppression and those with power to oppress. Think of a group locally that

is experiencing the consequences of that oppression. Together with your partner develop an action plan to address that oppression. Who would you need to talk to? What would you need to know?

    a. How would you measure the impact of the action on empowerment?

    b. How would you plan to prove that the project empowered the identified oppressed group?

143

The constructivist researcher is the most distinctively different of all four kinds of researchers that are described in this book. Constructivists are so attentive to subjective data that they even count their own constructions of reality as one of the data sources. When setting up the research plan, therefore, as constructivist researchers, we devise a strategy for finding all possible constructions of our research focus. Methods of identifying and engaging key players are thought through as well as a strategy and time line for participants to develop and share their constructions of the research focus. To do this we identify a "**hermeneutic dialectic circle**" of key informants who will jointly build a construction of the research focus. The circle is **hermeneutic** because each person brings their own construction to the research project and **dialectic** because each person is informed of other participants' constructions and given the opportunity to further develop a construction as a result of reflecting on other perspectives. The framing of the issue and the membership of the circle will constantly change as the study progresses. This is a planning stage rather than a mapping stage. To offer an explanatory metaphor, the positivist researcher develops a map before embarking on the journey of the research project, assuming that a good researcher's map will exactly portray the territory to be covered during the journey. The map is not changed once the journey begins. In contrast, the constructivist researcher develops a map for the journey assuming that a good researcher will change the map once the journey starts because the territory that is encountered during the journey will probably be different to the territory that was anticipated when the map was made before the journey started. Thus according to Erlandson et al. (1993), when designing a research project the constructivist researcher plans for negotiating conditions of entry, purposive sample selection as described in Chapter II, data collection, data analysis, strategies for assessing the quality of the study, and dissemination of findings. However, all of this can change when we engage in an exploration of the subjective experience of study participants.

The plan for a constructivist study identifies the study site and the key players in that study site who are most likely to be productive members of the hermeneutic dialectic circle. This is done using maximum variation sampling which is defined by Patton (2002) as a process that identifies the diversity of experiences with a social phenomenon and gives in depth descriptions of unique cases as well as any important shared patterns that are common to diverse cases (p234-5). The phases of data collection for building individual and joint constructions are mapped out as well as strategies for data gathering and recording which are describe in detail in Part 3 However, this is not a fixed plan. Once the study starts, things could change. The best way to understand this is to return to our three example student constructivist studies.

Study of HIV-AIDS: Planning.

Hogan, the student researcher, planned to use purposive sampling to identify stakeholder groups in the community. She decided that maximum variation sampling would be used within each stakeholder group to identify individuals with contrasting constructions regarding services to people living with HIV-AIDS. However, once data collection began, this plan proved impractical. Because of the stigma and possible harm linked with being identified as HIV positive, many agencies that served the general population including people living with HIV-AIDS, did not know which of their clients were living with HIV-AIDS. Also, such agencies admitted that should they identify a client who is a person living with HIV-AIDS, they would refer this client to a specialist agency that intervenes with those clients only. Also, some respondents who initially agreed to be interviewed for the study, on reflection, decided that for reasons of personal or professional confidentiality they should withdraw from the study.

The final circle of participants was the circle of those remaining after this fallout. Some stakeholder-groups were represented by one person while others were represented by two or three people. The final circle of participants for the first stage of the study therefore totaled 22. Because of the sensitivity of the topic and requests for confidentiality, some participants were simply identified with a grouping name rather than personally identified. The plan was to gather data in two phases: first individual interviews and then a meeting of all participants to review the joint construction. However, the sensitivity of the topic, and the limited time frame for the student researcher meant that only the first round of data was collected. The accuracy of these constructions was checked by sending the written account of the interview to participants in the mail and then following up with phone calls to discuss any modifications. The final report was sent to stakeholders separately.

Study of Homeless Children: Planning.

The plan for this study was more ambitious than the above study and in the end, more successful in achieving a shared construction of the problem and action needed to address the problem. As noted in Part 1, successive students planned to carry out this study over two years. The first student would develop the study and conduct the first round of interviews. After the first student had graduated, the second student in the next year of the M.S.W. program, would continue the study, do a second round of interviews and hold a meeting of all participants to review the joint construction and develop an action plan. For the student in the first year of the study, an initial circle of stakeholders was identified and interviewed as noted above. In the second year of the study, this circle was expanded upon and constructions were revisited and further developed. This new circle included:

1. Homeless Shelters

2. Domestic Violence Shelters

3. School Districts

4. Public Health Department

5. Local Church Based Soup Kitchen

6. Transportation and Food Distribution Center

145

7. One member of the Board of County Supervisors (an elected official)

8. A member of city government (an elected official)

9. The Sheriff's Department

10. Child Protective Services

11. The Regional Child Abuse Council

12. The County Department of Social Services

13. A Mental Health, Substance Abuse Treatment Agency

14. Mental Health Department

At the end of the second year of the study, this group met, reviewed their shared construction and developed an action plan to address the needs of homeless children in the Coachella valley.

Study of Spirituality: Planning.

Brown (2011) states that,

"Though the dialectic nature of the constructivist paradigm requires that the participants or stakeholder group may expand and change throughout the inquiry process, the initial stakeholder group or categories of participants are those who will either implement (agents), become the recipient or beneficiary of, or contribute to the practice or policy changes that this research seeks to initiate (Guba & Lincoln, 1989). The initial stakeholder groups for this study included Riverside County Children's Services staff including administrators, supervisors, and social workers and African American parents. Though community service providers were initially thought to be a key stakeholder, as data collection and cursory coding occurred, it was determined that community members would not be able to add to the questions most relevant to the study.

Selection of participants was conducted serially, meaning that new participants were not nominated or selected until the previous participant had been interviewed and an initial analysis of their data had occurred (Rodwell, 1998). In this way participant nomination and selection was more focused to provide the widest variation of constructs.

The first interview was scheduled with the Assistant Director of Children's Services as the identified agency gatekeeper. The Assistant Director was asked to recommend other members of the CSW stakeholder group who may have a divergent construct. Those recommended individuals were then be asked to participate as stakeholders in this research and once consented and interviewed, were asked to provide a referral to another participant or stakeholder who may add a different perspective or view point regarding spirituality/religion and its role in child welfare practice with African American families. This sampling strategy though similar to snowball sampling, has as its focus to provide divergent rather than similar perspectives. Participant recruitment continued until the data reveals no new stakeholders or additional constructs, also known as redundancy or saturation (Guba & Lincoln, 1989). Though there was no maximum number of participants targeted, it was expected that the number of child welfare staff and African American parents interviewed would be balanced to provide an equal voice to the major stakeholder groups. There were 26 participants, 16 CWS staff and 10 African American parents.

The child welfare staff interviewed included the Assistant Director, two Deputy Directors, five Regional Managers, one Assistant Regional Manager, two Supervisors and five line level Children's Social Service Workers. The ethnic makeup of the staff was seven African American/Black Americans, one Latino American, and eight European Americans.

African American parents were recruited to participate in this study through a list of contacts provided by the child welfare agency. That list initially included only those African American parents who have been involved with CWS, had their case or investigated referral closed within the last 12 months, and who lived in Moreno Valley. The contact list was expanded to include a larger geographic area within Riverside County in order to gather a larger sample of parents. Though it was expected that those parents who agreed to participate would provide referrals to other African American parents that might have a different perspective although not necessarily prior involvement with child welfare services, that did not occur. Parents with open cases were not selected due to the potential fear of retribution and/or the effects of the perceived and real power differential.

Of the ten parents interviewed, three were European Americans who were either married to an African American parent, or had a child with an African American partner when involved with the child welfare system. These parents were interested in participating in the study with the understanding that the focus of the study was on African American families. Nine of the ten parents were women. Parent interviews occurred either in the parent's home or in a neutral setting of their choosing. Parents who attended the final group meeting were compensated for their time and participation with a $25.00 gift card." (pages 65-69)

We can see that for the constructivist researcher, planning is intertwined with Engagement and Assessment.

According to Erlandson et al (1993), the plan for the study at this stage should include:

1. *Plan for Engagement*: How will we engage the setting? It could be through a letter of introduction into a formal setting or through personal contacts with trusted key informants in a more informal community setting. In our example studies, the researchers were already living and/or working in the community, so they already had a relationship with some participants, and were referred to participants they did not know.

2. *Plan for renegotiation or terms of engagement with the research site*: as the project starts and people start talking, unexpected issues may surface and we need to be alert to any need to revisit the terms that were agreed at the beginning of the project. In our HIV-AIDS study, prejudices against people with HIV-AIDS were surfacing within the social work community and this client group was expressing unexpected anger with the profession. The researcher needed to revisit the comfort of the gatekeepers with these conversations and this changed participation in the study

3. *Plan for purposive sample selection*: as far as possible, we need to anticipate those who are likely to have constructions of the research focus. In addition, we need to have a plan for including a wide range of differing constructions of the research focus. As can be seen in our sample studies, either the sensitivity of the topic or pragmatic time constraints can make some stakeholder groups reluctant to participate in the study.

4. *Plan for data collection*: At this stage we need to think through the combination of interviewing, observation, and review of additional artifacts that will most comprehensively address the research focus. As data gathering progresses, this will change, but a starting point where as much has been thought through as possible is important. In our sample studies, data was gathered by interviews only. This was partly due to the students' time constraints but also the result of a plan where various entities needed to be brought together to plan action. At the planning stage of each of these studies, additional sources of data were not considered to be a priority.

5. *Plan for analysis*. As with post positivist and critical theory research, data collection and analysis are parallel processes. We need to develop a process and time line for both that is realistic and fruitful.

6. *Plan for trustworthiness and authenticity*. In a large scale, fully-funded constructivist study, there would be funding for an outside auditor to check the researcher's journal on data gathering and the steps of data analysis. Usually, the student researcher does not have such funding and must turn to

the research advisor for the audit. This auditing process needs to be negotiated at the start of the project.

7. *Plan for dissemination.* We need to anticipate the likely audiences for the project findings. Of course, the members of the circle of informants are the first audience but are there others? Will there be a wider community meeting? Is the media interested? Is there an academic setting where results must be displayed? Who will be involved in the action plans? For our example studies, the HIV-AIDS study was too sensitive for dissemination beyond sending the report on the joint construction back to individual participants for their own reflection. In addition, a summary of the findings was displayed at a poster session on campus for social work student research. The study of homeless children was able to move further forward with the constructivist process. It included a meeting of all stakeholders where findings were reported and action plans were developed. It too was reported at a poster session on campus for student projects. The study of spirituality was reported back to the administration of the Children's Services Department that was the focus of the study, as well as the workers and families who took part in the study. This process of dissemination is discussed in more detail in chapter 6

The planning identified in the steps above facilitates thoughtful entrance to the research setting and appropriate invitations into the circle of informants, whether the research site is a formal agency setting or a more loosely defined community. Thinking through this plan helps us understand the dynamics of the setting and answer questions from participants such as why they should participate in the study and what they may gain from the study. It also develops our awareness of the agendas of participants and their motivations for taking part in the study, which may range from airing grievances to an interest in improvement and change.

Often, in student projects, with limited time and resources, our plan can only be approximated. However, even with the approximated plan, our example studies show that useful research that impacts service delivery in the research site can be carried out. Constructivist research is a process and an outcome. The process of being engaged in developing constructions, although truncated in the HIV-AIDS study, still brought a meaningful review of this issue to a community that was being heavily impacted by this client population. The study of homeless children both engaged key participants in building a joint construction and resulted in action to improve service delivery. The study of spirituality created a useful dialogue between key participants that facilitated input to the administration of a County Children's Services department on working with an important aspect of African American family life. This ends our discussion of the Planning stage for constructivists. A summary of the chapter follows below with some constructivist learning assignments. Important cross cutting issues are similar to those discussed in Part 1. Additional diversity and technology issues are discussed in Chapter V.

- Each constructivist study is considered unique to its time and place

- The quality of a constructivist study is measured by its credibility, transferability, dependability and confirmability

- Constructivist studies ask exploratory, explanatory and action questions

- A constructivist study demands an intensive commitment of time and energy

- Constructivist studies focus on problems, evaluands or policy options.

- Initial engagement of research sites needs to be thoughtful, well planned and persistent

- The plan for a constructivist study includes strategies for collecting all possible interpretations of the research topic

- The research plan identifies a "hermeneutic dialectic" circle of key informants, In addition, the researcher plans for negotiation of conditions of entry, purposive sampling, data collection, data analysis, assessment of quality of the study, and dissemination of the findings

- The research plan will change once the project begins and the reality of engaging the research site and gathering data is encountered. Constructivist researchers anticipate such changes and build flexibility into their approach to research.

Constructivist Learning Assignments

1. Think of a topic that you are interested in. How would you study it using a constructivist approach? Where and when would you carry it out? Who would be included in your hermeneutic dialectic circle?In pairs, discuss your possible projects. How would you engage the circle of key informants?

In the planning stage the important cross cutting issues are similar to those discussed in Part 1 However, there are some additional diversity and technology issues to be considered.

Diversity Issues

In her book on feminist research methods, Reinharz (1992) reviews various approaches to research and suggests modifications that are sensitive to the needs of women. Her discussion suggests that feminist research, rather than being critical theory research only, is any research project carried out by those who identify themselves as feminists and/or those who are focused on an aspect of a feminist agenda. The methodologies she reviews are traditional positivist designs. When discussing survey research and experimental designs she suggests that, although such approaches may not be sensitive to women in their conceptualization and data collection modes, they provide quantitative data that can be used to document the oppression and empowerment of women. She makes the same argument for positivist experimental designs when she references Lenore Walker's (1979) use of animal experiments to illustrate learned helplessness. These findings have been used to develop behavioral theories of how women develop learned helplessness in battering relationships. She also notes that many feminist researchers believe that experiments can be used to address feminist topics if a contextual explanation of the observed behaviors is added to the study (V aughter, 1976). In the design stage, both between and within group comparisons raise questions about stereotyping of ethnic groups. Between-group comparisons in the pat have stressed deficits in various ethnic groups, while within-group comparisons have not been generalizeable because of differences in conceptual and measurement equivalence between various ethnic groups. For example, comparisons on indicators such as poverty and child abuse stress the over representation of certain minority groups in poor and abusing populations. However, comparisons on community commitment or ability to collaborate to solve problems would show strengths. Or, in another example, comparisons between middle class Latinos and working class Latinos in California are not generalizeable to similar groups in, say, Mexico.

Technology Issues

For planning, again the phones, emails and computer cams noted in Part 1 can assist efficiency. Fascett et al, again offer some useful web based resources such as the Network for Good (http://www.networkforgood.org) that offers information and strategies for advocacy for community change. These authors' own web based Community Took Box (http://ctb.ku.edu) offers assistance with: building capacity for community change, learning and adjustments to be made during the process of community change, and evaluation and analysis of the contribution made by the intervention to community change.

This concludes Part 2. We have seen how Planning is a very different enterprise for each of our paradigms. Sometimes we set up a plan in advance that will not change no matter what happens during the Implementation of the study. Other times we have a plan that may well need to be modified as the study progresses. Each of these approaches is supported by a worldview and rationale that justifies such differences. Having thought about our plan, we can now move on to a discussion of the Implementation of our research project.

References

Brown, L.E. (2011) Spirituality's Role in the Interaction Between Child Welfare and Black Families. San Bernardino: Loma Linda University, social work student doctoral dissertation.

Cohran, W.G. (1954). Some methods for strengthening the common X2 tests. *Biometrics* 6: 426-443.

Christopulos, J. (1995) Oppression through Obsession: A Feminist Theoretical Critique of Eating Disorders. San Bernardino, CA: Student research project

Durkeim, E. (1938). *The Rules of Sociological Method*. New York: Free Press. First published, 1895.

Erlandson, D. A., Harris, E. L., Skipper, B.L., Allen, S. D. (1993). *Doing Naturalistic Inquiry.* Thousand Oaks: Sage.

Fawcett, S. B., Schultz, J.A., Carson, V. L., Renault, V.A., Francisco, B.T. (2003). Using internet tools to build capacity for community based participatory research and other efforts to promote community health and development. In M. Minkler & M. Wallerstein (Eds.) *Community-based participatory research for health.* Pages 155-178. San Francisco: Josey-Bass.

Frankel, M. (2010) "Sampling Theory" In, Marsden, P.V. & Wright, J.D. (Eds.) *Handbook of Survey Research*. Bingley, UK: Emerald Publishing

Guba, E.G. & Lincoln, Y.S. (1989) *Fourth Generation Evaluation* Newbury Park: Sage

Hogan, P. (1995) *A Constructivist study of Social Work's Involvement with HIV-AIDS.* San Bernardino, CA: School of Social Work, CSUSB,

Johnsen, H. C. G, & Norman, R. (2004). When Research and Practice Collide: The Role of Action Research When There Is a Conflict of Interest With Stakeholders. In *Systemic Practice and Action Research,* Vol. 17, No. 3, June.

Kirst-Ashman, K. K. Hull, G.H. (2009) Understanding Generalist Practice. Florence, KY: Cenage.

Land, K. C., & Zheng, H. (2010). "Sample Size, Optimum Allocation, and Power Analysis". In Marsden, P.V. & Wright, J.D. (Eds) *Handbook of Survey Research*. Bingley, UK: Emerald Publishing.

Mach, E. (1959). *The Analysis of Sensations*. New York: Dover. First published in 1883.

Manicas, P.T. (1988). *A history and philosophy of the social sciences*. Oxford, U.K.: Blackwell.

Millet, K. R., and Otero, L. R. (2011) The North Shore Public Transportation Dilemma: How Local Sociopolitical Ideologies, Ethnic Discrimination And Class Oppression Create Marginalization, And A Community's Quest For Social Justice. San Bernardino, CA. CSUSB, a social work student research project.

Moustakas, C. (1990) *Heuristic research: design, methodology, and applications*. Newbury Park: Sage.

Patton, M.Q. (2002) *Qualitative research and evaluation methods*. Thousand Oaks: Sage.

Reinharz, S. (1992) *Feminist Methods in social research*. New York: Oxford University Press.

Riech, J. R. (1994). Psychotherapy Encounters Curanderismo: Implications for Clients Treated in the United States by Culturally Insensitive Social Workers. San Bernardino: Student Project at CUSUB

Rodwell, M.K. (1998) *Social Work Constructivist Research*. New York: Garland Publishers.

Rubin, A & Babbie, E (2011) Research Methods for Social Work. Belmont, CA: Brooks Cole.

Ruttman, D., Hubberstey, C., Barlow, A., & Brown, E (2005). Supporting young peoples' transitions from care: reflections on doing participatory action research with youth from care. In, Brown and Strega (Eds.) *Research as Resistance.* Pages 153-180Canadian Scholars' Press: Toronto.

Schulz, A., Israel, B.A., Parker, E., Lockett, M., Hill, Y., Wills, R. (2003) Engaging women in community based participatory research for health. In Minkler, M. & Wallerstein, N. (Eds.) *Community based participatory research for health.* San Francisco: Jossey-Bass

Skinner, B.F. (1953). *Science and Human Behavior*. New York: Macmillan

Spencer, H. (1902) *Principles of Psychology*, 3rd Edition, New York: Appelton.

Strauss, A & Corbin, J. (2008) Basics of Qualitative Research. Thousand Oaks: Sage (3rd Edition)

Stringer, E.T. (2007). Action Research. Thousand Oaks:Sage.

Sudman, S. (1983) "Applied Sampling". In Rossi, P.H., Wright, J.D., & Anderson, A.B. (1983) (Eds.) Handbook of Survey Research. Orlando, FA: Academic Press.

Vaughter, R. M. (1976). "Psychology" in *Signs: Journal of women in culture and society* 2, pp 120-146.

Walker, L (1979) *The Battered Woman*. New York: Harper Row

Watson, J.B. (1963) Psychology as the behaviorist sees it. In W. Dennis (ed*.). Readings in the history of psychology*. New York: Appelton-Century-Crofts.

Weinberg, E. (1983) "Data Collection: Planning and Management" In Rossi, P.H., Wright, J.D., & Anderson, A.B. (Eds.) Handbook of Survey Research. Orlando, FA: Academic Press.

Weiss, H.B., Jacobs, F. H. (1988) Evaluating Family Programs. New York: Aldine de Gruyter.

Young, M.L. and Creacy, M. (1995) *Perceptions of Homeless Children*. California State University, San Bernardino: Masters Research Project.

Attachment A

INSERT THE NAME OF YOUR

PROJECT ON THESE TWO LINES

_____

A Project Proposal

Presented to the

Faculty of (Insert University Name)

_____

In Partial Fulfillment

of the Requirements for the Degree

Master of Social Work

_____

by

First, Middle, and Last Name

First, Middle, and Last Name

June 2006

Note: Spell out middle name NO initials

155

INSERT THE NAME OF YOUR

PROJECT ON THESE TWO LINES

_____

A Project Proposal

Presented to the

Faculty of

(Insert University Name)

_____

by

First, Middle, and Last Name

First, Middle, and Last Name

June 2003

Approved by:

, Proposal Supervisor Social Work   Date
I.M. Encharge, L.C.S.W., Big County
Agency
M.S.W. Research Coordinator

ABSTRACT

PROPOSAL: TABLE OF CONTENTS

CHAPTER ONE

ASSESSMENT

(Problem Focus and Literature Review)

In this section you address questions such as, what is your research focus or question. What is the perspective you are brining to the research focus, which paradigm are you adopting? Why is this one the most appropriate paradigm to use for this study? What does the literature say about this focus or question and how does that relate to your study? How will a study of this research focus add to our knowledge of social work practice at the micro and/or macro levels of human organization? Use the following headings

Introduction

One paragraph outlining what will be covered in this chapter.

Research focus and/or question

Paradigm and rationale for chosen paradigm

Literature Review

Theoretical Orientation

Potential Contribution of study to micro and/or macro social work practice

Summary

One paragraph outlining what was covered in this chapter.

CHAPTER TWO

ENGAGEMENT

(Initial Engagement of Study Site Gatekeepers and Preparation for Study

In this section you address questions such as:what is your study site, where is your study site, what services does it provide, who are its clients, and who are the gatekeeper? How will you engage the study site gatekeepers in the initial development of the research question or focus? How will you prepare yourself to carry out this study? Which diversity issues do you need to be aware of and trained for? What are the ethical issues that your study will introduce? What are the political issues that your study will introduce? Is there a role for technology during this initial phase of engagement?

Introduction

One paragraph outlining what will be covered in this chapter.

Study Site

Engagement strategies for Gatekeepers at Research Site

Self Preparation

Diversity issues

Ethical issues

Political issues

The Role of Technology in Engagement

Summary

One paragraph outlining what was covered in this chapter.

CHAPTER THREE

IMPLEMENTATION

(Methodology)

In this chapteraddress questions such as, who will be in your study? How will you select study participants? Why will you use this approach? How will you gather data: interviews, observation, social artifacts, other? What are the phases of data collection? How will you record your data? How will you analyze your data: quantitative, qualitative, power analysis? How will you communicate your findings to the study site and study participants?How will you terminate the study? What will your ongoing relationship be with study participants? What is your plan for dissemination of the study findings?

Introduction

One paragraph outlining what will be covered in this chapter.

Study participants

Selection of Participants

Data Gathering

Phases of data collection

Data recording

Data Analysis

Termination and Follow Up

Communication of Findings and Dissemination Plan

Summary

One paragraph outlining what was covered in this chapter.

APPENDIX A

DATA COLLECTION INSTRUMENT(S)
(including informed consent, questions, debriefing)

REFERENCES

Part 3

Implementation

Quantitative and Qualitative Data Gathering

Contents

Part 3 discusses Implementation in relation to positivism, post positivism, critical theory and constructivism. Each paradigm is discussed in a separate chapter and important cross cutting themes are discussed in the final chapter:

Chapter I: Positivism
Chapter II: Post Positivism
Chapter III: Critical Theory
Chapter IV: Constructivism
Chapter V: Important Cross Cutting Themes

However, there is some overlap between the paradigms. Where an overlap is noted, there are links to the shared information.

Having engaged the research site, assessed the research question, focus or statement and made a plan for the study, we can begin carrying out the data gathering stage of the study. If we are implementing a positivist research project, then we are gathering quantitative data. This means that we are gathering data that will be translated into numbers. If we are carrying out a post positivist research project, then we are gathering qualitative data. Our data will be in the form of words and sentences. If we are carrying out a critical theory research project we will gather mostly qualitative data but we may have a reason to gather quantitative data when evaluating the success of the action taken to empower. If we are carrying out a constructivist research project, we will be gathering qualitative data. In this part of the book, **quantitative data gathering** is described with reference to the positivist and critical theory paradigms and **qualitative data gathering** is described with reference to post positivism, critical theory and constructivism as shown in Table 1.1

Table 1.1
Data Gathering for each Paradigm

	Quantitative (information represented in numbers)	Qualitative (information represented in words)
Positivism	X	
Post Positivism		X
Critical Theory	X	X
Constructivism		X

To gather quantitative data we need to develop a data gathering instrument, decide whether we will administer that instrument via face to face interviews, group interviews, or through a self administered process and also decide how we will manage the data. To carry out precise measurement, make probabilistic statements about causality and correlation, and generalize findings from a sample to a broader population; we translate information about human behavior into numbers that can be manipulated by statistical procedures. To make this translation reliable and valid, we develop and test measurement instruments before data gathering begins. Such instruments will perform the pretest and/or posttest for causal studies or be the standardized questionnaire that will measure the variables to be correlated.

Developing the Data Gathering Instrument

Sheatsley (1983) (page 201) notes that a well-designed questionnaire should meet the objectives of the research, obtain the most complete and accurate information possible, and do this within the limits of available time and resources. This author also suggests five simple steps for constructing a questionnaire (page 202). These are,

1. Decided what information is required

2. Draft some questions to elicit that information

3. Put them in a meaningful order and format

4. Pretest the result

5. Go back to step 1.

When we start considering the questions for our measurement instrument, the first issue to be address is whether they should be open or closed ended. **Open-ended questions** let the respondent verbalize the answer. **Closed ended, or multiple choice, questions** ask the respondent to choose an answer from a list of alternatives which have been developed by the researcher. While open ended questions encourage respondents to answer in their own terms, they can lead to repetition, the gathering of irrelevant information and misunderstandings about the intent of the question. They also lead to considerable additional coding work in the analysis phase of the study. Closed ended questions limit respondents' input into the wording of answers but ensure that the interviewer or anyone else is not influencing the answer by randomly encouraging elaboration or making suggestions for answers. Sometimes we can combine closed and open-ended questions by giving a list of possible responses to a question and then adding a section where other comments can be made if desired. Generally though, as positivist researchers of causal and correlational questions, we will favor closed ended question wherever possible so that our quantitative data is consistently and accurately gathered.

It is a common practice to use **scaling techniques** when developing closed ended questions. The most common types of scales are **Guttman scales** and **Likert scales**. Gutman scales measure cumulatively while **Likert** scales measure dimensionally. A **Gutman** scale of items measuring supervision might include a list of statements that are ordered so that each one gradually describes a more authoritarian style of supervision. Supervisors would be asked to select the item that reflects his or her supervision style. A **Likert** scale of supervision might list the same items but instead, ask supervisors to strongly agree, agree, disagree or strongly disagree with each statement. These scales would be measuring the same concept but the conceptualization of measurement of the concept of supervision would be slightly different. For example one item in a **Guttman** scale for supervision might be:

1. When providing supervision I *(circle one choice only)*,

2. Encourage the supervisee to suggest the discussion topics in an open ended free flowing discussion

3. Suggest that the supervisee come prepared with some talking points that he or she would think we need to discuss

4. Have some key talking points that I think we need to discuss

5. Have a clear agenda with detailed descriptions of the learning that should take place during the session

However a **Likert** scale using the same items would ask a slightly different question as we see below, *(circle one response to each item)*

1. In supervision the supervisee should suggest the discussion topics in an open ended free flowing discussion

    Strongly agree   agree   disagree   Strongly Disagree

2. In supervision the supervisor should suggest that the supervisee come prepared with some talking points that he or she would think we need to discuss

    Strongly agree   agree   disagree   Strongly Disagree

3. In supervision the supervisor should provided some key talking points that need to be discussed

    Strongly agree   agree   disagree   Strongly Disagree

4. In supervision the supervisor should have a clear agenda with detailed descriptions of the learning that should take place during the session

    Strongly agree   agree   disagree   Strongly Disagree

Another form of **Likert** scale is a semantic differential where we ask respondents to choose between opposite poles on an issue. For example, if supervisees were being surveyed they might be given an instrument with the following instructions and format,

On the items below circle the number on the continuum that best reflects the supervisory style that you experience in this organization

positive feedback									negative feedback
1	2	3	4	5	6	7	8	9	10
Makes you feel like you make a positive Contribution									Never Comments on Your Contribution
1	2	3	4	5	6	7	8	9	10
Responds to your Stress level									Never comments on Stress Level
1	2	3	4	5	6	7	8	9	10
Helps you learn About best Practice									Never addresses practice learning
1	2	3	4	5	6	7	8	9	10
Helps you reflect on Your practice									Never encourages Reflection
1	2	3	4	5	6	7	8	9	10

Certain principles should guide the writing of questions and scales and certain mistakes should be avoided according to both Sheatley (1983) and Krossnick and Presser (2010).

1. Keep it simple

2. Avoid lengthy questions, keep it to 25 words or less

3. Specify alternatives, don't just give one side of the issue. For example, my supervisor is dictatorial: strongly agree, agree, disagree, strongly disagree.

4. Avoid loaded questions. For example, most experts think that a facilitative style of supervision is most effective, what do you think?

5.

Common mistakes when wording questions include:

1. Writing a double-barreled question, where a respondent is asked about two different things in the same question. For example, how satisfied are you with your supervisor both as a colleague and as a manager? The respondent may have different feelings about the two roles

2. Assuming a false premise, where the respondent is thought to have an opinion that he or she might not have. For example, what should be done to

solve the problems with supervision? This may leave the respondent wondering "what problems?"

3. Writing a question that is vague and ambiguous, when the meaning of the question is not clear or can have several interpretations. For example, do you get supervision? This leaves the respondent to define supervision and to define what "getting" it means

4. Writing a question that includes overlapping alternatives, where the alternatives in the question are not mutually exclusive and respondent could truthfully answer yes or no to them all. For example, are you generally satisfied with supervision in this department or are there some things you do not like about it? The respondent maybe both satisfie2d and have some concerns.

5. Writing questions that include double negatives, where the respondent is asked about not doing something where the meaning of answering "yes" or "no" is not completely clear. For example, would you be in favor of not training supervisors?

6. Asking about intentions to act, where the respondent is asked what they would do in a hypothetical situation. For example, if group supervision were offered would you go to it? Such statements are poor predictors of actual behavior.

Having decided on our questions, our next step is to decide on the structure of the data collection instrument. We should start with a brief introduction explaining the study, the questionnaire, who the study is for, and who we are. The opening questions should be easy and non-threatening and any difficult or controversial questions should come later. We need to make sure the instrument is not too long and justify every item. Also, we need to be sure that we are asking the right person the question; that is, someone who is knowledgeable and interested in the topic.

To decide which questions should be included in our data gathering instrument, we need to review the variables in our question (s) and hypothesis (es) and think about the best questions that would measure those variables. Variables can be measured at four levels: **nominal**, **ordinal, interval** and **ratio**. It is important to understand levels of measurement because later, this will influence the appropriate statistics to be used when analyzing our data. **Nominal** measurement is simply categorization of data with no real numerical value for the number given to each category. The number is simply used as a way of identifying each different category of the variable. Thus the values cannot accumulate. In our example studies, approaches to training, permanent employment, families, and mental health clinics are nominal variables.

Figure I.1, Examples of Nominal Variables

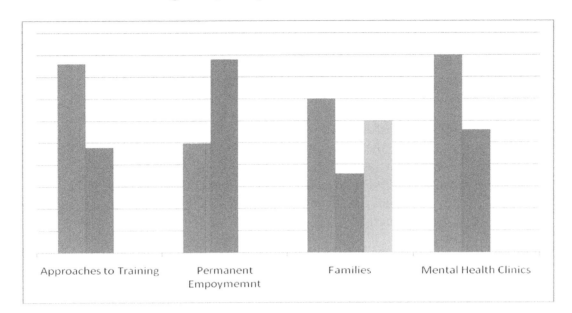

As we can see in figure I.1, there are 2 approaches to training, 2 levels of employment, 3 kinds of families and 2 kinds of mental health clinics. Adding the values for dimensions of any of these variables makes no sense. The total would tell us nothing.

Ordinal variables have levels of measurement that identify different values of the variable and can be added but these values have been assigned for non-mathematical reasons. In our example studies both items on the FAD and Supervision are ordinal variables (see column 3 of Table I.2 in Part 1). The levels of the dimensions of these variables have value relative to each other; a score of 1 on the FAD items denotes more agreement with an item on that instrument than a score of 3. A score of 3 on supervision variable denotes a more authoritarian supervision style than a score of 7. But the size of the difference between these scores is unknown. Two is not necessarily twice as high as one and three is not necessarily three times as high as one. This is illustrated in figure I.2 where we can see that the differences between Strongly Agree, Agree, Disagree, and Strongly Disagree can be different.

Figure I.2 Illustration of Ordinal Variable

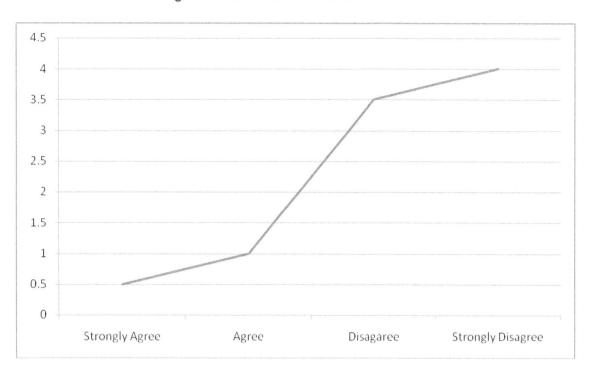

Moving to the next level of measurement, scores on **ratio and interval** variables *do* have equal mathematical relationships and for all practical purposes ratio and interval levels of measurement are the same. Just to be clear, though, age and money are variables measured at the ratio level because they have a true zero, you can have no money (right?) and you can be aged zero. However I.Q. is measure at the interval level since it has no true zero, you cannot have zero intelligence (yes, it's true!). In our examples both uptake of mental health services and staff retention rates are variables measured at the ratio level. This is illustrated in Table I.2 in Part 1 in relation to staff retention rates.

So now that we understand levels of measurement we are ready to decide how we will measure the variables in our study examples. For our nominal variables measurement it is quite straight forward, we simply count the numbers for each category. We add up the number of people who got training and we add up the number who did not get training or we add up the number of people in the Anglo ethnic group, in the Hawaiian American Ethnic group and in the Japanese American ethnic group. For our ordinal variables we have one preexisting instrument (FAD) and one instrument that needs to be created for this study (measurement of supervision style).

As we create our new instrument we must remember that it should be both reliable and valid. **Reliability** is the consistency with which the instrument measures the variables. That is, if the same situation recurs will the instrument give that situation the same score each time it is measured? The best way to explain this idea is to think of a decision you might make to lose weight. You step on your weighing scales one day and you are shocked at the number you see on the scale. You are sure it could not be correct, so you go to a friend's house and use the weighing scales in her bathroom. You see the same number staring back at you. Both these scales are giving you the same message, and it turns out that your scale is **reliably** measuring your weight. So, you go on your diet and you lose 10lbs in the first week. Low and behold, when you stand on your weighing scale, it shows a number that is 10lbs less than a week ago. You know this is true because you know that your weighing scale is reliable. Whatever you weigh, your scale reliably reflects that number of pounds, no matter how many times you step on and step off of the scale.

To return to our social work practice example then, given a series of supervisors with similar characteristics, we need to know if our instrument will give each of those supervisors the same score on supervision style. So, if there is a group of supervisors with authoritarian approaches to supervision, does our instrument label each one as having that style? Or, does it assess them as having a lot of different styles when this is not true? That is, does it measure the same thing the same way every time?

The concept of reliability becomes clearer when we contrast it with validity. **Validity** refers to the accuracy with which a measurement instrument reflects the variable or concept that it is measuring. If we return to our dieting plans: imagine that your weighing scale is actually calibrated incorrectly. Imagine that when you stepped on the scale it measured you as 10lbs heavier that you actually are. Every time you step on the scale it gave you that extra weight. Now your scale is reliable, because it measures you with the same weight every time you step on the scale, but it is not a valid measure of your weight because the weight the scale registers is wrong (thank goodness).

To use our pre-existing instrument measuring family functioning as an example, the FAD assesses families on problem solving, communication, roles, affective involvement, affective responsiveness, behavior control and general functioning. Does this instrument appear to address all dimensions of family functioning? This is **face and content validity**. Does this instrument measure the same way as other measures of family functioning or predict accurately how "problem free" a family might be? This is **criterion related validity**? Does this measure of family functioning measure the same way as other aspects of family functioning, for example, family violence? This is **construct validity**. For this pre existing instrument the **reliability and validity** can be given since it has been used in other studies and it is reported in articles which used that instrument. For the instrument we intend to create we will need to assess validity and reliability before and during the study.

To create the instrument assessing supervision styles we would need to look at definitions of supervision. Since we are studying the difference between two contrasting styles, a semantic differential Likert type scale would be a good choice. Gibbs (2001) suggests that elements of effective supervision include: acknowledgement of the emotional intrusiveness of the work; building resilience in workers; and, adopting the principles of adult learning theory that include reflective supervision. She suggests that an effective supervisor will move beyond a focus on the tasks to be completed and become a messenger who sends and receives messages to and from workers, affirming both the merit and necessity of exploring the impact of feelings and thoughts on action and perception. She suggests that supervisors must affirm the value of individual workers to the organization, building self-esteem and self-efficacy. These findings suggest dimensions that we might build into our supervision scale as follows.

In supervision we *(circle one number)*

Concentrate on the task	1	2	3	4	5 Reflect on the Task to be done
Never address emotions	1	2	3	4	5 Acknowledge emotional impact of the work
Concentrate on	1	2	3	4	5 Acknowledge issues professional judgment

Accountability

Feel blamed for failure	1	2	3	4	5 Learn about assessing and learning from each situation

These items can be pre-tested with respondents that are similar to but not included in the study sample and modified accordingly.

Managing and Implementing Data Collection

Having found a valid reliable existing instrument or developed our own new instrument, the next step is to actually collect the data. The first decision is whether to administer the surveys in a face-to-face situation or adopt one of many self-administered questionnaire strategies. This decision will depend upon sample size, time and resources. The larger the sample size and the less time and resources we have, the more likely we are to choose a self-administered strategy. However, if we have the time and resources, the face-to-face strategy ensures that we have control of the interview setting and can immediately clarify any misunderstandings about the intent of questions.

Face-to-Face Interviews

Personal Interviews: Schaeffer et al (2010) note interviews are one of several possible modes of data gathering. In a personal interview, as we work our way through the data collection instrument, we can see the person, we can make a non-verbal assessment of how things are going and decide whether the respondent is offering reliable and valid information. Also, personal interviews are a more sensitive way to make contact with culturally diverse populations, poorer groups, older people and those who live in more isolated communities. Recently, there has been a focus on how study participants often give incorrect information in an interview. This is not to accuse study participants of telling lies, it's just that often, in any situation, when someone asks us a questions we unintentionally give incorrect information. This reality has led to a recent focus on cognitive processes in answering survey questions.

Tougrangeau and Norman (2010) in their discussion of the psychology of responding to survey questions, note that a person's response to survey questions entails four things:

1. **Comprehension of the question**: Often the study participant does not understand the words in the question in the same way that the interviewer understands those words. For example we might ask a study participant "Do you have supervision?" A person responding to this question will have to make up their own mind whether we are including informal conversations with more experienced colleagues or formal session with designated mentors. This will depend on context, is this a new employee being interviewed in a study of employee morale or a middle manager being interviewed in a study of leadership succession? This context also allows an interviewee to make assumptions about the intent of the question. Tourangeau and Bradburn (2010) give four tips for improving comprehension:

    a. Provide as much information as is necessary for the purpose at hand and no more

    b. Be truthful

    c. Stick to the topic

    d. Be clear. (page 320)

2. **Retrieval:** When trying to remember something we access our long term memory and our working memory. Our long term memory stores general information we have gathered about the world around us and how to do things that we have learned, like riding a bike (or not). It also stores information about specific events in our lives. Working memory is our ongoing cognitive processing of things as they happen. It works quickly but has limited capacity, while long term memory works more slowly but has unlimited capacity. To answer a question, we need to remember something and that means moving information from long term memory to working memory. So the person asking the question needs to offer retrieval cues. For example, if we ask the question "Did you get supervision in the last six months?" a respondent's mind might go blank and he or she might not be able to think of anything. Then we need to offer cues that assist retrieval of that information and "activate the pathways of association leading to the desired information" (page 322). For example, "Do you usually have supervision in your office or somewhere else? Which day of the week do you usually have supervision?

3. **Judgment/Estimation**: When formulating an answer to a question, there are four processes that we might use:

a. *Direct retrieval of an existing answer.* For example, the respondent's age or the number of years he or she might have worked at a particular agency

b. *Retrieval of general information from which an answer can be constructed or inferred.* For example, when asked how many times he or she had a supervision session last year, the respondent might not remember but they may know that they have supervision sessions once a month and so they may give an answer based on that information.

c. *Retrieval of specific memories form which an answer can be derived.* For example, when asked the question about supervision sessions, a respondent might remember one session and then count up the number of times a session like that is remembered.

d. *Retrieval of an impression.* This is a vaguer process. When asked about supervision sessions, a respondent may have a vague idea of when they happen and give an answer base on that idea.

The decision a respondent makes about which of these strategies to us may depend on how seriously the interviewee is about the topic or how much energy he or she is willing to put into answering questions.

4. **Reporting an answer**. When we use quantitative survey instruments, we structure the form and range of answers a respondent can make. We ask if they strongly agree or agree and often a respondent does not have an opinion about the question we are asking or has opinions that one person might consider strong while another might consider not so strong. So often, the answer is edited and, according to Tourangeau and Norman (2010), the main reason for this is to avoid embarrassment in front on the interviewer.

It is clear that we need to be aware of the psychological processes that are associated with answering interview questions so that we can gather accurate data. This not only reemphasizes the need to be aware of mistakes in wording of questions noted above but also, according to Tourangeau and Norman (2010) respondents' potential to:

1. not take in or, misinterpret, the information we are asking about;

2. misunderstand questions;

3. have difficulty with retrieving information from memory;

4. have difficulty with correctly estimating data about events in the past;

5. be influenced by the questions that preceded each question;

6. edit responses on sensitive topics; and

177

7. round down rather than up when giving numerical estimates in open ended questions, avoid extreme ratings on rating scales, and be influenced by the order of choices when given a list of alternative of responses.

Individual interviews are clearly expensive and time consuming. It takes time to set up the interview, travel to the interview site and generally engage someone in a personal exchange. A one-hour interview can take three or four hours when all of this is taken into account. One way to maintain the face-to-face contact with respondents but, at the same time, gather data more efficiently is to use a group interview strategy.

Group Discussion This is an effective quick way to pre test an interview instrument. A group of people who are not in the sample but who have similar characteristics to those who will be in the sample can be brought together to review and respond to the instrument.

Group Interview A way to solve the problem of the time consuming nature of personal interviews is to organize group interviews. A pre existing group such as a group of workers can be brought together at a regular meeting time such as a staff meeting to complete questionnaires. In this way the researcher controls the data-gathering setting and any clarification questions can be answered but several questionnaires are completed.

Telephone Interviews

A compromise between face-to-face interviews and the use of self-administered questionnaires is the telephone interview. If participants are informed about the study, knowledgeable and interested in the topic, and are willing to put some time into an interview this can be an effective strategy. Lavrak as (2010) offers the following guidelines:

1. Decide on a sampling method for selecting telephone numbers;

2. Decide on the time period, days of the week, and time of day for data gathering;

3. Decide on the maximum number of attempts for each telephone number;

4. Set up a procedure for logging contact with each telephone number;

5. Draft a survey, including an introduction, that is not too long for a telephone conversation, not longer than 15 to 20 minutes;

6. Decide on the language to be used and translate all materials to that language;

7. Decide on whether to make advance contact with possible participants via mail or email and whether there will be an incentive for being in the study; and

8. Try some practice interviews with friends or acquaintances who will not be in the study

Face-to-face strategies for gathering data include personal interviews, group discussions and interviews, and telephone interviews.

Each approach has pros and cons. The face to face interview gives us the most complete control over the interview and the context of data gathering but it is time consuming. Group strategies facilitate more data gathering in a shorter period of time but the researcher does not always have complete control over the data gathering process. Telephone interviews are even more efficient, it terms of time, but they cannot last much longer than 15 to 20 minutes and it is very easy for someone to just hang up the phone when asked to participate in this kind of data gathering process.

Self Administered Questionnaires

Because of the above issues with face-to-face data gathering strategies, many studies use self administered questionnaire to gather data and web based internet surveys have become a most popular approach to this data gathering strategy. We can make a relatively inexpensive subscription to a web based service and then upload our instrument into a professional, easily accessible format that study participants can access via a web link in an invitational email. According to Couper and Bosnjak (2010) web based internet surveys have the following advantages:

1. They are self administered and, therefore, the affect of the interviewer on the study participant is removed. This is particularly true in relation to participants feeling the need to give socially desirable responses.

2. They are computerized, and so quite sophisticated data gathering strategies such as:

    a. variations in question types,

    b. customizing questions

    c. word fills using previously uploaded information about the study participant or previously answered questions,

    d. branching questions depending on study participants' answers,

    e. correct incorrect entries with automatic error messages, preventing the study participant from skipping to the end before answering certain questions,

    f. randomizing the order of questions

3. They can be interactive giving study participants the opportunity to respond to tailored text or hints about the meanings of certain terms. They can even include motivational messages such as "we are nearly done" to keep the study participant engaged

4. They are easily distributed. However, technical issues with study participants' computer hardware and/or software can interfere with this ease of access.

5. They offer the opportunity to include rich graphics such as drawings, photographs and videos.

There are other internet strategies for gathering data such as the use of "apps." on smart phones, downloadable surveys attached to emails, and the use of online text or voice tools. This is a constantly changing environment that we can only acknowledge and then negotiate at the time of data gathering.

A more old fashioned approach to self administered questionnaires is the paper questionnaire that is mailed out. Harrison (2010) notes that, since the researcher is not present when the study participant receives this questionnaire, attention should be paid to the visual layout of each page and the format of each question. Harrison (2010) outlines the following principles regarding visual presentation of questionnaires

1. Response boxes are typically simple squares so that they are easily and quickly comprehended

2. Items in the same group are spaced together. For example a rating scale may have a larger space between the "don't know" option and the actual scale

3. In general, items on addressing the same topic should be grouped together

4. Text and shading can be used to enhance understanding. One convention suggests that bold type should be used for questions, plain text for response choices, and italics for instructions or clarification. Sometimes the background of the question is lightly shaded while the response area is white

5. Ordinal scales should be place horizontally. If choices are place vertically, there should be only one column, multiple columns can be confusing

6. If there are navigational paths that the respondent needs to follow depending on answers to certain questions, need to include visual aids marking the beginning and end of separate sections and using arrows to guide the study participant to the desired section of the questionnaire.

7. Questionnaire booklets should have a cover page with the study title, a short explanation of the study, contact information for the researcher, and survey return instructions.

The other organizational tasks of data collection include monitoring the return of questionnaires and any follow up mailings and emails that might improve the response rate. This brings us back to a consideration of sampling and probability theory. From the discussion of Planning in Chapter 3we can see how crucial it is that a random sample is surveyed so that probability theory and sampling theory can be used as rationales for generalizing the results of our analysis to a wider population of interest. However, most surveys get a response rate of approximately 25%; a 50% response rate is considered good but even if we manage to gather data from 50% of our original sample we no longer have a probability sample, but we are still estimating the likelihood that our statistics, which are estimates based on probability theory, are accurate estimates of the characteristics of the population of interest. One solution to this problem is to use replacement sampling where we would continue down our list and add people to the sample as respondents fall out of our sample. However, these replacement members of the sample have an equal likelihood of not responding. There comes a point where we have to end data collection and use the sample we have.

The implementation stage for positivist involves developing data gathering instruments before data gathering begins and using either face-to-face or self administered strategies for gathering the data. These procedures are designed to give the study strong quantitative validity and reliability. Important cross cutting issues of ethics, politics, diversity and technology or similar to those discussed in Part 1 and Part 2. However, additional diversity and technology issues for the Implementation stage are discussed in Chapter 5. Below is a summary of this chapter and positivist learning assignments. We can now move on the Chapter II and the post positivist approach to Implementation.

Summary of Chapter I

- Since quantitative data is needed for positivist research, standardized instruments are developed

- The favored form of instrument is one containing closed ended questions using Guttman or Likert scaling

- When writing items for a questionnaire, be careful to follow suggested guidelines and principles with relation to item construction and diversity.

- When creating items for surveys we need to understand the difference between nominal, ordinal, ratio and interval levels of measurement

- We also need to address reliability and validity

- When organizing data collection, we need to decide on a mode of communication with the respondent that is either face-to-face or at a distance.

- We need to track the response rate.

- We need to consider diversity issues when developing data gathering instruments

1. For the questions you developed in Part 2, for either the causal or correlational question, think of 10 questions you could ask a study participant. Remember the answers to these questions will provide data that answers your overall research question and tests your hypothesis.

2. Get into pairs, and ask your partner the 10 questions. Did you get data that answered your research question? Was the data nominal, ordinal, interval or ratio? Did your data allow you to test your hypothesis? If so, did your data confirm or reject the null hypothesis?

3. Ask your partner to give you feedback on the actual questions you used. Were they easy to understand? Could there have been a better way to ask these questions?

As post positivist researchers, we gather data in naturalistic settings by,

1. engaging people in conversations via **interviews** or group meetings; and/or

2. **observing** people interacting with each other; and/or

3. studying **documents** and social artifacts.

So we now consider approaches to gathering **qualitative data** Skilled questioning, active listening, focused observation, and disciplined reading will all facilitate the collection of valid qualitative data. There are various ways that we can organize our thinking as we prepare for these activities. We might ask ourselves core questions Why, What, How, When and Where (Stringer 2007) in relation to the topic we are studying; we might use foci such as: meanings, practices, episodes, encounters, roles, relationships (Lofland and Lofland 1995); or we might use case study structures or ethnographic frameworks. All of these strategies will assist us in our interviews, observations, and document review.

Interviews

As post positivists we approach interviews in a different way to positivists. Unlike positivists we acknowledge the inevitability of the impact of tour own values and biases on the interview and on data collection in general. We are searching for regularities and patterns that will emerge from the data and be assembled into a theory. So we comfortable with preparing a structured set of questions before the interview because this will make sure that all interviewees experience the same or a similar interview and common patterns regarding similar research foci will be addressed. However, we are also comfortable with changing this set of questions as the study progresses because ongoing data analysis may lead to ideas we had not considered. We do accept the positivist assumption that previous knowledge is the foundation for our data collection and we have looked to previous knowledge in the form of readings and the opinions of key players and experts to identify the topics and questions to be addressed at the beginning of the study. However, we are anticipating incremental changes during the data gathering phase of the study.

We do not see the topics addressed in these interviews as variables to be identified, measured and tested but rather foci to be explored, reexamined, perhaps redefined, and eventually connected with each other. Thus we use strategies aimed at identifying patterns and regularities. Crabtee and Miller (1999) suggest three categories of questions that explore a person's understanding of a research focus and assist in the process of sorting data for later analysis. These are **descriptive, structural** and **contrast** questions.

Descriptive questions are over arching questions such as: what is your day-to-day experience with homelessness? What do you do in a typical day spent in the shelter? More focused descriptive questions might be: What things do you like about the shelter? How do you spend your weekends at the shelter? Who are your friends there and what do you do together? What is your vision for your future?

Structured questions expand understanding of a particular topic. They can be: **inclusion questions, verification questions**, or **substitution frame questions**. Inclusion questions expand a particular topic, verification questions assess a researcher's understanding of a topic and substitution frame questions remove a piece of information from a question and invite the respondent to replace the piece of information with his or her understanding or reaction. Using our sample phrases from the literature review process described in chapter 2, they might be: How has the shelter helped your family **(inclusion)**? Since you live in the shelter, do you even see yourself as homeless **(verification)**? When I think of the future of these homeless children I feel powerless, *substituted with*, When I think of the future of these homeless children I feel...**(substitution frame)**.

Contrast questions develop criteria for inclusion and exclusion for a category of knowledge. For example the interviewer might ask, with reference to the shelter, what is it about the shelter that makes you feel like you have a home and family? Is there anything about the shelter that makes you feel like you do not have a home and family? These are "pile sorting" and "set sorting" questions where various topics are labeled as respondents report agreement on information that should be included in each topic. Topics are then grouped into sets and labeled as concepts. For example children may repeatedly report that shelter life makes them feel like they are not homeless anymore but does makes them feel deprived because they can't invite friends over to their house. This might be used to build a definition of a continuum of homelessness, ranging from being on the street to having a home, where being in a shelter is at a midpoint of that continuum. At this midpoint on the continuum, the shelter and basic food needs are met but developmental and social needs are not met. However, at the "being on the street point of the continuum is a point where none of these needs are met and the point of the continuum where the family has its own home is a point where all of these needs are met. This continuum might then be combined with other continua, which address feelings of self-esteem at various stages of homelessness and family functioning at various stages of homelessness, to form a rough draft of the set of homelessness continua shown in Table 4.1 that will guide further thinking and question development. All of this synthesis of data is built from descriptive, structured and contrast questions that are used throughout the interview process as appropriate.

Table II.1
Possible Synthesis of Interview Data

	Living on Street or in a car	Living in Homeless Shelter	Living in Permanent Home
Basic Food and Shelter Needs met	No	Yes	Yes
Developmental Needs of Children Met	No	Sometimes	Yes
Social Needs of Family met	No	No	Yes
Level of Children's Self Esteem	Low	Low-Medium	High
Level of Family Functioning	Dysfunctional	Stable but not yet Functional	Functional

As well as deciding on questions for the interview, we also anticipate the various stages of an interview. Tutty et al. (1996) suggest the following steps in the interviewing process.

1. <u>Preparing for the interview.</u>

This includes preparation for both the interviewer and the interviewee. As post positivist interviewers we prepare ourselves by being knowledgeable about the topic and having a set of prepared questions. We also work on developing a consciousness of our own biases and values regarding the research topic and "controlling" the influence of these biases and values on the data gathering process. The earlier we develop the habit of recognizing and controlling the influence of our values and biases on the research project, the more credibility the data and findings will have. One place where this process takes place is in the research journals discussed in <u>Part 1</u> as we record our thought processes and reasoning as the study is implemented. This journal writing also facilitates the reflection on, and stepping back from the data, so favored by Strauss and Corbin (2008).

When preparing the interviewee, we make sure that the he or she is properly oriented to the research study and this interview. We secure the participant's informed consent, ensuring privacy and confidentiality, ensuring that no harm will come to the interviewee and answering any questions the interviewee might have. Formal Human Subjects approval for the study will have included a sample informed consent letter. However, since qualitative interviewing for post positivist research purposes involves a more intense engagement with the interviewee, phone calls and letters offering extra explanations about the study are important. Our aim is to put the interviewee at ease so that reliable, valid and comprehensive data is collected during the interview.

2. <u>Choosing a recording mode</u>

Having completed preparation tasks successfully, we must now establish a method of making accurate records of data collected during the interview. Videoing or sound recording would offer the most fidelity but may well, even with the miniaturized cameras and microphones we have today, make an interviewee uneasy. Taking notes during the interview may be distracting and taking notes after the interview may result in the omission of important data this is simply forgotten or ignored. Every method has its strengths and drawbacks. We are aiming to get the most accurate record of everything that is said during the interview and thus would favor a form of sound recording at least. However, note taking assists us in processing and clarifying responses during the interview. Whatever the decision, it is important to negotiate the recording mode with the interviewee before, or at the start of, the interview and establish a comfort level during the interview that facilitates valid data gathering.

If recording or note taking during the interview is not an option, then a record of the interview must be developed immediately after the interview and Neuman and Kreuger's (2003) advice on how to recall important information is useful. Some of their hints are listed and modified here:

- Make notes as soon as possible after the interview, a laptop computer or electronic tablet with a keyboard would be the most efficient mode for doing this.

- Make sure you have included identifying information: time, place, interviewee name, role, etc

- Record the conversation in the order it happened including everything that you can remember, even if it seems irrelevant right now.

- Record your reactions and feelings at this point and any insights that come into your mind as you write.

- Make diagrams, charts or tables if they explain ideas

- Try not to evaluate what was said, simply record without commentary

- Make sure you have a backup copy of the record you develop.

Additional issues associated with recording data are discussed in Chapter IV with reference to constructivist interviews

3. Conducting the interview

Generally, like any conversation with another person, the interview is divided into phases that build comfort and familiarity. These are usually **engagement, development of focus, maintaining focus** and **termination**. However, it would be useful to be aware of various individuals' reactions to these stages. Some people or cultures may not see the need for the engagement stage given the informed consent process. Others may need a long period of engagement. And still others may be conscious of the gender and ethnicity of the researcher and need to take time to react to and process the prospect of being interviewed by a particular interviewer. Regardless of order of stages of the interview, or the interview questions, Berg (2009) notes that in order to obtain the most complete data from an interview, four types of questions to assist the interview process should be included:

> **Essential Questions:** These are questions addressing the specific research topic, they can be grouped together or scattered throughout the interview. (What is it like to live in the shelter? What are your three wishes for the future? What would your dream home look like?)

> **Extra Question:** These are questions that are similar to essential questions but worded slightly differently to check on the consistency of responses to the same inquiry. (Do you enjoy living in the shelter? What do you think you will be doing in five year's time? Where would you like to live?)

> **Throw Away Questions**: These maybe demographic questions or general questions used at the beginning of the interview to establish rapport. They may also be scattered throughout the interview to assist a change in focus or to calm things down if a sensitive topic has been broached. Berg refers to this as "cooling out the subject" (Where were you born? Did you like it there? What do you remember about that place? What is you favorite food? Who is your best friend?)

> **Probing Questions**: These are simply requests for elaboration such as "tell me about that" or minimal encouragers such as "ah ah" or "I see". Again, these might be scattered throughout the interview depending on needs for clarification and elaboration.

Berg (2009) describes the interview as a drama or a scene from a play where one person has a script and the other does not. He suggests that as interviewers we should be aware of our changing roles as actor, director and choreographer. He also suggests that the more practice or "rehearsal" that you have, the better interviewer you become. In time you start to sense which role to play and how to sequence questions.

We signal the termination of the interview by offering an overall summary of our understanding of what has been said. This is a time to ask the interviewee for feedback on the interview and to address any concerns that might be voiced. It has been an intense "conversation" and it is important that we ease out of the interview in the same way that we eased into it. It is a good idea to gradually reduce the intensity of questions, and include non-threatening throwaway comments as the exchange ends. The interviewee should know how to contact us if he or she has further questions. The likely use of the data should be clarified as well as the source of information about the findings of the study.

4. Reflecting about the interview

After the interview it is important to take time to write in the research journal about reactions, both thoughts and feelings, to the experience. We should decide if the data gathered was important or irrelevant to the study. This is the time to evaluate the interview, what worked and what did not work? Was there a functional balance between types of questions? How did our values and biases affect the interview and how were these values and biases challenged by the interview? What can be improved next time?

To summarize guidance for interviewing, the checklist below combines Berg's ten commandments of interviewing with some important reminders to give you guidance on carrying out your post positivist interview.

1. Never begin an interview cold, make sure there is an initial engagement phase. In addition to gaining formal consent, continually strive to keep the person you are interviewing engaged and interested in the interview.

2. Remember your purpose, don't get distracted by something the interviewee is excited about but has nothing to do with the study. Make a decision about whether a tangent in the interview conversation is an important addition to the development of your theory or a completely different topic.

3. Present a natural front. Jean Giraudoux (1882-1944) said once that, "The secret of success is sincerity. Once you can fake that you've got it made". You need not be this cynical but you do need to put your interviewee at ease by being relaxed and informal.

4. Demonstrate aware hearing. Use non-verbal cues or minimal encouragers such as "I see" or "Is that right?" to communicate that you have heard what has been said and are interested in hearing more. Reflect back what you have heard and check that you have understood correctly

5. Think about your appearance. What is the appropriate dress in this setting and how will the interviewee react to how you look? Think about the range of possibilities from formal to informal clothing and find out what is appropriate and acceptable.

6. Interview in a comfortable place. Where is the interview most relaxed, in your office or at a coffee shop? Find out.

7. Don't be satisfied with monosyllabic answers. Prompt for reflection from your interviewee. You have put a lot of work into organizing this interview; make sure you actually gather quality data.

8. Be respectful. Your mother told you first. Make sure you are polite and show appreciation for the time and effort the interviewee is putting into your project.

9. Practice, practice, and practice some more. Remember, you have the script and make sure you know it and deliver your lines well.

10. Be cordial and appreciative. See 8 above, this person is doing you a favor; let him or her know you appreciate it.

11. Make sure you prepare well for the interview and follow the stages of the interview identified above.

Observations

Although the usual source of information for a post positivist researcher is the interview, this has its limitations. The interview data gives us a firsthand report of the interviewee's own perceptions and knowledge but it is a second hand report, filtered by the interviewee, of the context and activities associated with the interviewee. Since accurate collection of data on an objective reality is our goal, as post positivists, then we may also need to make observations at the site of the research project and directly observe the context and activities at the study site. The ethics of some approaches to observation have been questioned and these are addressed in more detail in the discussion of critical theory observation in Chapter III. However, for the post positivist, the opportunity to observe objective data is a powerful motivation to proceed with this approach to data gathering.

The discipline with most experience of direct observation of human phenomena is anthropology and generally anthropologists refer to the practice of such observation as "Ethnography". Wolcott (1973) defines ethnography as "the science of cultural description". Berg (2009) notes that it "places researchers in the midst of whatever it is they study" and suggests that a new ethnography has emerged in the last 20 years that has "highly formal techniques designed to extract cognitive data."

Like interviewing, ethnography has stages which are: the beginning stage engaging people at the observation site; the process of gathering data; and the ending state of termination with the people at the site:

1. Accessing a Field Setting: "Getting in"

Like the interview, the beginning of observation has an engagement phase. We need to remember that this is an imposition on people and an intrusion into their daily lives, appreciation and thanks should be offered. Our personal motivations need to be faced as well. Is there some personal agenda for choosing to observe this situation? Is there some theoretical reason that makes this observation necessary or is it simply convenient? We should think through the purpose of the observation. Since, as post positivists, we do not want to influence the situation being observed, we must find ways to "become invisible" Berg (2009) offers six insightful strategies for doing this. These are:

189

i. Dis-attending by becoming invisible, or just being present in the setting over a long period of time so that eventually people do not pay any unusual attention to us;

ii. Dis-attending by making no symbolic attachments to activities being observed;

iii. Dis-attending by making symbolic attachments so that after initially being aware of a new member of the group, the role of observer becomes less important;

iv. Dis-attending by personalizing the ethnographer-informant relationship so that people simply just like having the observer around as a friend and colleague;

v. Dis-attending by masking the real research interest, thus the ethnographer pretends to be studying one thing but is actually studying another thing;

vi. Dis-attending by not revealing the ethnographer as a researcher and pretending to be simply a new member of the group.

The last two options, of course, would need to be thoroughly justified to a human subjects committee so that no harm results from such deception, and debriefing is carried out. In addition, the impact of any deception being revealed and potentially harming the researcher would need to be evaluated.

2. <u>Watching, Listening, and Learning</u>

Having entered the observation site we can begin to gather data. While in the observer or ethnographer role, we must be disciplined onlookers. This discipline includes:

- Taking in the physical setting, which includes mapping it out, deciding on the most significant places in the setting for the research focus, and developing a planned timetable for observing various areas;

- Developing relationships with inhabitants of the setting, which includes both casual conversations as well as conversations that may later be revisited for interview purposes;

- Tracking people, which includes observing individuals in a planned way for reasons associated with the purpose of the study, and eavesdropping; and finally,

- Locating subgroups and key players, which includes noting who the opinion leaders are, who the organizational leaders are, and identification of subgroups formed around both informal and formal issues and activities

Throughout this process we should take notes by recording key words and phrases while in the field, making notes about the sequence of events being observed, limiting the time in the setting so that only short periods of time need to be recalled for note taking, writing the notes immediately after leaving the field and writing the notes before discussing observations and conclusions with others.

3. Disengaging: "Getting Out"

Like approaching the ending of an interview, we must plan the process of terminating the observation period. This can be done by negotiating time lines at the beginning of the study but will still need our personal attention at the end of the study. People have been observed and are aware of us; they will react negatively if we just stop turning up. We and they will regret that. Talking to people about the study coming to an end is important or, if we have disguised that role, talking generally about leaving and the reasons for leaving is important. We and the study participants must be prepared for an ending and exit. The same issues that were discussed in the section on interviews need to be resolved with observations when it comes to recording the data we collect during observations. We need to decide if we are going to video or audio record or take notes and we need to address informed consent issues reviewed in Part 1

Documents and Social Artifacts

A third source of data is documents and social artifacts such as symbols or rituals that are talked about or observed in the research setting. These are sources of data and they can be analyzed using the approaches discussed in Part 4. However, for the post positivist there is a warning here. Documents are constructions of events. Indeed historical research is the research of those constructions, rather than the research of historical facts. There is a difference between historical data such as the Declaration of Independence and the Magna Carter and historical facts such as the dates of these documents. Thus documents used as data, reports or mission and goals statements, are not really appropriate for post positivist research since they are data on subjective understandings of an event or entity. They may enrich a concept or theory but, as subjective constructions, for the post positivist, they are a weak source of data. They are not a record of an objective reality and its regulatory mechanisms. Before using these documents as data, the post positivist needs to think about what they represent and how "accurate" the data is for an objective post positivist scientist.

To sum up, we have reviewed interview, observation, and a review of documents and artifacts as methods of data gathering for post positivists. The important cross cutting issues are similar to those discussed in Part 1 and Part 2. However, additional diversity and technology issues for Implementation are discussed in Chapter V. Below are a summary of this chapter and learning assignments. We can now move on to consider critical theory Implementation in the next chapter.

- Data can be gathered by means of interviews, observations or review of documents and artifacts

- Interviews have structures for both process and content

- We need to prepare for an interview

- We need to analyze each interview before moving on to the next interview

- We need to understand the psychological and social context of our interviews

- Both interviews and observations are carried out by means of a series of stages from beginning to ending the data gathering process

Post Positivist Learning Assignments

1. For the research topic you developed in Part 2, develop 2 descriptive, 2 structured and 2 contrast questions, also, develop 2 essential, extra, throw away, and probing questions.

2. With your partner, practice asking these questions and get feedback on how comfortable your partner is with your approach to interviewing.

As critical theorists we can gather quantitative data to support our ideological positions and proposed action plans. We can also use these methodologies to gather data on needs or to evaluate the effectiveness of a particular action plan. However, gathering qualitative data is our primary vehicle for developing the collaborative teaching/learning relationships between ourselves and study participants. We have three main goals for our critical theory data gathering:

1. looking and developing the ideological analysis;

2. organizing and implementing action;

3. evaluating the impact of action.

Interviews for Looking and Developing the Ideological Analysis

At this stage we are refining our ideological position as it relates to the focus of the study. We collect data for the ideological analysis from the literature as well as from interviews with key informants and any supporting observations. The literature on the ideology is reviewed using the synthesis techniques for any literature review and the ideological analysis described in Part 1. As social work researchers we may be addressing a topic at the micro or macro practice level. Thus the literature on the ideology and the research topic should be reviewed with this in mind. What does it say about social work interventions with individuals, families, groups, organizations or communities and their relationship with power and oppression? In our example studies, the Millet and Otero (2011) study of transportation needs showed us the social and economic impact of public transportation on low income communities, the Riech study of Curanderismo alerted us to a strategy for being culturally sensitive when intervening with a particular population of individuals and families. The Christopulos (1995) study of eating disorders alerted us to an aspect of human development that affects women and may well need to be included in a micro practice client assessment protocol.

Our interviews with key informants carried out at this stageaim to understand the interviewee's perception of the ideology and its relevance to him or her. Just to clarify, key informants are "individuals who possess special knowledge, status, or communication skills, who are willing to share that knowledge and skills with the researcher and who have access to perspectives or observations denied the researcher" Crabtree & Miller (1999). Interviews can be with individuals alone or with groups of participants. When carrying out these one-on-one interviews the best practice techniques, according to Evans et al (2004) include the following skills.

*   Listening Skills to draw out experiences, issues and problems

    o   Attending Behaviors (listening, eye contact, appropriate verbal and non-verbal responses)

- Effective Questioning: (timing open and closed questions appropriately and using minimal encouragers appropriately)

- Reflecting Content (hear and clearly describe to the interviewee what your are hearing)

- Reflecting Feeling (identify and reflect emotions)

- Helping interviewees to Understand and Expand Their Experiences

  - Communicating and sharing the interviewers own immediate feelings and reactions

  - Confronting. In a therapeutic interview this relates to client behavior. In the critical theory interview, this relates to labeling and exploring power relationships that affect the interviewee

  - Self-Disclosing: Again, this is not the same as a therapeutic interview. It relates to interviewers, appropriately, disclosing the oppression they have identified and their reasons for adopting the ideology that is guiding the study.

  - Information Giving. This includes the results of the ideological analysis of the literature and preliminary analysis of interviews with other key informants.

In these interviews we should follow the same planning, processing stages, and recording options that were described in the discussion of post positivist interviewing. However, an additional issue for deciding on the data recording mode will depend on the negotiated comfort we have developed while talking about sensitive political issues. Video or audio recording an interview may well inhibit the interviewee's willingness to explore power relationships and oppression. The same may be true for taking notes during the interview. We may well need to develop notes after the interview. Since this is an ideological analysis, below are some questions that will help us recall what was said about oppression and structure this process as we develop our notes.

- What was the interviewee's personal experience of the power relationship and its oppression? What is his or her history with this?

- What is the interviewee's perception of the group awareness and experience of this power relationship and oppression?

- What did the interviewee say about how this power relationship and oppression affects his or her ability to

  - Meet basic physical need

  - Relate with people

- Participate in decision-making processes and structures

- Have experienced a full formal education

- Reflect on how he or she was socialized

- Have access to recreation

- Develop trust, acceptance and belief in the society he or she experiences

- What are his or her demographic characteristics?

As well as interviews with individuals, we can carry out interviews in group settings. Fontana and Frey (1994), offer a typology of such interviews (page 365), shown in Table III.1

Table III.1
Types of Groups

Type	Setting	Role of Interviewer	Question Format	Purpose
Focus Group	Formal-Preset	Directive	Structured	Exploratory Pretest
Brainstorming	Formal or Informal	Nondirective	Very Unstructured	Exploratory
Nominal/Delphi	Formal	Directive	Structured	Pretest Exploratory
Field, Natural	Informal, Spontaneous	Moderately Nondirective	Very Unstructured	Exploratory Phenomen ological
Field, Formal	Preset, but in Field	Somewhat Directive	Semi-structured	Phenomen ological

In this early phase of the study we are pre-testing an ideological position and so we should choose either the focus group or nominal/delphi group. With the focus group, all group members address a preset list of questions developed by the researcher. With the nominal/Delphi method, there is a preset list of questions, but there is the opportunity to respond to other participants' answers to the questions. With these processes in mind, as facilitators we need to apply our group work skills. We need to watch for:

- those who are playing potentially positive roles (information seeker, collaborator, energizer, encourager, tension reliever, listener, etc); and

- those who are playing potentially negative roles (dominator, blocker, aggressor, recognition seeker, etc) (Kirst-Ashman & Hull, (2009).

Obviously the best strategy is to encourage the positive behavior and ignore the negative behavior. Since critical theory research addresses sensitive political topics, we may well need to deal with group conflict. Kirst-Ashman & Hull suggest that when a conflict emerges, the facilitator can adopt the following strategies.

- Ask participants to listen and then paraphrase what they heard

- Role play a participant's behavior so that they can see how they are being perceived

- Use a board or butcher's paper display to list areas of agreement and disagreement

- Remind participants of the common goal of addressing oppression

- Move the discussion to a discussion of facts rather than opinions and emotions

- Negotiate agreements and concessions for the common good.

The researcher, in this context, is the facilitator of a discussion that should not deteriorate into argument but also should not be constrained. Data gathering for looking and developing the ideology is the foundation of the critical theory study. We build trust through personal exchanges with individuals and groups and collaboratively develop an understanding of the ideology and its associated empowerment and oppression.

A final comment on group interviewing is offered by Kamberelis and Dimitriadis (2011) who alert us to the overall functions of such groups.

1. The pedagogical function

2. The political function

3. The research and Inquiry function

The pedagogical function is "collective engagement designed to promote dialogue and to achieve higher levels of understanding of issues critical to the development of a group's interests (page 546). The political function is to "transform the conditions of existence for particular stakeholders" (page 546) and the research and inquiry function is to "to achieve richer, thicker, and more complex levels of understanding" (page 546).

Interviews for Organizing and Implementing Action

The action phase will be a time where key players are engaged in action for empowerment. At this stage, presentations of materials that will communicate the analysis and alternative actions strategies are developed. This could happen in a task group meeting. However, if scheduling such a meeting becomes difficult, then these materials can be posted on a website and key players can respond individually or in internet "chat rooms". Also, the materials could be distributed through email and, again, individual reactions could be given. Regardless of how the process is set up, the key to the communication is a learning conversation rather than an expert to non-expert interview or lecture. The goal of this process is to engage key players in an ideological discussion that will result in action strategies to address oppression.

Data gathering, at this stage, is a process of recording and transcribing individual or group discussions and noting organization of action plans. Stringer (2007, page 129) suggests developing action plans with objectives and organizational charts as in Table III.2. The researcher in collaboration with key informants reviews plans for strengths, weaknesses, opportunities and threats.

Table III.2
Action Planning Chart

TASKS	STEPS	PEOPLE	PLACE	TIME	BUDGET
1	a. b. c.				
2	a. b. c.				
3	a. b. c.				

Using this chart, the task group can identify the action tasks, the steps to be taken, who will be responsible for tasks and steps, where and when the action will happen and the resources that will be needed. In our study of Transportation needs (Millet and Otero, 2011) action included setting up meetings, inviting politicians to meetings, organizing a petition, attending the transit authority's board meetings and organizing a demonstration. These activities were carried out in the community by community leaders and the student researchers. This is described in Table III.3 taken from the students' (final report, page 119)

In the Curranderism study (Riech, the task would have included negotiations with the local social work program(s), development of curriculum on folk healing, negotiating the curriculum review process, and ensuring implementation of the curriculum in social work education and training. Steps for the task would have included identifying the people to be negotiated with, and timelines. The people responsible for identifying and implementing these steps would have included students, academics and experts in Curranderism. The time would have included scheduling of meetings, and the budget would have included travel and expenses. This is illustrated in Table III.4.

Table III.3
Action Plan for Transportation Study

Task	Steps	People Responsible for Task	Place	Date	Budget
1. Petition	a) Contact Community Leaders b) Meet with Community c) Consult Experts d) Develop next plan	Researchers Community Members Professionals	North Shore Yacht Club	January 2011	Travel, refreshments other supplies
2. Community Meeting with Key figures	a) Contact Community Leaders b) Meet with Community Representatives c) Consult Experts d) Develop next plan	Researchers Community Members Elected Representatives	North Shore Yacht Club	March 2011	Travel, refreshments other supplies
3. Petition Results to the press	a) Contact Community Leaders b) Find Contacts with the Press c) Consult Experts d) Develop next plan	Researchers Community Leaders	Press Offices	April 2011	Travel, Cell Phones

Table III.4.
Action Plan for study of Curranderismo

Tasks	Steps	People Responsible for Task	Place	Time	Budget
1. Negotiate with social work Program	a. Contact Program Head b. Contact Faculty Members c. Contact students	a. Researcher and experts in Currnaderismo b. Students c. Students	At the Program's offices	In the fall at the beginning of the academic year	Travel
2 Develop Curriculum for training and education	a. Experts in Curranderismo work with key faculty b. Experts in Curranderismo work with key trainers	Curanderismo experts, faculty and students.	At any place where participants are comfortable	During fall and winter depending on complexity	Travel
3 Guide curriculum through curriculum review process	a. Find schedule of committee meetings b. Identify key faculty member who sill sponsor the curriculum c. Identify someone to check progress	a. Social Work Faculty b. Social Work faculty and students c. Researcher and Curranderism experts	Wherever meetings are held	As scheduled by process	Travel

For the eating disorders study the tasks could have been, negotiating with high school administrators for inclusion of eating disorder groups on high school campuses, development of program, organizing the groups. The steps could have been meetings with principles and female students as well as contacting experts in group facilitation, the people could have been the researcher, students, parents and teachers. The time could have been a goal of implementing the groups at the end of one year and the budget would have been travel to meetings and the cost of materials for the group sessions. See Table III.5.

Table III.5
Action Plan for Eating Disorders Study

Tasks	Steps	People Responsible for Task	Place	Time	Budget
1 **Developing program for eating disorder groups**	a. Contact experts on eating disorders b. Search for current programs c. Consult with parents and students and teachers	a. Researcher b. Students and Teachers c. Researcher, students and teachers	At school or in homes.	Start in fall at beginning of academic year	Travel
2 **Negotiating for groups in high schools**	a. Meet with school administrators b. Develop plan for number of groups and when to be implemented c. Negotiate resources for groups	a. Researcher, students. b. Researcher, students. c. Researcher, students, teachers, administrators	In schools	First groups to start mid year	Travel
3. **Implementing groups**	a. Scheduling b. Advertising c. Evaluation	a. Administrators b. Researcher, students, parents c. Researcher	In identified school sites	Monthly	Supplies Payment for facilitators and organizers

All these plans identify tasks to be carried out so that action for empowerment is carried out as well as responsibilities, costs and scheduling. When considering action plans in general, we need to be clear about the level of human organization that is the focus of the action. Is it individuals, families, a particular group, an organization or a community? The transportation study had a community focus while the Curranderismo study had an organizational focus (social work programs) and the eating disorders study had an individual focus. The target will dictate data gathering for action. For example, Van Olpen and Freudenberg (2002, 2004) in their description of a policy change campaign to promote community reintegration of drug users leaving jail in Central and East Harlem in New York City concluded that such reintegration would be facilitated by targeting:

- Policies and programs within prisons so that a comprehensive discharge plan is developed that links offenders to support services and treatment in the community.

- The communication between prisons and community health care centers so that medical records are shared.

- Medicaid policies so that waiting periods are waived

- Housing policies so that shelters do not refuse to accept people coming out of prison.

- Individual employers who discriminate against former inmates so that strategies of rewards can be developed to change these practices.

- Employment training programs so that they are encouraged work with former inmates.

- City government entities so that a coordinated community re-entry program is developed

Data gathering for action is the core of the critical theory study. This is when we articulate the purpose of the study. At this stage of the study, both the researcher and study participants now have a strong enough collaboration to commit to addressing empowerment and oppression together

Interviews for Evaluation of the Impact of Action

Once a critical theory process is started it potentially has no end, so we should identify a time when evaluation of the impact of action should commence. This evaluation can be either positivist orconstructivist. The positivist approach assesses the process and efficiency of a program through a **formative (process)** evaluation and the impact of a program by means of a **summative (outcome)** evaluation that generally uses a pretest posttest assessment of change. This is the equivalent of a one or two group design and program evaluation that was discussed in Part 2. Constructivist evaluation or "Fourth Generation" evaluation as identified by Guba and Lincoln (1989) is an approach that requires key players to collaboratively identify claims, concerns and issues regarding a program and its effectiveness. The group then decides together on the appropriate assessment of the program and any future program development as described in Part 2.

The audience for the evaluation and the function of the evaluation will guide our decision about which of these evaluation approaches we should take. In our example studies, the authors of the transportation study opted for an informal discussion of the impact of the study with community members while the authors of the other studies opted for positivist outcome evaluations of their presentations of the ideological analysis using pretest posttest comparisons. Funded projects may also opt for a positivist evaluation, since this generates statistics indicting progress that sponsors can quickly and easily understand in a chart or table. However, if the evaluation is for study participants or members of the general public, then the fourth generation constructivist approach will probably offer more useful findings. This approach will offer participants meaning, a process of reflection, and a future action strategy for the project that requires participant "buy-in" to the proposed action.

The most rigorous form of positivist outcomes evaluation is the outcome/impact evaluation using the experimental design described in Chapter 3. This is extremely directive and creates artificial groups and power relationships between the researcher and study participants that would not be feasible in a study that has developed with the critical theory approach and culture. A non-experimental outcome/impact design would be more feasible. According to Neuman and Kreuger (2003), non-experimental evaluations begin with a description of the ideal situation and then proceed to an assessment of how far the activity has progressed towards that ideal. For a critical theory evaluation of action, the steps are to,

1. Describe the ideal empowered power relationship for this topic

2. Explain the activity, why it was chosen and how it will affect empowerment

3. Describe the target organizational entity of the activity

4. Report progress of activities

5. Report whether activity achieved desired outcome

Table III.6
Assessment of Action Resulting from Example Student Studies

	Millet and Otero study of Transportation	Riech study of Curranderismo	Cristopolus study of eating disorders
1. Ideal Situation	Community gains public transportation in the form of a bus service	Social Work students know about Curandersimo and refer to a Curanero when appropriate	Young women make their own decision about body image and eating habits
2. Activity	Community Meetings, lobbying elected representatives, petition, attending board meetings, demonstration.	Infusion of Folk Healing in social work curriculum to inform students	Self help groups in High schools to promote women's "healthy" body image and eating habits
3. Target	Transit authority	University	High School
4. Report on Progress	Company has committed to special meeting to address community concerns	Identification of achievements using action planning tables	Identification of achievements using action planning tables
5. Did activities achieved desired outcomes	Progress was made on empowering community. Bus service is now policy priority	Comparison of scores on students' knowledge of folk healing before and after curriculum	Comparison of female H.S. students perceptions of body image before and after participating in self help groups

In two of our sample studies (Curranderismo and Eating Disorders), if the students had more time and resources, the evaluation approaches shown in Table III.6 would have taken place. It also suggests the potential outcome of the studies were to empower students through knowledge of folk healing and young women by consciousness of healthy decisions regarding body image. The activities to achieve this would have involved community action, curriculum development and self help groups in universities and highs schools respectively. In a formal positivist evaluation, the action planning tables would have been used to show activities and progress and pretest posttest data would have been gathered to identify whether the desired empowerment was achieved. However, the results shown for the transportation study are the actual achievements of the transportation study where the transit authority has moved forward with paying attention to the community need for a bus service. Indeed, 2 years after the study was completed, a bus service was established.

In the constructivist approach to evaluating the critical theory activity, the circle of key informants is interviewed separately after completing the activity and asked about their claims, concerns and issues regarding the activity. They are asked what they liked about the activity and what they did not like about the activity. As these "constructions" are shared, a joint construction emerges noting areas of agreement and issues of disagreement. When all stakeholders have been interviewed separately and been given the opportunity to respond to others' constructions then a "member check" meeting is held to finalize the joint construction of the impact of the activity. As a group the key players decide what worked, what did not and what further action needs to be taken. A modified version of this approach was used in the Millet and Otero (2011) study of community transportation needs.

Observations

During the ideological analysis stage a third source of data, beyond individual and group interviews and discussions, is formal or informal observation. For critical theorists, observation, whether in person or by means of small unobtrusive cameras, can be at least uncomfortable and at most an imposition, no matter how much informed consent is given. In these days of heightened security and various anti-terrorism measures we have all become more accustomed to being observed in public places. Beyond public safety, though, as critical theory researchers we must ask ourselves, what gives one person the right to observe and interpret another person's behavior? To simply answer by saying that the observations are necessary for research purposes is not a good enough. Not only is the data that is collected using this method subjective; it is a demonstration of power, since it usually does not take into account the perceptions of those being observed. Also, it would be inappropriate, since it suggests that the observer is somehow outside the experience in which he or she is participating. As critical theorist we would argue that none of us is outside social experience. Critical theorists engage study participants rather than observe them from afar. These issues have been expanded and underlined by Angrosino and Rosenberg (2011) who suggest that observation based research is in a postmodern period were social justice requires that collaborative observational techniques are used such as those developed by the service learning movement.

Given this orientation, the only ethical observation we can make is in settings were the observation is obvious, those being observed give their consent, and the report of the observation is shared with participants for feedback, interpretation and comment. For example at family events, group meetings, organizational meetings, or community events, we could identify ourselves as observers and explain the focus of the enquiry. We would then gain informed consent with the condition that there is a commitment to share the record of the observations with participants and partner with participants to interpret the meaning of the behaviors that were observed. With this understanding, we could carry out participant observation and use the following stages of observation adapted from those offered by Adler & Adler (1994)

1. Select the Setting

2. Gain entrée

3. Decide on how to record (camera or personally)

4. Develop structure for recording observations

    ■ Where are you and what is the name and purpose of the activity?

    ■ Who is present?

    ■ What are their power relationships with each other? (formal and informal)

    ■ What incidents happened that illustrate their understanding of the ideological focus of the study?

    ■ What are your conclusions about their understanding of the ideological focus of the study

5. Decide how and when observations will be shared with participants for joint interpretation

6. Present the interpretation of the observation to participants in an easily understood format.

7. Engage in a discussion of the interpretation using the teaching-learning philosophy. Modify the interpretation in the light of the consensus reached on its meaning during the discussion

8. Decide how this interpretation will inform the thinking and the action stages of the project?

Having completed these steps we would now have useful data that was collected in the spirit of a critical theory approach.

Documents and Social Artifacts might well be useful to critical theorists in developing the ideological position and developing appropriate empowerment action plans. Participants might mention influential reports, rulebooks, or legislation. Picture on the walls or posters may point to a significant issues or important shared understandings. Such nonhuman data sources, for the critical theorist might illustrate oppression and empowerment.

To sum up, we have discussed interviews, observations, and the consideration of documents and social artifacts as approaches to data gathering for critical theorists. The important cross cutting issues of ethics, politics, diversity, and technology for critical theorists are similar to those discusses in Part 1 and Part 2 Additional important cross cutting issues at the Implementation stage are discussed in Chapter V. Below is a summary of this chapter and critical theory learning assignments. We can now proceed to a discussion of Implementation for constructivists.

Summary of Chapter III

- Implementation consists of three types of data gathering: data gathering for the ideological analysis, data gathering for action, data gathering for evaluating action

- Data gathering for ideological analysis, beyond the literature, includes individuals and groups and observational data collected under clearly defined conditions.

- In the looking phase researchers carry out interviews that not only follow the usual phases of an interview but also address the interviewee's experience of oppression and empowerment.

- In group interviews, as well as using the usual group work skills, researchers should adopt strategies to address conflict.

- Observational data can be collected under specific circumstances of full disclosure.

- Data gathering for action includes development of work plans with assigned tasks, timelines and budgets.

- Data collection in the evaluation stage will either follow the traditional positivist techniques or constructivist techniques

Critical Theory Learning Assignments

1. Form small discussion groups. Imagine you are a community group discussing the ideology you identified at the end of chapter ten. One group member should take on the role of the researcher and the others are community members who are not clear about the ideology or are not sure if

they are oppressed by it. Have a discussion with the goal of coming to a consensus about the impact of the ideology

2. After the discussion, make notes on the discussion. Record data that was gathered and your rationales for any ideological statements, action strategies and evaluation decisions. Then get together with the other members of the group and compare notes. Did you manage to remember everything?

As noted in Part 2 the initial hermeneutic dialectic includes the gatekeepers' constructions, the researcher's construction and the construction identified in the literature. It really doesn't matter which gatekeeper is interviewed first because all members of the circle get the chance to respond to each other's construction. These constructions are gathered via interviews, which are the most important form of data gathering for us as constructivists. During constructivist interviews we ask each participant in the hermeneutic dialectic circle of stakeholders for his or her construction of the research focus. In addition, we share the constructions of other interviewees and the literature so that participants have an opportunity to refine their constructions after hearing other points of view. We ask participants to identify any other relevant and important sources of information that might contribute to the joint construction such as social artifacts, reports and documents. At the end of initial interviews, we ask participants for the names of key players who are likely to have a completely different perspective on the research focus. Thus the **Hermeneutic Dialectic** is set in motion. Participants build their own initial constructions and also engage in a dynamic process of developing and refining the joint construction over time with additional input from others and as a response to any events that maybe happening during the study. Initially, interviews take place separately then, after each study participant has been interviewed once, we bring the circle of study participants together at the **member check meeting** to review the group's current joint construction and to give feedback on areas of agreement, areas of disagreement, and action steps that might be needed.

Initial Individual Interviews

Having gained initial trust and agreements with the gatekeepers of the setting, we build the Hermeneutic Dialectic Circle of study participants. The gatekeepers are asked to nominate stakeholders who should be invited into the circle. This is a starting point, as the study proceeds, we ask each participant in the study to nominate other stakeholders who should be included in the circle. Guba and Lincoln (1989) suggest that stakeholders can be divided into agents, beneficiaries and victims of a particular research focus. In the Hogan (1995) study of HIV-AIDS, the agents of services were the human service professionals, the beneficiaries were those who successfully received services, the victims were not only those who did not successfully received services but also other members of the community that were opposed to services to HIV-AIDS clients and perhaps prejudiced against this population. In the study of spirituality (Brown, 2011) the agents were the child welfare workers and administrator, the beneficiaries were client families, and the victims were children and in African American families in the child welfare system. Patton (2002) suggested fifteen types of sampling as described in Part 2. As constructivist researchers, we keep all these possibilities in mind, but we tend to use a combination of maximum variation and snowball sampling. We aim for a diverse set of perspectives and develop the sample by means of recommendations of interviewees.

Theoretically, our stance is to enter an interview with a blank sheet of paper having no preconceived questions. The first question to a participant in this ideal world of constructivist research would be "What do you think are the key questions regarding this research topic and what do you consider the answers to those questions to be?" However, to actually do this would not only be anxiety generating for the researcher but a little disconcerting for the participant. So, we have this "bank page" notion in mind when starting the interview but we also have some general questions prepared so that the study participant can be engaged and both the interviewer and interviewee can start to relax with each other. The constructivist interviewer can lean from the post positivist interview structure and questions described in Chapter II. In addition to this, Erlandson et al. (1993) give us a structure for the constructivist research interview divided into four stages:

1. preparing for the interview,

2. beginning the interview,

3. maintaining productivity during the interview, and

4. closing the interview.

The major difference between the constructivist interviewer and other interviewers is that the constructivist researcher **is** the interview data-gathering instrument not the questions on a piece of paper. When preparing for the interview, as constructivists, we need to hone all five senses as well as anticipate the need to use intuition and thought during the interview. We need touse micro social work practitioners' interviewing skills when preparing to gain a valid, comprehensive account of a study participant's constructions. For example, we should learn the vocabulary and terminology of the setting. It may well be useful to spend some time in the interviewee's setting to gain an experiential understanding of how he or she may perceive the research topic. This will help us with preparation of a pool of questions that might or might not be used in the interview. Patton (2002) lists several types of questions that can focus on the present, the past or the future. These are:

1. *Experience/Behavior Questions*: What is your experience with this topic? What do you do each day in relation to this topic? If I were to follow you around, what would I see you experiencing in relation to this topic?

2. *Opinion/Values Questions*: What do you think about this topic? What do you believe is happening with this topic? What would you like to see happening with this topic? What is your opinion about all of this?

3. *Feeling Questions*: To what extent do you feel pleased, confident, satisfied, unhappy or dissatisfied with this issue?

4. *Knowledge Questions*: What is your understanding of this topic? Which parts of it do you know most about? What do you know about those parts?

5. *Sensory Questions*: When you are engaging in this topic, what do you see? What do you hear people saying?

6. *Background/Demographic Questions*: What is your age, education, occupation, mobility, residence, and ethnicity?

Having developed a pool of questions, the next decision is how to record data gathered in interviews. This is discussed above in Chapter II. In addition to those considerations, as constructivist researchers, we focus on a balance between the fidelity of data recording and the comfort of the interviewee. Methods of data recording range from the absolute fidelity achieved by videoing each interview or observation to the limited fidelity achieved by making notes after an interview or observation. Videoing can be an uncomfortable situation for participants, but according to Erlandson et al. (1993) if used, it should be set up and left running for a period of time before data collection begins. At first participants tend to be conscious of the camera and will perform for it rather than continue with their normal behavior, but after a while the camera becomes part of the setting and tends to be ignored. Also, with easily accessible miniature cameras, videoing can take place unobtrusively. This may be the case in non-threatening situations but in interviews with professionals about, for example, discomfort with providing services to people living with HIV-AIDS the use of cameras may well inhibit open frank discussion and development of an authentic construction of the research topic.

If videoing is not a feasible option, then the next most reliable method is audio recording. Again, like the camera, a recorder is something that people tend to be conscious of at first and then ignore. Patton (2002) offers some pragmatic tips for using recording equipment: check equipment; choose a quiet place to record; test voice of respondent before starting; speak clearly; don't make any unnecessary rustling noises; identify the interview on the recording; and if using a transcriber, listen to the recording afterwards and erase any unnecessary conversation; finally, label all recordings.

If video or audio recording of the interview is too obtrusive then we must rely on note taking, either during or after the interview. Erlandson et al (1993) suggest the use of critical incident reporting as a way of recalling the key facets of someone's construction when taking notes after the interview. They suggest that as soon as possible after the interview, the researcher should make a list of critical incidents. A critical incident is something that "either highlights the normal operation of the (setting) or contrasts sharply with it" (page 103). At first we might not know if the incident is typical or not, however, trying to discover the answer to this question will help us build the joint construction. A description of a critical incident should:

1. *Contain one event or description.* What was the event or main point made by the interviewee? Why was it important to him or her?

2. *Identify specific persons, locations, and times.* Who were the key players in the incident or point being made? What do they do and when do they do it?

3. *Be observed by the researcher or verified by more than one other source* What is the interviewee describing as evidence for the incident or point of view? Is this evidence accurate?

4. *Should help build the joint construction by identifying typical or atypical features.* What has the interviewee said that agrees with other study participants' constructions and what has been said that is unique to this interviewee.

A final consideration when preparing for the interview is presentation of self and orientation of study participant. We need to decide on the appropriate style of dress and level of formality. We should contact the participant and tell him or her about the study, what to expect, and any formal informed consent procedures. If possible, the study participant should choose the setting for the interview.

When beginning the interview, we should orient the interviewee once more to the aim of the project as well as its approach noting that it entails open sharing. We need to address any concerns such as the likelihood of not having anonymity. We should explain the logistics of the project, including any possible follow up contact, other interviews, any possible meetings, proposed length of data collection period, any payments and who has final control over the data and the research report. Having completed these initial negotiations and understandings, it would be best for us to begin with some broad experience/behavior questions that put the interviewee at ease and keep the conversation in familiar territory. The aim is to establish a relaxed rapport between interviewee and researcher. At this point, we will be asking general questions about the interviewee's background and experiences in general and perceptions of the study topic in particular. These are "getting to know you" questions rather than data gathering questions. When we sense that the interviewee is ready, we can ask the data gathering questions. We should be alert to any tangents that the participant seems to be interested in at this point, and encourage exploration of those tangents. For example, in Hogan's (1995) HIV-AIDS study focus questions included:

1. What is your experience of HIV-AIDS?

2. How would you define AIDS?

3. In your opinion, what causes AIDS?

4. Have you ever worked with social workers?

5. In your opinion how might the social work profession best make a contribution to the field of AIDS in this region?

6. What factors might facilitate this involvement?

7. What factors might inhibit this involvement?

For Kelly's (1995) Homeless Children study these questions included:

1. In your opinion, what are the key issues in meeting the social and educational needs of homeless children in this region?

2. How do you think these needs are being met?

3. How do you think these needs are not being met?

4. What, in your opinion, can be done to improve services aimed at meeting these needs?

5. What do you see as barriers to successfully meeting the needs of homeless children in this region?

For Brown's (2011) study of spirituality, questions for parents followed this process:

Engagement Questions

1. How long have you lived in the M. V. area? What do you enjoy most about living in this area? What do you least enjoy about this area?

2. What about this topic caused you to agree to participate in this study?

Topic Questions

3. Given the topic of this research, can you tell me what has been your experience with spirituality or religion? (all groups)

4. What do the terms "spirituality" and "religion" mean to you? (all groups)

5. What has been your experience with child welfare workers asking about your spiritual or religious beliefs and values?

6. What do you think about child welfare social workers asking about spirituality or religion as an aspect of family life?

7. If spirituality or religion is important to a family, what do you think are some of the ways that child welfare social workers might use this information to assist families?

8. What would the inclusion of spirituality or religion sound like in order to be effective in engaging and assessing African American families?

9. Do you feel there are some benefits that might occur as a result of including spirituality and religion in the conversation between child welfare social workers and African American family members? Are there some negative consequences you can think of?

Termination Questions

10. Are there any questions or concerns regarding this issue that I have overlooked or that you want to add?

11. Is there someone else that you know who may have something different to say about this topic that you think I might talk to?

As the interview proceeds, we can explore tangents by using probes and prompts and being as natural and relaxed as possible. Prompts or "minimal encouragers" (Evans et al, 2004) let the interviewee know that we are interested and would like to hear more. Lincoln and Guba (1985) suggest encouragers such as a wave of the hand, sounds such as "…umm or uh-huh", or simply reflecting back by restating an understanding of what has just been said. Interviewee needs to get the message that the focus is on them and that we are genuinely interested in making sure that they say all they have to say and that we understood correctly.

The usual and most effective way for us to close the interview is to review and summarize what has been said. This may lead to further clarification and conversation but it also starts the process of ending the interview. One last question is to ask if there is anyone else who might have something to say about the topic. Also, we should thank the interviewee both at that time and with a follow up note. Always leave the door open for further contact between the researcher and the participant.

After the interview the transcript of the recording, or the notes on the interview, are analyzed using the procedures described for constructivist analysis in Part 4. This analysis is then sent to the respondent for review and confirmation of the validity of the construction. The respondent may make additions or changes as needed. Once the respondent has agreed that the analysis accurately represents his or her construction we move on to interview the next member of the circle and follow the same process. However, now we will first gather that respondent's construction, then share the literature construction, then the previous respondent(s)'s constructions and then our construction. This sounds like a process that makes interviews get longer and longer until they reach to infinity. However, redundancies and repetitions will occur in respondents' constructions so that our representation of other constructions, after a few interviews, can be structured into a kind of checklist of questions. As it evolves, this checklist can also be shared with the first interviewees via email, phone or mail so that all participants have the opportunity to respond to all constructions individually.

Groups Interviews: The Hermeneutic Dialectic Circle and the Member Check Meeting

After competing our individual interviews and verifying the individual constructions we move on to developing the joint construction. We write the first draft of the group's joint construction and share it with the circle at a meeting known as a "member check meeting". The function of this meeting is to ensure the "credibility", "dependability" and "confirmability" as discussed in Part 1 of the shared construction. The meeting will identify **claims, concerns** and **issues**; i.e. areas of agreement, areas of disagreement and issues to be addressed and acted upon (Guba & Linclon, 1989). The unique commitments that participants make when agreeing to take part in a constructivist study are described in Part 1. As the study moves into this stage that brings the group together to review and finalize the joint construction, it would be useful for us to review these commitments with participants. Such reflection will assist us all to truly perceive how constructivist research is both process and product. Data gathering has generated a process, which hopefully will have a life of its own beyond the official end of the research project, and a product, which will be a report on a shared construction at one point in time.

The member check meeting is an important stage of the constructivist project. At this point, we will, not only validate the joint construction with the study participants but also, motivate circle members to collaborate in taking an active part in continuing the project into its action stages. We have been careful about giving every group member a reason to believe that his or her constructions are understood, valued and included in the final joint construction. When contacting group members to schedule the meeting this engagement of participants is reinforced by accommodating schedules and setting a meeting place that is familiar and comfortable for as many of the circle as possible. Before the meeting, we share the joint construction and the meeting agenda with circle members and encourage questions and clarifications. This pre-meeting preparation can be carried out via email, and phone conversations.

At the meeting the researcher becomes, not only the reporter of data but also the group facilitator. At this meeting, we adopt social work group work skills to facilitate understanding of the joint construction and consolidate motivation and commitment to action. Using a generalist approach (Kirst-Ashman et al., 2009), engagement, assessment, planning, implementation, evaluation, termination and follow up are necessary stages for the meeting. Members should be introduced to each other, the purpose of the meeting should be reviewed and clarified, issued to be discussed should be prioritized, action plans should be identified, and the credibility of the group's final construction should be evaluated by group members. Termination of the meeting should be accompanied by a commitment to send the final report to all group members and the allocation of action tasks and roles to group members. This is basic team building where there is a need for organizational support for the project and strong leadership of the team. This group is the entity that is going to carry the project forward. By the end of the meeting group members should have understood and taken ownership of the shared construction. They will also have adopted their new roles as leaders of the project. To illustrate this stage, we can review our example student studies.

Study of Spirituality (Brown, L 2011)

The member checking meeting for this study was attended by family members who were former clients, child welfare workers and child welfare administrators. A summary and comparison of different key player groups' constructions is given in Table IV.1

Table V.1
Parent/Staff Construction Comparison[1]

Major Categories	Parents	CWS Staff
Spiritual/Religious Experience	⊙ Almost all those interviewed had some spiritual/religious upbringing. ⊙ That spiritual/religious upbringing impacted current spiritual/religious expression. ⊙ How that upbringing impacted current spiritual/religious expression varied by person.	⊙ Almost all those interviewed had some spiritual/religious upbringing. ⊙ That spiritual/religious upbringing impacted current spiritual/religious expression. ⊙ How that upbringing impacted current spiritual/religious expression varied by person.
Spirituality/Religion and Parenting	⊙ Spiritual/religious values, beliefs and practices were seen as important in raising children. ⊙ These spiritual/religious values, beliefs and practices were seen as important in parenting in that they gave children; (Stability, security, strength, moral guidelines, sense of thankfulness.)	⊙ Spiritual/religious values, beliefs and practices were seen as important in raising children. ⊙ These spiritual/religious values, beliefs and practices were seen as important in parenting in that they gave children; (Stability, security, strength, moral guidelines.)
Defining Spirituality/Religion	⊙ 2 major constructs ▪ Spirituality/religion the same ▪ Spirituality/religion connected	⊙ 3 major constructs ▪ Spirituality/religion the same ▪ Spirituality/religion connected ▪ Spirituality/religion distinct

---

[1] Brown, L. (2011) pages 116 to 118

Functions of Spirituality/Religion	◉ Organized religion or the church serves several functions;
	  ▪ Social support (connection, nurturance), counseling, rules and expectations regarding lifestyle.
	◉ Faith or Belief;
	  ▪ Strength, purpose, motivation, hope.
	◉ Religion;
	  ▪ Guides decision making, purpose, power and protection.
		◉ Organized religion or the church serves several functions;
		  ▪ Social support (connection, mentoring, nurturance), soft and concrete services (counseling, education, food, clothing, etc.) rules and expectations regarding lifestyle.
		◉ Faith or Belief;
		  ▪ strength, security, purpose, motivation.
		◉ Spirituality;
		  ▪ Identity, internal resource, guidance, moral compass.
		◉ Religion;
		  ▪ Guides decision making, purpose, power and protection.

Spirituality/Religion and African Americans		◉ The African American community is unique in terms of connection to the church(organized religion) ◉ African Americans even when not connected to organized religion tend to be spiritual or have a strong belief in God.
Engagement and Spirituality/Religion	◉ Key to engaging families in CWS process includes gaining knowledge about the family, their strengths/needs, connecting with the family and building trust with the family. ◉ Asking the family about strengths, supports, values, which may include spirituality/religion, are some ways to engage the family.	◉ Key to engaging families in CWS process includes gaining knowledge about the family, their strengths/needs, connecting with the family and building trust with the family. ◉ Asking the family about strengths, supports, values, which may include spirituality/religion, are some ways to engage the family.
Assessment and Spirituality/Religion	◉ Asking about supports, strengths is important in making a good assessment.	◉ Asking about spirituality/religion should be part of a holistic assessment of the family. ◉ Asking about spirituality/religion crosses church/state and or personal/professional boundaries.
Placement and Spirituality/Religion	◉ Asking about the spiritual/religious beliefs and practices of the family of origin, youth and foster family may be important in making placement decisions.	◉ Asking about the spiritual/religious beliefs and practices of the family of origin, youth and foster family may be important in making placement decisions.

215

Services and Spirituality/Religion	⊙ Church or faith based services are preferred as these services are based on a similar belief system and established trusting relationships.	⊙ Church or faith based services are preferred as these services are based on a similar belief system and established trusting relationships. ⊙ Church or faith based services may not be appropriate to provide formal services such as counseling, parenting, drug treatment. ⊙ Work needs to be done to develop and maintain understanding and communication between CWS and faith based community.
Concerns	⊙ No concerns about CWS including spirituality/religion in their practice. ⊙ Concerns about worker bias.	⊙ Concerns about professional/personal and church/state boundaries. ⊙ Concerns about worker bias. ⊙ Concerns about system barriers (guidelines, policies, Court, admin support, liability)
Social Work Skills		⊙ Additional education, training and support needed. ⊙ Buy in regarding rationale, expectations, within and outside CWS. ⊙ Clear guidelines, procedures, direction. ⊙ Knowledge about available resources. ⊙ Administrative support and flexibility.

Brown (2011) gives the following summary of the meeting

The group was presented with areas where there was agreement or shared constructs, as well as the categories where there were different or conflicting perspectives. Though there was no further negotiation of constructions where there was not agreement at the comprehensive member check, the discussion that occurred during the meeting indicated that sharing the constructions with the group led to increased understanding and appreciation of differing perspectives and the group confirmed that the research presented an accurate portrayal of participant constructions.

With regard to action planning, the participants determined at that meeting that they will continue and intensify work with members of an ongoing faith based collaborative which they are a part of. Intensified work includes encouraging members of the African American faith organizations to join the collaborative. It also includes developing a resource list of services that the faith organizations currently provide and the group determined that additional services may need to be developed that would meet the needs of the families served by CWS, including the credentialed services necessary for Court mandated services. The group also agreed that further discussion, training and work with staff around engaging families in identifying strengths and supports including spirituality/religion needed to occur in the agency. They are anticipating structural changes that they hope will allow CWS workers more time and opportunity to engage families in these types of discussions. (pages 107-108)

Study of Homeless Children (Becker, J., 194: Kelly, G., 1995)

The study of homeless children, carried out over two years, was able to complete much more of the constructivist research process. Participants in the original hermeneutic dialectic circle were interviewed in year one. In year two, as a result of these interviews, the circle was expanded and everyone in the final circle was interviewed twice. More was achieved in the second year because interviews became more focused as redundancy and repetition within constructions was identified. At the end of year two all participants were invited to the member checking meeting. This is described in her report by Kelly (1995), the student researcher, and is reproduced here in full:

The networking meeting was held at a city hall, located mid valley, which was easily accessible to all participating agencies. Meeting time and date was scheduled to accommodate the local member of the county board of supervisors, who was interested in the issues addressed in this research report. The meeting agenda was as follows:

Homeless Children Research Networking Meeting
May 24th, 1995
Agenda

Introductions
    Agency and Information Sharing
    Discussion of Identified Issues
        Families
        Adult Literacy
        Job Skills Training
        Mental Heath Outreach Services
        Additional Health Services
    Transportation
    Affordable Housing
    Shelters
        More Shelters
    Schools
        Identifying and Monitoring Homeless Children
        Funding
    Global Issues
        Agency Restrictions and Policies
        Community Awareness
        Prevention Through Policy Changes
    Suggested Solutions

Networking Regularly
Sharing Resources
Liaison, inter-agency representatives
Expansion of Services
Future Networking Meetings?

Participants from the two separate research inquiries who attended the meeting represented the following agencies: drug-free community based intervention program for the nine valley cities, domestic violence shelter, Western Valley Homeless Shelter, a soup kitchen, a food distribution and transportation resource center, Child Protective Services, The Department of Public Social Services, Riverside County Regional Access Project, Riverside County Office of Education, Riverside County Supervisor, Desert Sands Unified School District, Palm Springs Unified School District, Coachella Valley Unified School District, and the academic tutors for the two participating school districts of the Stewart McKinney Grant Program. Also attending was the professor and research advisor for this project and the former graduate student who was the original researcher for the first round and peer debriefer for this project,

Agency participants who agreed to participate but had to cancel due to last minute emergencies were representatives of law enforcement, the Eastern Valley Homeless Shelter, representatives of the Public Health Department, representatives of City Government, representatives of the Mental Health Department, and representatives of the regional Child Abuse Council. These participants indicated interest in attending future networking meetings and asked to be kept informed of this meeting outocome.

The first part of this meeting focused on information sharing, with most agencies supplying handouts about their organization and having a question and answer period about various agencies services. (This was a need that had been identified during interviews)...

The discussion phase of the meeting focused on issues of lack of community awareness about homeless children and their families and barriers that school districts have created in the past by "turning children away" because they did not have a permanent address. One tutor participant indicated a concern that many homeless children presently are "out there in a nonexistent" home and are not receiving academic services. School district representatives shared that homeless children is a "new" issue for them and they are still in the process of learning how to deal with this problem. Respondents admitted many school personnel within their school districts do not know how to work with this population and are often insensitive to their needs. AS a result of this discussion, the county board of education representative suggested that t his office could provide in-service trainings to all three school districts when requested.

Upon further discussion of identified issues, agency participants focused on possible joint networking meetings with the east and west valley networking groups already in existence. Additionally, shelter and child protective service representatives addressed the need for sharing affordable housing information resources with other agencies...Participants agreed to compile a "housing list" of the entire valley and bring it to the next meeting...

Representatives also agree dot participate in future networking meetings and suggested inclusions of G.A.I.N (the local "welfare to work" program) and the Housing Authority in this group...Agency participants agreed to meet in mid-July with this researcher coordinating time, location and date with follow-up communication to all participating agencies.(pages 49-53)

It is clear here that the project moved a long way towards understanding the issue and taking action to address the issue. The researcher was not able to completely hand over the project to the group but several participants had taken on responsibilities for additional training, information, and contact to other stakeholders.

Study of HIV-AIDS (Hogan, P., 1995)

In the HIV-AIDS study because of concerns regarding confidentiality and stigma, members of the group were reluctant to attend a member-checking meeting. The researcher was not able to bring together enough of the participants for the meeting to be able to achieve "credibility", "dependability" and "confirmability" The researcher thus, confirmed the trustworthiness of individual constructions with individual participant via mail and phone calls (at this time, email was not so prevalent as now) and then wrote a final report, or case study, which she sent to participants. The study had to end there. It began a process of reviewing services to people living with HIV-AIDS and produced a report but was not able to facilitate continuation of the project into the action state at that time. For the constructivist researcher, this was not failed research but a statement of the joint construction in this research context at a certain point in time. Stakeholders in this setting were at a point of acknowledging an issue but not yet able to move forward with joint action to address the issue.

Observations

As constructivist researchers we not only interview key informants in the research site, we also have the opportunity to observe the site. As noted in the discussion of post positivist observation, such observing or fieldwork, has stages:

1. preparing for the field,

2. entering the field,

3. routinizing observation, and

4. leaving the field.

However, like the critical theorist, we have certain issues to resolve in relation to observing study participants. In a constructivist study, joint constructions of a research focus are being developed. The only justification for gathering observational data is that it has the potential to add new dimensions to the joint construction. We and study participants may gather observational data. However, such data is considered to be each person's subjective understanding of what was observed and must be shared with the circle of study participants for review and possible modification.

Preparing for constructivist field observation includes negotiating and explaining the terms and uses of such observation. We would not disguise our role, but would openly acknowledge that a research observation is taking place, that the making of the observation is influencing the activities being observed and that the record of the observation is a subjective account of activities at one time in one particular setting. The site for the observation could be a micro or macro practice setting. Thus it could be the home or other meeting place of families, groups or individual(s) or it could be an agency or community setting. These are not anthropological study settings but practice settings where researchers cannot really become insiders and, as outsiders, seriously affect the nature of the activity being observed.

In our example HIV-AIDS study, the researcher could have observed the experiences of HIV-AIDS clients seeking services. The presence of the researcher may well have increased the likelihood of the client getting services. The description of these observations would have acknowledged and reviewed the implications of such observer effects. The observer could be behind a one-way mirror but for a constructivist, this would be an unsatisfactory form of observation since the equal partnership strived for in constructivist research would be lost. A comment on modern technology: indeed it would be possible to make observations with miniature hidden cameras, should the resources be available. However, for the constructivist, data collected in this fashion would be of limited value. The camera does not allow the observer to engage all five senses. There is partial visual and auditory data but that is all. The constructivist is not fully engaged in the process of observation.

Thus the observer role, for constructivists, is generally a secondary role to the interview role and any observations are generally made while carrying out an interview and included in the written account of the interview. However, should the constructivist decide to gather observational data, the structure offered by Bogdewic (1992), will help focus such data collection. They suggest that the observer should ask him or herself:

1. Who is present? What are their roles? How did they enter the setting? Why is each person present? Who seems to be in charge?

2. What is happening? Who is involved? What is the tone of the communication? Is it routine or unusual?

3. When does this happen? Is this the regular time for this occurrence? How long does it last?

4. Where is this happening? Is this the usual place? How is the spaced used? Who seems to be comfortable here and who is not?

5. Why is this happening? What precipitated this occurrence?

6. <u>How is this activity organized?</u> What are the rules? How are various events observed connected?

Using this structure to record observations, we can make observations that contribute to the joint construction being developed. When these are shared with participants for reflection on and development of constructions there is an interaction between interviews and observations where observations can suggest questions and informants' constructions can suggest foci for further observation.

Documents and Social Artifacts

Documents and social artifacts found in the research setting might well be useful in developing the construction. Participants might mention influential reports, rulebooks, or legislation. Picture on the walls or posters may point to a significant issues or important shared understandings. Such nonhuman data sources, for the constructivist, would provide context since they are not open to a dialectic that builds and changes the construction but they can affect the development of individual and joint constructions.

This concludes our discussion of constructivist approaches to data gathering. Important cross cuttings issues of ethics, politics, diversity and technology are similar to those discussed in Part 1 and Part 2. Additional important cross cutting issues at the Implementation state are discussed in Chapter 5. Below is a summary of this chapter and a constructivist learning assignment.

Summary of Chapter IV

- Data gathering generally begins with separate interviews with members of the hermeneutic dialectic circle of study participants

- Sampling of participants usually uses maximum variation and snowball procedures

- The constructivist interview is open to exploring tangents and the interviewer perceives him or her self as the interview instrument rather than questions on a questionnaire or interview protocol

- Interviews proceed through stages: preparing for the interview, beginning the interview, maintaining productivity during the interview, and closing the interview

- Observations follow stages: preparing for the field, entering the field, routinizing observation, and leaving the field. There are constraints, related to openness and partnership, for the constructivist researcher wishing to collect this data.

- Methods for recording data include recording or taking notes during the interview or observation, or writing notes immediately after the interview

- The hermeneutic dialectic circle is developed from individual interviews where constructions are shared and a joint membership checking meeting where agreement is reached on claims, concerns and issues.

- Evaluation, or analysis, of the data requires identifying units and categories of data that should be included in the joint construction.

Constructivist Learning Assignments

1. Form a small discussion group of about six participants. Assign a community member role to each member of the group. With the study you identified in Part 2 in mind, share your constructions of the topic. Identify areas of agreement, and areas of disagreement. Identify action that the circle would take about the issue being discussed.

The important cross cutting issues for the Implementation stage of our study are similar to those discussed in Part 1 and Part 2. However, there are some additional diversity and technology issues to be considered.

Diversity issues

Rubin and Babbie (2011) offer some guidelines for addressing diversity for positivists when pre-testing our data-gathering instrument:

1. Immerse yourself in the culture to be studied before constructing instruments

2. Use pre existing instruments that have been tested for reliability and validity with the culture you are studying

3. Use key informants to get advice on the cultural sensitivity of an instrument you plan to use

4. Use bilingual interviewers or interpreters

5. Use the processes of back translation where an instrument is translated from English into a desired language and then translated back to English by a second translator to check for accuracy of meaning.

6. Pretest the instrument with members of the culture being studied who will not be participants in the proposed study.

We use these surveys to gather data that is translated into numbers. When developing items for a survey instrument, we review validity and reliability and we review validity by considering face, content, criterion, and construct validity. When making such assessments we need to:

- ask a diverse group to assess face validity;

- consider if the content includes items that address diversity when considering content validity;

- review whether the comparison criteria being used in tests of criterion validity acknowledge diversity; and

- consider if all the indicators measure the same way for various diverse groups when assessing construct validity.

For example, when we assess the face and content validity of a survey instrument measuring social work knowledge of micro practice we should consult a diverse group of experts to see that interventions unique to certain cultures are at least considered for inclusion. If we are assessing criterion and construct validity, we should use instruments and indicators that include interventions that have been found to be effective with diverse groups.

The conceptualization and measurement techniques that are adopted for surveys can frequently be of concern to certain groups of participants. Martin and Knox (2000) discuss the measurement tools for sexual orientation that assume mutually exclusive categories of sexual orientation. They suggest that this may not be true since a person may fall into several categories of sexual orientation. Feminist researchers such as Graham and Rawlings (1980) have gone so far as to insist that quantitative research cannot address feminist research issues because the use of quantitative data reflects a patriarchal definition of science that categorizes numbers rather than words as "hard" facts. Clearly, we need to pay attention to these issues when gathering data for a positivist study.

When carrying out interviews, the impact of differences between the interviewer and interviewee, as discussed in Part 1, needs to be reviewed and included in any preparation for the interview. Generally according to Neuman and Kreuger (2003), interviewees are more truthful with interviewers that look and sound similar to them. However, if such matching is not possible then reviewing guidelines for effective interviewing included in this chapter and the following Implementation chapters is crucial for the gathering of authentic data. In addition, on the one hand, the intense involvement with participants that is required by the forms of qualitative research describe here acknowledges the unique contribution each participant will make to the data set; on the other hand, this involvement can be a major intrusion into someone's private opinions and feelings. When Armitage et al (2002) talked about a methodology for taking women's oral histories they noted that researchers and academics tend to focus on activity and generalizations. Thus when someone reveals feelings about a topic, they tend to disregard such an expression as irrelevant to the research topic or assume that it is not a "fact" and thus ignore or dismiss such data during the interview. These authors, therefore, noted that research interviewers should learn how to listen actively. Dana Jack (2010) talked about interviewing depressed women and realizing that she needed to acknowledge that definitions of maturity and health imply self reliance and autonomy and exclude some female notions of maturity that include connection and relationship to others. She worked to avoid interpreting women's stories for them and encouraged the female interviewees to be the experts on their own experience and its meaning. Reinharz (1992) discusses feminist interviewing and concluded that a feminist approach to interviewing assumes that interviewees are human beings to be engaged rather than subjects with identification numbers who are a source of predetermined data. She also notes that the interviewer needs to reflect on the implications of his or her relationship with the interviewee. Is the interviewee perceived to be a friend or a stranger? One suggested answer to this question was to call the interviewee the "knowledgeable stranger;" someone who is between a friend and a stranger. With this notion of a relationship between the interviewer and interviewee, some feminists have made commitments to interviewing practices that would not be accepted by traditional positivists. For example, some believe that, during an interview, the interviewer should intervene with the interviewee if her or she has a problem or a need for information (Webb, 1984). Many believe that the interviewer should self disclose during the interview (Melamed, 1983: Bristow and Esper, (1988); Bombyk et al, (1985), although Bombyk et al. felt that such disclosures should be paced and timed appropriately.

Observation, as a data gathering method, has been criticized for its subjective quality and expression of a power relationship between the observer and the observed. As stated in Chapter III, we need to discuss the implementation of observation and the use of the resultant data needs with those who are being observed if it is to be an ethical and sensitive process. The diversity issues for this mode of data collection, namely, the impact of the differences between observer and observed and how this impact can be understood and addressed, returns us to the emic and etic concepts derived from Anthropology. As a reminder, the emic perspective is the perspective of the insider of a particular social setting, while the etic perspective is that of the outsider. Do we have the right to say that we have gathered data on the insider's (the person being observed) reality just because we have observed him or her? Or do we only have an "etic" understanding of what has been observed; a setting viewed and interpreted using an outsider's orientation? The implications of these questions are illustrated in the famous controversy about Margaret Mead's work in Samoa. The Australian, Derek Freeman (1973), challenged the validity of Mead's work and her findings regarding adolescent promiscuity as described in her book "Coming of Age in Samoa: A Psychological Study of Primitive Youth for Western Civilization". His account of the reasons why he believed her to be wrong about her accounts of promiscuity in adolescents in Samoa makes the following points.

- "First, she brought with her to Samoa a belief in ideology, impressed upon her by her mentors Franz Boas and Ruth Benedict, that human behavior is determined by cultural patterns.

- Second, her involvement with ethnology studies for the renowned Bishop Museum created a crisis regarding her original research of adolescence and she turned to informants in Samoa such as Fa'apua'a and Fofoa in hopes of finding a cultural pattern that would allow her to solve the problem that Boas had sent her to Samoa to investigate.

- Third, she arrived in Samoa with a false preconception from Edward Handy, director of the Bishop Museum, that she would find premarital promiscuity as the cultural pattern in Samoa.

- Fourth, she idolized Franz Boas and wanted to reach a conclusion that he would find acceptable.

- Fifth, Mead had inaccurate knowledge of the responses she received from Fofoa and Fa'apua'a when she asked them about their sexual behavior. (page "*The Fateful Hoaxing of Margaret Mead*" (1999) pgs. 12-15).

Freedman himself has been criticized for the methodology he used to conclude that Mead had gathered inaccurate data. However, the rights and wrongs of this debate need not concern us here. It is the above list of potential mistakes that give us pointers

225

to the personal reflection we need to make when we gather observational data. He is giving several good reasons to wonder whether Margaret Mead, wedded to an "etic" perspective, could have misinterpreted what she saw and heard. He notes her biases, her need to please her mentors, and the potential for her to misinterpret humorous responses to her questions from two study participants. If Margaret Mead can be accused of making such mistakes, then we mere social work researchers need to beware.

When we review artifacts, documents and secondary data, of course, we need to include an acknowledgement of the context of such sources, their history and their authors' perspectives so that the reader can assess the import of that data. Howard Zinn's (2001) approach to writing history in his "A People's History of the United States: 1492 to Present" clearly reminds us that, when looking at any document, we need to reflect on who's perspective is being portrayed and who sponsored the document before we assess the authenticity of the data in the document. His history gives us perspectives of the recent history of the United States from the point of view of Native Americans, various ethnic groups, women and the poor. So, to sum up, we need to pay attention to sensitivity to diversity when gathering both quantitative and qualitative data.

Technology Issues

Before we move to consider data analysis in the Evaluation state in Part 4, it would be useful to comment on technology and the data gathering that we carry out during Implementation. Digital recorders and cameras can immensely assist us as we gather this data, Indeed, the participatory, partnership oriented approaches to research have chosen to put the recorders and cameras in the hands of study participants. Wang (2003) defines "photovoice" as a "process by which people can identify, represent, and enhance their community through a specific photographic technique." (page 179). It has three goals:

(1) to enable people to record and reflect their community's strengths and concerns,

(2) to promote critical dialogue and knowledge about important community issues through large and small group discussion of photographs, and

(3) to reach policy makers and others who can be mobilized for change." (page 179).

In the case study described by this author, homeless people are given cameras, trained, and then sent out to take pictures of homeless issues in their community that they consider to be important. These researcher/photographers are asked to explain each photo and describe: what is happening in the photo, how it affects the lives of local homeless people, and resultant suggestions for any action that should be taken in relation to the issue being illustrated in the photo. After discussion with the research partners, the information from the photos is shared with policy makers, journalists and the wider community so that action can be advocated for and later assessed.

Another technology that has begun to assist data collection is the use of internet surveys (Couper and Bosnkak, 2010). While this has the limitation of only being accessible to those who can log onto the Internet, and there are sampling issues to be addressed, there are advantages to this mode:

- Web surveys are self administered

- Web surveys are computerized

- Web surveys are interactive

- Web surveys are distributed

- Web surveys are rich visual (graphical and multimedia) tools (page 540)

A number of software programs have been developed to promote such methods of data collection and web sites such as http://lap.umd.edu/survey_design/tools.html that provide design guidelines and principles for web-based survey instruments. This particular web site designs survey instruments based on the principles of cognitive psychology, heuristics, and design theory. However many other for-profit and non-profit sites can be found giving a range of resources and software.

To conclude Part 3, we have reviewed quantitative and qualitative approaches to gathering data. We have linked the quantitative approaches to positivism and the qualitative approaches to our other paradigms. Again, we see the potential for gathering a comprehensive set of data when we adopt a range of worldviews. We can now move on to Part 4 and a discussion of the Evaluation, or data analysis stage of our project.

Angrosino, M and Rosenberg, J. (2011) "Observations on Observation" in (Eds.) Denzin, N.K. and Lincoln, Y.S. *The SAGE Handbook of Qualitative Research.* Thousand Oaks, CA: Sage

Adler, P.A. & Adler, P. (1994). "Observational Techniques" In (Eds.) Denzin, N.K. and

Lincoln, Y.S. *Handbook of Qualitative Research.* Thousand Oaks, CA: Sage

Armitage, S. H, Hart, P. and Weathermon, K. (2002) *Women's Oral History.* Los Angeles: Frontiers Publishing Becker, J. E. (1994) *A Constructivist study of the social and educational needs of homeless children.* San Bernardino, CA: School of Social Work CSUSB

Berg, B.L. (2009). *Qualitative Research Methods for the Social Sciences.* Boston: Pearson.

Bogdewic, S.P. (1992) Participant Observation. In Crabtree B.F & Miller, W.L. *Doing Qualitative Research.* Newbury Park: Sage.

Bombyck, M., Bricker Jenkins, M., & Wedenoja, M. (1985). Reclaiming our profession through feminist research: some methodological issues in the feminist practice project. Paper presented at the Annual Program Meeting of the Council of Social Work Education.

Bristow, A. R. and Ester, Esper, J.A. (1988). A feminist research ethos. In The Nebraska Sociological Feminist Collective (Eds.) *A Feminist Ethic for Social Science Research.* Lewiston, NY: The Edwin Mellen Press

Brown, L.E. (2011) Spirituality's Role in the Interaction Between Child Welfare and Black Families. San Bernardino: Loma Linda University, social work student doctoral dissertation.

Christopulos, J. (1995) Oppression through Obsession: A Feminist Theoretical Critique of Eating Disorders. San Bernardino, CA: Student research project

Corbin J. & Strauss, A. (2008) *Basics of Qualitative Research.* Thousand Oaks: Sage (3rd Edition) Couper, M. P. and Bosnjak, M. (2010) " Internet Surveys" ". In Marsden, P. V. & Wright, J.D. (Eds.) *Handbook of Survey Research (second edition).* Bingley, U.K.: Emerald Group Publishing (pp 527-550)

Crabtree, B.F., Miller, W.L. (1999). *Doing Qualitative Research.* Newbury Park, CA: Sage

Couper, M.P. and Bosnjak, M. (2010) Internet Surveys. In Marsden, P. V. & Wright, J.D. (Eds.) *Handbook of Survey Research (second edition)*. Bingley, U.K.: Emerald Group Publishing (pp 527-550)

Erlandson, D. A., Harris, E. L., Skipper, B.L., Allen, S. D. (1993). *Doing Naturalistic Inquiry.* Thousand Oaks: Sage.

Evans, D. R., Hearn, M.T., Uhlemann, M.R., Ivey, A.E. (2004) *Essential Interviewing: A Programmed Approach to Effective Communication.* Belmont, CA: Brooks Cole-Thomson Learning

Fontana, A. & Frey, J. K. (1994). "Interviewing: The Art of Science". In (Eds.) Denzin, N.K. and Lincoln, Y.S. *Handbook of Qualitative Research.* Thousand Oaks, CA: Sage

Freeman, D. (1983) *Margaret Mead and Samoa: The making and unmaking of an Anthropological myth.* Cambridge, MA: Harvard University Press

Freeman, D. (1999) *The fateful hoaxing of Margaret Mead: A Historical Analysis of Her Samoan researches.* Boulder, CO: Westview Press

Gibbs, J.A. (2001) "Maintaining front line workers in child protection: A case for refocusing supervision" In *Child Abuse Review* Vol 10 pp. 323 335.

Graham, D & Rawlings, E (1980) "Feminist Research Methodology: Comparisons, Guidelines and Ethics. Paper presented at the Annual Meeting of the American Psychological Association.

Guba, E.G. & Lincoln, Y.S. (1989) *Fourth Generation Evaluation* Newbury Park: Sage

Hogan, P. (1995) *A Constructivist study of Social Work's Involvement with HIV-AIDS.* San Bernardino, CA: School of Social Work, CSUSB,

Harrison, C. H. (2010) "Mail Surveys and Paper Questionnaires". In Marsden, P. V. & Wright, J.D. (Eds.) *Handbook of Survey Research (second edition)*. Bingley, U.K.: Emerald Group Publishing (pp 499-526)

Jack, D. and Ali, A (2010) *Silencing the Self Across Cultures: Depression and Gender in the Social World* New York: Oxford University Press

Kamberelis, G. and Dimitriadis, G. (2011) "Contingent Articulations of Pedagogy, politics, and Inquiry". In Denzin, N.K. and Lincoln, Y.S. (Eds) The Sage *Handbook of Qualitative Research (fourth edition)* Los Angeles: Sage.

Kelly, G. (1995). *A Constructivist Second Year Study of the Social and Educational Needs of Homeless Children.* San Bernardino, CA: School of Social Work, CSUSB.

Kirst-Ashman, K.K. & Hull Jr., G. H. (2009). *Understanding Generalist Practice*. Belmont, CA: Brooks Cole

Krossnick, J. & Presser, S. (2010), "Questions and Questionnaire Design". In Marsden, P. V. & Wright, J.D. (Eds.) *Handbook of Survey Research (second edition)*. Bingley, U.K.: Emerald Group Publishing (pp 263-314)

Lavrakas, P. J. (2010) "Telephone Surveys" In Marsden, P. V. & Wright, J.D. (Eds.) *Handbook of Survey Research (second edition)*. Bingley, U.K.: Emerald Group Publishing (pp 471-498)

Lincoln, Y.S. & Guba, E. G. (1985) *Naturalistic Inquiry.* Newbury Park: Sage

Lofland, J & Lofland, L.H. (1995). *Analyzing Social Settings: A guide to Qualitative Observation and Analysis.* Belmont, CA: Wadsworth.

Martin, I. M. and Knox, J. (2000) Methodological and Ethical issues in research on lesbians and gay men. In *Social Work Research* 24 (1) pp. 51-59.

Melamed, E. (1983) *Mirror mirror: the terror of not being young.* New York: Simon & Schuster.

Millet, K. R., and Otero, L. R. (2011) *The North Shore Public Transportation Dilemma: How Local Sociopolitical Ideologies, Ethnic Discrimination And Class Oppression Create Marginalization, And A Community's Quest For Social Justice.* San Bernardino, CA. CSUSB, a social work student research project.

Neuman, W.L. and Kreuger, L.W. (2003) *Social Work Research Methods: Qualitative and Quantitative Applications.* Boson: Allyn and Bacon.

Patton, M.Q. (2002) *Qualitative evaluation and research methods. Thousand Oaks*: Sage.

Reinharz, S. (1992) *Feminist Methods in social research.* New York: Oxford University Press.

Riech, J. R. (1994). Psychotherapy Encounters Curanderismo: Implications for Clients Treated in the United States by Culturally Insensitive Social Workers. San Bernardino: Student Project at CUSUB

Rubin, A & Babbie, E (2011) *Research Methods for Social Work.* Florence, KY: Cenage.

Schaeffer, N.C., Dykema, J., Maynard, W. (2010) "Interviews and Interviewing" In Marsden, P. V. & Wright, J.D. (Eds.) *Handbook of Survey Research (second edition)*. Bingley, U.K.: Emerald Group Publishing (pp. 437-470)

Sheatsley, P.B. (1983) "Questionnaire Construction and Item Writing" In Rossi, P.H., Wright, J.D., & Anderson, A.B. (Eds.) *Handbook of Survey Research*. Orlando, FA: Academic Press.

Strauss, A & Corbin, J. (2008) Basics of Qualitative Research. Thousand Oaks: Sage (3rd Edition)

Stringer, E. T. (2007). Action Research (Third Edition). Thousand Oaks: Sage

Tourangeau, R & bradburn, M. M. (2010) "The Psychology of Survey Respponse" "In Marsden, P. V. & Wright, J.D. (Eds.) *Handbook of Survey Research (second edition)*. Bingley, U.K.: Emerald Group Publishing (pp 325-346)

Tutty, L. M., Rothery, M.A. Grinnell, Jr. R.M. (1996). *Qualitative Research for Social Workers.* Boston: Allyn and Bacon

Van Olphen, J. (2002). "Adopting a community-based participatory approach to advocate for policies to promote community reintegration of drug users leaving jail". Paper presented to the 130th annual meeting of the APHA,

Van Olpen, J. and Freudenberg, N. (2004). "Harlem service providers' perceptions of the impact of municipal policies on their clients with substance abuse problem". *In Journal of Urban Health* Vol 81, Number 2 pp 222-231

Wang, C.C., & Pies, C.A. (2004) Family, Maternal, and Child Health Through Photovoice. In Maternal and Child Health Journal, Vol. 8, No. 2, June 2004

Wang, C.W. (2003) Usingphotovoice as a participatory assessment and issue selection tool; a case study with the homeless in Ann Arbor. In M. Minkler & M. Wallerstein (Eds.) Community-based participatory research for health. Pages 179-196. San Francisco: Josey-Bass.

Webb, C. (1984), Feminist methodology in nursing research. Journal of Advanced Nursing, 9: 249–256.doi: 10.1111/j.1365-2648.1984.tb00368.x

Weinberg, E. (1983) "Data Collection: Planning and Management" In Rossi, P.H., Wright, J.D., & Anderson, A.B. (Eds.) *Handbook of Survey Research.* Orlando, FA: Academic Press.

Wolcott, H.F. (1973) *The man in the principal's office: an ethnography* (Reprint, 1984), Prospect Heights, IL: Waveland Press.

Weinberg, E. (1983) "Data Collection: Planning and Management" In Rossi, P.H., Wright, J.D., & Anderson, A.B. (Eds.) *Handbook of Survey Research.* Orlando, FA: Academic Press.

Zinn, H. (2001) *A People's History of the United States.* New York: Harper Collins

Part 4

Evaluation

Quantitative and Qualitative Data Analysis

Contents

> *Part 4 discusses Evaluation in relation to positivism, post positivism, critical theory and constructivism. Each paradigm is discussed in a separate chapter and important cross cuttings issues are discussed in the final chapter:*
>
> > *Chapter I: Positivism*
> > *Chapter II: Post Positivism*
> > *Chapter III: Critical Theory*
> > *Chapter IV: Constructivism*
> > *Chapter V: Important Crossing Issues*
>
> **However, there is some overlap between the paradigms. Where an overlap is noted, there are links to the shared information.**

Having engaged the research setting, developed our research focus or question, made a plan to carry out our study, and collected our data; our next step is to analysis our data or, in other words, evaluate what our data means. To do this we carry out quantitative and qualitative analysis. Quantitative analysis interprets the meaning of data gathered in the form of numbers. Qualitative analysis interprets the meaning of data gathered in the form of words. If we have completed a positivist study then we need to use quantitative statistical procedures. If we have completed a post positivist, critical theory or constructivist study, we will be using qualitative analysis procedures as shown in Table 1.1

Table 1.1
Data Analysis for each Paradigm

	Quantitative Analysis	**Qualitative Analysis**
Positivism	X	
Post Positivism		X
Critical Theory		X
Constructivism		X

Positivist researchers develop an understanding of the data and its meaning through hypothesis testing using statistical procedures. Hypothesis testing is the key to finding causality and correlation as defined by positivist thinkers. So we need to look a bit more closely at hypothesis testing to make sense of quantitative analysis. In the eighteenth century (bear with me) the Scottish philosopher David Hume (1711-1776) developed laws of cause and effect which became the foundation for the scientific method. These laws were that,

1. The cause and effect are contiguous

2. The cause is prior to the effect

3. There is a constant union between the cause and the effect

4. If there are several causes of the effect, they have a common feature

5. If causes have different effects, then they are different

6. If a correlation is observed between cause and effect, this correlation is derived from the relationship between cause and effect

7. If a cause appears to have no effect at certain times it is because that cause only creates the effect in combination with other causes.

Thus we had a set of principles aimed at determining causes and correlations so that scientific knowledge could be advanced. In the nineteenth century in the United States this thinking was combined with the pragmatist school of thought that led to empirical testing being the proof of the truth of knowledge.

To operationalize this scientific method, in the social sciences, psychologists have developed the experimental design while sociologists have developed the survey design. The experimental design addresses causality while the survey design addresses correlation. These deterministic designs have been combined with sampling and statistical procedures based on probability theory, not without controversy (Cohen, 1994), to make the case for a "scientific" approach to research aimed at gathering knowledge and making predictions about people.

Hume did not considerprobability when developing his principles of causality. He was assuming an absolute statement of fact, not a percentage probability of causality or correlation. He was assuming that to prove cause and effect we would need to observe the relationship between them every time we observed them together. This would mean that we would never be sure of the proof because there would never be an end to such a study. The concept of probability allows us to end the study by suggesting that we can estimate the likelihood that we have proved the cause and effect. This modification was made during the debates at the beginning of the twentieth century that extended the logic of Bertrand Russell's (1872-1970) work linking mathematics to philosophy and suggesting that the logic of philosophical propositions could be proved mathematically. This entry of mathematics into proofs meant that confirmation of causality, which was originally framed as needing absolute proof, could be reframed to mean verification of the probability that a cause had an effect.

So, who made this conceptual leap from the need to prove absolute causality to the need to prove probability or likelihood of causality? **Probability theory** was developed by a French civil servant named Pierre Fermat in the 1620s, for whom mathematics was a hobby. Later Thomas Bayes (1702-1761) who lived in England set out his theorem of probability in his papers "Essay towards solving a problem in the doctrine of chances" published in the Philosophical Transactions of the Royal Society of London in 1764. At about the same time, according to Charles Hull (1914), Achenwall invented the word **"statistics"** from the Italian word for a statesman. The term referred to information needed by statesmen and those in public life. Such information was gathered in numerical form but with no commonly accepted methodologies.

The statistical methodologies emerged in the nineteenth century when a Belgian Astronomer named Felt Quetelet developed *"social physics"* and the idea of the *'statistical man"* to make predictions about society as a whole. He claimed that we can identify **"laws deduced from inference"** (Hull, page 36). Thus a natural scientist transferred the methods of the "hard" sciences to the study of society. This assistance from their natural science benefactors gave the newly developing social sciences of *"folk-psychology and sociology"* an improved prestige. Meanwhile, according to Stephan (1948), in the United States there was an extensive use of **sampling**, where inferences were made about a larger phenomenon from a selection assumed to represent that phenomenon in: agricultural crop and livestock estimates; economic statistics of prices, wages and employment; social surveys and health studies; and public opinion polling.

According to Stephan, though, the application of **probability theory** to the selection of **samples** was not made until the twentieth century with Arthur Bowley's (1869-1957) sampling of bonds and their interest rates in 1906 and Student's ("Student" was the "nom de plume" of William Sealy Gosset [1876–1937]), testing of the t-distribution in 1907. Then Leonard Tippett's (1902-1985) table of random numbers was published in 1927. It was Bowley and his colleagues who estimated errors associated with various approaches to stratified random sampling. The students of Bowley working for the Russell Sage foundation and influenced by the Social Science Research Council, gave serious attention to **sampling methodology** especially with the demands of the social programs developed under the New Deal in the 1930s. From then until now sampling and statistics based on probability theory have been the accepted methodologies for studying society.

In the middle of these developments, though, critics noted that probabilistic statements could not be made on the basis of the finding of one study since this would be making the assumption that one can generalize from the specific case to all cases. Karl Popper (1934) stepped into the breach at this time and suggested that since a hypothesis cannot be confirmed, because of this problem of induction, then lets us simply reverse the logic and, rather than confirm the hypotheses, let us **reject the null hypothesis**. To clarify, since we cannot generalize a finding about one relationship (e.g. effective parenting skills in one particular sample of parents reduced child abuse) from one study to the general population (effective parenting skills causes a reduction of child abuse in all families), we can assess the absence of the finding in our study (is it true that there is no relationship between effective parenting skills and child abuse in this particular sample of parents?). If we can reject this null hypothesis then the relationship must hold (if we can say no, there is not no relationship between effective parenting skills and child abuse in this particular sample of parents). This is illustrated in Table I.1 where we can reject the null hypothesis because we can reject the idea that parenting classes did not affect child abuse

Table I.1
Rejecting the Null Relationship between Parenting And Child Abuse

	Received Parenting Class	Did not Receive Parenting Class
Child Abuse Increased	NO	YES
Child Abuse Decreased	YES	NO

Karl Popper's methodology for this "logical empiricism" was:

1. Formulate a Hypothesis

2. Test the consequences of the hypothesis experimentally

3. Show if the hypothesis is false

4. Formulate predictive principles

If we can repeat this study and reach the same conclusion then we have a logical empirical proof of the relationship between cause and effect. Again, this position is controversial but it has gained acceptance.

The last step in this line of thought is the *linking of probability statements, and testing the null hypothesis, to quantitative methods*. If positivist, logical empiricism aims to make probabilistic statement about the absence of a relationship between cause and effect, the only way to do this is to gather data in terms of numbers that can then be manipulated via statistical procedures based on probability theory. Therefore, the only way to faithfully carry out this methodology and meet the requirements of positivist logical empiricism is to gather quantitative data to test hypotheses about the absence of a relationship or correlation between cause and effect. Data collected in the form of numbers, facilitates probabilistic statements, data collected in the form of words does not facilitate statements about the precise relationships between cause and effect as specified by Hume.

We now have the conceptual clarity we need to understand quantitative analysis. Positivist data analysis uses statistical procedures appropriate to the level of measurement (nominal, ordinal, interval, ratio) to manipulate the data as we discussed

237

in Part 3. **Inferential statistics** give estimates of whether a finding in our study sample (for example, that the TANF training program led to permanent employment) is indeed true. There are two kinds of inferential statistical tests: **parametric** and **non-parametric**. **Parametric** statistical tests are mostly used to test relationships between variables measured at the **interval** or **ratio** levels. There is some discussion of using such parametric statistics with variables measured at the **ordinal** level according to Weinbach and Grinnell, (2004) but to do this we would need to find a way to show that there was an equal distance between the levels of the scale being used. Thus **non-parametric statistical tests** are generally used to test relationships between variables measured at the ordinal and nominal levels. Parametric tests are considered to be more powerful tests than nonparametric tests, since they rest on more stringent assumptions of probability and statistical theory.

There are three stages to carrying out quantitative analysis

1. Enter our data into a statistical software package

2. Run **descriptive** statistics which summarize the data.

3. Run **inferential** statistics to assess the strength of relationships between independent and dependent variables. This will allow us to reject the null hypothesis and explain as much of the relationship between variables as possible.

Data Entry

Generally a statistical package such as the Statistical Package for the Social Sciences (SPSS) is used to analyze quantiative data. Although there are other packages, this is the one most commonly used by social workers and it will be the illustrative package used here to explain data entry and analysis. To understand data entry we need to remember our unit of analysis and observation units, which we discussed in Part 2. Our observation unit is the source of our numerical data and thus our data will be entered for each of these *cases*. For example, in our four example positivist studies the observation units are:

- *Individuals*, for out study of TANF;

- *Counties*, for our study of mental health service uptake;

- *Individuals*, for out study of the FAD; and

- *Individuals*, for our study of supervision.

However our unit of analysis for each of these studies is different. For the study of TANF it is the *programs*, for the study of Mental Health services it is *counties*, for the study of the FAD it is *families* and for the study of supervision it is *departments or agencies*. Thus our data will be entered according to our observation unit but our analysis will be organized in terms of our units of analysis. To clarify, the data entry screen for SPSS looks like table I.2 where *variable* needs to be replaced by the names of the variables in our study and the numbers down the side identify each person who has participated in the study.

Table I.2
Data Entry Screen

	Variable	Variable	Variable	Variable	Variable	Variable	Variable
O.U. 1							
O.U. 2							
O.U. 3							
O.U. 4							
O.U. 5							

If we use our study of the FAD as an example, where individuals are asked to report on their family's functioning on a scale of 1 to 4, then data entry would be as shown in table I.3. There are hypothetical scores for three participants in the study; one person from each of the designated ethnic groups. Remember, the scores are derived from the operationalization of concepts into variables and their dimensions that was explained in table I.2 in Part 1

Table I.3
Entered Data

Identification number	Problem Solving	Communication	Roles	Affective Responsiveness	Behavior Control	General Functioning	Ethnicity
1	2	3	4	2	1	3	1
2	4	2	1	4	2	3	2
3	4	2	3	2	4	1	3

Once the data has been entered, we need to check for errors. Errors are most often made when transcribing the data from the questionnaire to the computer screen. They are detected when frequencies show values that we did not assign, or we have some cases in our sample with a pattern of responses that is very different from other members of our sample. Karwell and Meyers (1983) suggest five options for **cleaning the data** and correcting errors in data entry:

1, go back and check the original questionnaire;

2, if you can, contact the respondent and try to correct the error;

3, estimate a corrected response by, for example, substituting scores from a case with similar characteristics;

4, discard the error and label it as missing data; and

5, discard the entire case.

Once errors in data entry have been addressed we can proceed with data analysis.

Descriptive statistics describe and summarize data; they do not test the null hypothesis. There are two kinds of descriptive statistics, **measures of central tendency and measures of dispersion.** Measures of central tendency are the **mean, median** and **mode,** and the measure of dispersion is the **standard deviation.** These are discussed below in terms of univariate statistics. **Univariate** statistics analyze one variable at a time.

Univariate Statistics

The first analysis we run is usually a **univariate** analysis so that we can look at the distribution of the values of each variable. Running this analysis is simply a "point and click" procedure in SPSS, where we click on analysis, then descriptive, and then frequencies while selecting all variables to be included in the analysis[1]. This will give us percentage and numeric frequencies for each value of each variable. As we look at the output for frequencies we will notice that it gives us a lot of detail. Reporting data in this kind of detail would be cumbersome and confusing to consumers of our research. So we need a way to graphically display the data using histograms or pie charts or other such charts and we need a way to show summaries our data. We summarize our data by reporting each variable's **central tendency.** There are three measures of central tendency: **mode, median** and **mean.** The **mode** is the value of the variable that is most frequent. It can be used with all four levels of measurement (nominal, ordinal, interval and ratio) but is usually used with nominal variables since more accurate summaries of data at the other levels of measurement can be given by the median or the mode. The **median** is the halfway point in a distribution of values. Half the values fall below the median and half the values fall above the median. Thus extremely high or extremely low scores have little effect on its value. It is always in the middle. The **mean** is calculated by adding up all the values of the variable for each person in the study and dividing that number by the number of people in the study. This measure of central tendency can misrepresent data, if there are a number of extremely high or low scores. For example, if 20 students took an exam and 6 students scored 100 while the other 14 students scored between 0 and 60. The mean student score would be 42.55 which is *skewed* towards the high scoring students, as you can see in figure I.1 where 40% of the students are above the mean and 60% below the mean. In this case, the median would offer a more representative summary of what happened.

---

[1] If you are interested in finding out about SPSS right now go to
http://calcnet.mth.cmich.edu/org/spss/toc.htm and run the "getting started" tutorial.

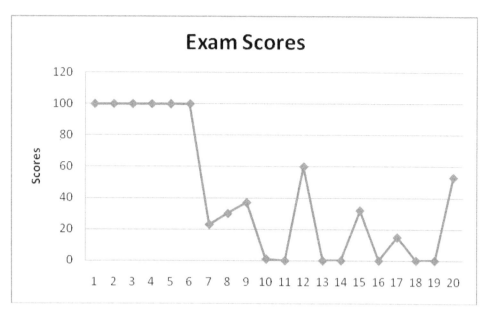

You can get the mode, median, and mean for any variable by simply pointing, clicking and selecting these options in the analysis window of frequencies in SPSS.

The measure of central tendency is a nice brief summary of the values for a variable but we may also want to report the distribution of values around the measure of central tendency. For modes and medians, the usual way of doing this is to report the inter-quartile range of values of a variable. This is the range of values for the lowest 25% of cases, the range of values for the next 25% of cases, the range for the next 25% of cases and the range for the highest 25% of cases. For example, if we carried out our study using the FAD and 50 families had a score of 1 and 50 families had a score of 4; we would have multiple modes of both 1 and 4 and multiple medians of both 2 and 3. To explain these results we would also explain that the lowest 25% of cases had a value of 1 as well as the next 25% of cases, while the top two quartiles had a value of 4.

For an interval or ratio variable there is a more sophisticated way of explaining the distribution of the values of the variable around the mean: the **standard deviation**. This was introduced when we discussed random samples and standard error in Part 2. This statistic not only reports the distribution of scores on a variable but also opens the door to more complex inferential statistics which are described below in the next section. **Probability theory** assumes that values for all variables in the population of interest are equally distributed around the mean: i.e. they have a normal distribution. The **standard deviation**, because of the properties of a randomly selected sample based on probability theory, is based on the assumption that the values for each variable in the sample are equally distribution around the mean; i.e. the values of the variables in our studies also have a normal distribution. In a normal distribution, 68.6% of the values for a variable are one standard deviation above and below the mean, 95.4% of the distribution of the values for the variable are two standard deviations above and below the mean and 99.9% of the values for the variable are three standard deviations above and below the mean. If the standard deviation is small, then the values are closely cluster around the mean and the mean is an accurate representation of the average value for the value. If the standard deviation is large, then the distribution of the values for the variable is spread out and the mean is not a good representation of the values for the variable. This is illustrated below in figures I.2 and I.3. In figure I.2, the sample is 100, the mean score is 50 and the standard deviation is 2. So we can see that the mean is a good summary of the data because 95% of the data is between 44 and 56 and very close to the mean score. However, in figure I.3 the mean is till 50 but the standard deviation is 10.

In this example, 95% of the scores are between 20 and 80. The distribution is much more spread out and the mean is not a good summary of the data.

To sum up, in our example studies, to carry out univariate analysis, we would run frequencies for our variables: approaches to training, permanent employment, all items of the FAD, families, mental health clinics, uptake of mental health services, supervision, and staff retention. We would also run frequencies on any variables that described the participants in the study such as demographics and characteristics of agencies and counties. We would then report the mode, median or mode depending on whether the variable was nominal, ordinal, interval, or ratio. We would also report the inter-quartile range and the standard deviation.

The standard deviation is calculated by subtracting all values of the variable from the mean, squaring those values and then adding them up (this is the sum of squares) and then dividing the sum of squares by the number of respondents in the sample and calculating the square root of that amount. In our hypothetical example using FAD scores where we had 50 families with a score of 1 and 50 families with a score of 4 the calculation would be $\sqrt{}$ ((2.5-1)*50 (squared)+(2.5-4)*50squared)/100=1.5. So this suggests that 68.6% of the distribution is between 1 and 4 and 95.4% of the distribution is between –0.5 and 5.5. Since the range is between 1 and 4, the distribution is too spread out for the mean to be a good representation of the score for that variable.

Figure I.2
Normal Distribution of 100 cases where the mean is 50 and the standard deviations 2

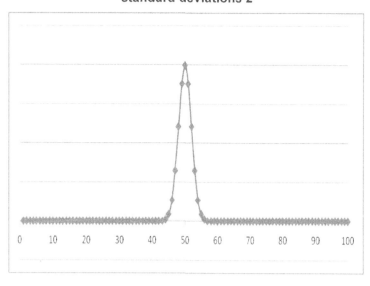

Figure I.3
Normal Distribution of 100 cases where the mean is 50 and the standard deviation is 20

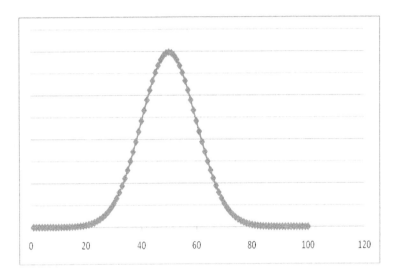

Inferential Statistics

The next step is to go beyond description of our data to interpretation of the meaning of our data. We do this by testing our hypothesis(es) using inferential statistics. These are **bivariate statistics** (testing the relationship between two variables) and **multivariate** statistics (testing the relationships between more than two variables).

Bivariate Statistics

With **bivariate** statistics we begin our hypothesis testing. Just as a reminder, we do this, *not* by actually testing if there is a relationship between our independent and dependent variables but, as we discussed above, by carrying out statistical procedures that indicate the likelihood that we can **reject the null hypothesis**. That is, that we can reject the idea that there is no relationship between the independent variable and the dependent variable. As the name suggests bivariate statistics simply address the relationship between two variables without consideration of the possible influence of other variables. They assess the likelihood of making **type I** or **type II** errors. A **type I** error is made when the null hypothesis is rejected and is should not have been rejected. For example, it may be true that in the real world TANF training has no effect on employment but, in our study, we conclude that this training does affect employment. Then we have made a **type I** error. A **type II** error is made when the null hypothesis is not rejected and it should have been. Again, to illustrate, if indeed in the real world TANF training does effect employment but in our study we conclude that it does not, then we have made a **Type II** error. According to Weinbach and Grinell

There is some discussion among mathematicians that nominal variables can have normal distributions because we could look at the proportion of the number "1" that responses to each category represent (e.g 40% employed and 60% unemployed). However, it is unclear if this argument is strong enough to warrant the use of statistical tests that assume normal distributions with nominal variables. We will therefore, use the currently accepted perspective on nominal variables. As an aside, there is some debate that variables measured at the ordinal level can be treated like ratio variables with a minimum of error and such means are often used for ease of understanding. However, the means of such variables cannot meet the assumptions of probability theory, this is simply a pragmatic practice.

(2010), the statistical test to be used for bivariate analysis will depend on

1. Whether the sample is randomly selected

2. Whether the variables have a normal distribution in the population of interest

3. The level of measurement of the variable (nominal, ordinal, interval or ratio)

4. The power that the statistical test has to avoid making a type II error

5. The degree to which a statistical test produces accurate findings when one or more of its assumptions are violated: the robustness of the test.

Since, only random samples can adequately meet the requirements of probability theory we will assume the selection of random samples for this discussion of our example studies. As discussed in Part 2, probability theory assumes that all samples of a particular size drawn from a population of interest have a normal distribution with a mean that is equal to the mean in the population of interest. Thus, any sample drawn from the population of interest measures variables whose mean scores' distance from the population mean can be estimated. Thus in our example studies all our ratio level variables are assumed to have a mean whose proximity to the true mean in the population of interest can be estimated. Using the Bayesian interpretation, we will assume that such estimates, or likelihoods, are normally distributed in the population of interest. Remember, the only variables within the sample that have the potential to have normal distributions in the population of interest are our ratio variables. Variables measured at the nominal and ordinal level do not have means because they do not have regular distributions; they are categorical or order variables. To illustrate this point, our variable, *approaches to training* has two values and therefore can only range between 1 and 2 and the same is true for our variable *permanent employment*.

Returning to our choice of bivariate statistical tests, we have variables at nominal, ordinal and ratio levels of measurements. Having discussed criteria 1, 2 and 3 above, we now turn to criteria 4 and 5. The choices for our example studies are tabulated in table I.4 below.

Table I.4
Bivariate Statistical Tests

	Causal (Explanatory)	Correlational (Descriptive)
Micro Practice (target is individuals, families or groups)	What is the differential effectiveness on TANF clients of two approaches to employment training where one group receives training and the other receives no training and is simply placed immediately into a job? **IV**= Approaches to Training (Nominal) **DV**= Permanent Employment (Nominal) **Appropriate Statistical Tests:** Chi-Square Fisher's Exact NcNemar's	How does a family assessment tool assess families from three different ethnic groups? **IV**=Families (Nominal) **DV**= Scores on FAD (Ordinal) **Appropriate Statistical Tests:** One way ANOVA or (if reject the idea that ordinal variables can be treated like ratio variables) Mann Whitney U Wilcoxon Sign Kruskai-Wallis
Macro Practice (target is organizations or communities)	What is the impact uptake of county mental health services where one county has neighborhood mental health clinics and the other has a central mental health clinic? **IV**=Mental Health Clinics (Nominal) **DV**=Uptake of Mental Health Services (Ratio) **Appropriate Statistical Test:** T Test One way ANOVA	How do the contrasting supervisory styles in two departments of children's services affect staff retention rates? **IV**=Supervision (Ordinal) **DV**=Staff Retention Rate(Ratio) **Appropriate Statistical Test:** Simple linear regression (or ordinal variable is treated like ration variable, otherwise) T test One Way ANOVA Pearson r

These tests compare the distributions of our dependent variables in the pre test and post test or in the two conditions that are being correlated and tell us whether we can **reject the null hypothesis**. They also tell us the likelihood of making a **type I error**. That is, rejecting the null hypothesis when we should not have done so. Generally the accepted likelihood that we have committed a Type I error is set at less than 5 times in 100. This means that if we repeated this study 100 times we would make a Type I error only 5 times. This is usually stated as $p<.05$. We could go as high as $p<.09$, which means that if we repeated this study 100 times we would make a Type I error 9 times, since the higher this number the lower the chance is that we will make a Type II error, which is the likelihood of failing to reject the null hypothesis when we should have done so. We can also avoid Type II errors by analyzing variables with small standard deviations and using larger samples.

To be more specific about table I.4, the chart tells us which bivariate tests to use to decide whether:

1. TANF training caused employment

2. The organization of mental health clinics caused uptake of services

3. The assessment of family functioning by the FAD correlated with ethnicity

4. The supervisory style correlated with staff retention rates

However, this is only the beginning. Bivariate analysis does not take into account the possible effects of other variables. If we have a concern that another variable maybe affecting scores on our dependent variable at the same time as our identified independent variable, or that there are many influences on our dependent variable then we need to carry out multivariate analysis using multivariate statistics

Multivariate Statistics

Multivariate statistics test the relationship between our dependent variable and several independent variables simultaneously. They control for the interaction between several independent variables. Rubin and Babbie (2011) explain this process by means of an elaboration model that shows how we can identify whether the relationship between the independent and dependent variable is indeed true or whether it is spurious or affected by other variables that specify or suppress the relationship we are testing. We do this by adding variables to our analysis as illustrated below in tables I.5 to I.7. Using the example of our TANF training study, we may begin by finding that the training program is ineffective as illustrated in table I.5. This data shows that the same percentage of clients gain employment regardless of training. However, in table I.6, when we add a third variable "age" to the analysis we find that training is effective with younger clients but not with older clients. However, when we add a fourth variable "having and undergraduate degree" as shown in table I.7 we see that the real determinant of getting a job is formal education rather than training.

Table I.5
Training program is ineffective

	Training	No Training
Employed	50%	50%
Not Employed	50%	50%

Table I.6
Training Program is effective with younger clients

	Younger Clients		Older Clients	
	Training	No Training	Training	No Training
Employed	75%	25%	25%	75%
Not Employed	25%	75%	75%	25%

These findings would be the result of various forms of multivariate analysis. We use **multiple regression** to assess the causal relationship between a ratio dependent variable and several ratio independent variables. We use **multiple correlation** to assess the correlational relationship between a ratio dependent variable and several ratio independent variables. We would use **discriminant analysis** to assess how a dependent variable measured at the nominal level is influenced by various independent ratio variables and we would use **multiple analyses of variance** to test the relationship between several dependent variables measured at the nominal and/or ordinal level and several independent ratio variables. There are other possibilities but the choice of multivariate analysis test will, again, depend on whether the sample is randomly selected, the distribution of the variables in the population of interest, the level of measurement of the variables to be included in the analysis, and the power and robustness of the test.

Table I.7
True relationship is between Formal Education and Employment rather than training and employment

	With undergraduate Degree			
	Younger Clients		Older Clients	
	Training	No Training	Training	No Training
Employed	75%	75%	75%	75%
Not Employed	25%	25%	25%	25%
	Without Undergraduate Degree			
	Younger Clients		Older Clients	
	Training	No Training	Training	No Training
Employed	25%	25%	25%	25%
Not Employed	75%	75%	75%	75%

Non Parametric Statistical Tests

All the statistics described above are **parametric statistics**, which means that they are based on the assumptions of probability theory and sampling theory. It has been assumed that as positivist researchers, we will always gather and analyze data using these theories to guide us because these are the principles that the positivist paradigm is based upon. However, positivist researchers have confronted numerous practical problems when carrying our research that remains true to the paradigm. We have noted some of these in our discussion of Planning and Implementation. Solutions to these problems include gathering data from non-random samples, gathering data from small samples, and measuring variables at the nominal and ordinal levels. These procedures are not based on probability theory or sampling theory and data collected using these approaches is analyzed using statistics known as **non parametric** statistics. Some of these are listed in table I.3. They are used to analysis variables that are not measured at the ratio or interval level and so do not have a mean and cannot be assumed to have a normal distribution clustered around a mean. The most commonly used non parametric bivariate statistical test is the Chi square which is used to test the relationship between two variables measured at the nominal level by comparing expected scores for each variable if the null hypothesis were true with the scores that were actually observed in the study. This test does not assume normal distributions of variables in the population of interest or the selection of independent samples.

It is as if the edifice of the positivist paradigm, having been built on a coherent scientific method and having been proposed as the touchstone for gathering knowledge, collapses with a muttered apology from its protagonists of "never mind" and the work and thought that we have discussed so far is forgotten. It would be more scientific to decide that, if a dependent variable needs to be measured at a nominal or ordinal level, positivism is not the approach that should be taken; alternative approaches such as post positivism, critical theory, and constructivism, which are based on other assumptions would be more appropriate.

To sum up our discussion of positivist analysis procedures for evaluating out data, we have reviewed the rationale for quantitative approaches to analysis and hypothesis testing. We have reviewed data entry into quantitative analysis software such as SPSS and then analysis procedures that can be used to both describe and interpret the data that we have collected using univariate, bivariate, and multivariate statistical tests, noting an objection to nonparametric statistics. Important cross cutting issues of ethics, politics, diversity, and technology are similar to those discussed in Part 1, Part 2, and Part 3. Additional important cross cuttings issues for the Evaluation stage are discussed in Chapter V. Below is a summary of this chapter and learning assignments. Next we move on to qualitative analysis of data that was collected using the post positivist approach.

Summary of Chapter I

- Quantitative analysis is the approach that positivists take to understanding the meaning of data

- There is a history and rationale for using probability theory and statistics to analyze data

- It is important to distinguish the units of observation and the units of analysis.

- Data can be entered in a statistical software package and frequencies can easily be run to check for any errors in data entry

- Descriptive statistics such as means, medians and modes summarize the data

- Bivariate analysis tests the relationship between an independent and dependent variable. Choice of a bivariate test depends on the characteristics of the measurement and distribution of the two variables

- Multivariate analysis is used to understand the relationship between more than two variables and measures such relationships simultaneously

- Non parametric statistical tests are used when the assumptions of parametric tests have not been met.

Positivist Learning Assignments

1. Go to http://calcnet.mth.cmich.edu/org/spss/toc.htm and run the "getting started" tutorial or click on http://calcnet.mth.cmich.edu/org/spss/V16_materials/ Video_Clips_v16/02getting_started/02getting_started.swf and run the tutorial

2. Or go to http://www.youtube.com/watch?v=eTHylEzS7qQ and watch the tutorial on utube.

3. Having gained this overview, go back to the first screen when you open the SPSS software package. You will see a data spread sheet layout. Click on the "variable view" tab at the bottom of the screen. Type in some imaginary demographic variables and variables that could be used as your independent and dependent variables in the left hand column (gender, ethnicity, age, years of education, whether TANF training was given, employment status). Now click on the "Data view" tab at the bottom of the screen and enter some imaginary scores for these variables. Now you have a data set

    a. Click on the "analyze" tab at the top, then click on "descriptive statistics". Run frequencies. What did you get? What does it mean

    b. Click on the "analyze" tab again and experiment with the various univariate and bivariate tests if offers you. Run them. What do they mean? Which tests were appropriate for your variables?

For the post positivist researcher data collection and data analysis are interwoven. Variables are not defined, measured, and then analyzed at the end of the data collection phase. Rather, as post positivists, we gather data in an interview, from an observation, or from a document and immediately analyze that data. The results of that analysis then inform the next round of data gathering. Thus, although analysis procedures that allow us to understand the meaning of the data are discussed here under a separate heading, they are in fact an integral part of the data gathering procedures described in Part 3.

As we have already discovered, data for post positivist research is collected in the form of words and is analyzed using qualitative analysis procedures. Two approaches to qualitative analysis are described here. The first is a "top down" approach where the same analysis framework is applied to all qualitative data collected in the study. It is rooted in linguistics and ethnography. We should use this approach when we are looking for patterns or describing processes. The second is rooted in Sociology. It is a "bottom up" approach to qualitative analysis, where the framework emerges from the data. We should use this approach when we are interested in developing theories about a particular topic

Qualitative Analysis using the "Top Down" Approach

The precise analysis and interpretation of meaning in language is rooted in linguistics and ethnography. Brown and Yule (1991), when discussing coherence in interpretation of discourse, tell us that linguists understand the meaning of language by analyzing sentences, identifying the format in which information is being conveyed, and using socio-cultural knowledge to make assumptions about what the speaker or writer is intending to say. They do this by,

1. Computing the communicative function: What is both the social and literal meaning of the communication? What is being said and how is the person behaving? Sinclair and Coulthard (1975) identified five categories of discourse: lesson, transaction, exchange, move, act. Sacks et al (1974) suggested that a better way to compute the communication function is to analyze "turn-taking" in conversations. Examples of forms of turn taking include: greeting-greeting (First person: Hi, how are you; second person answers: Fine how about you) or interrogative (First Person: Did you schedule another appointment for next week?; Second person answers: Yes, it's on Tuesday at 10.00am. Austin's (1962) theory of speech acts is another form of computation. The speech itself is an explicit or implicit act, such as asserting, congratulating, apologizing, and so on. All of these approaches give us some guidelines for understanding language. Although they lead us to categorization systems that sometimes appear to be arbitrary, they do give us a framework for our analysis of the interview or observation data.

2. Using general socio-cultural knowledge. What is the previously learned knowledge of context that is being used to predict what the next sentence will be and where the conversation is going? We do this using frames, scripts, scenarios, schemata, and mental models. Frames are simply preconceive understandings of a new situation (we have an appointment with a client); scripts are sequences of activities that we associate with particular situations (we have procedures that we follow when intervening with a client); scenarios are the components we anticipate for any new situation that has been given a label that we understand (we have an understanding of who and what should be present during the intervention); schemata are higher level knowledge that helps us understand a situation (our knowledge of theory and practice with this client); mental models are logical sequences of thought that explain a situation (the client cannot sleep and has a flat affect and is therefore depressed and we have decided to intervene with strategies that address cognition). There is some overlap between these terms but, again, they do give us a perspective from which to analyze our data.

3. Determining the inferences being made. How do we find the missing link, either automatically or with a conscious thought process that allows us to make an explicit link between statements? Automatic links would be made when, for example, a client who is depressed enters the room, sits down and begins to cry. We automatically interpret the crying as part of the depression. Conscious links are made when we step back from a situation and ask ourselves the questions; who is involved? What is involved? Where is this happening? When is this happening? We ask ourselves further question to elaborate and evaluate the situation; How is this happening? Why is this happening? Again these ideas give us guidelines for interpreting our data.

Coulthard (1985) in his discussion of the ethnography of speaking notes that ethnographers for all speech events need to provide data on:

1. The structure of the speech event (letter, song, hymn, poem, interview, conversation, meeting)

2. The setting of the speech event, both physical and psychological. That is a description of the physical surroundings in which the event is taking place and the cultural meaning of the setting.

3. Participants in the speech event, who can include

    i. Addressor or Speaker

    ii. Addressee

    iii. Hearer or Audience

4. The purpose of the speech event from the point of view of each participant.

5. The "Key" or the tone or spirit of the speech event as demonstrated by both verbal and non-verbal queues.

6. The channels of communication used in the speech event, which can be oral or written.

7. The message content giving all topics being addressed.

8. The message form, which can be informal or formal

9. The rule breaking being demonstrated in the speech event, where a statement of norms is given and an indication of if and when any norms are being broken.

10. The norms of interaction for the speech event, which includes how much silence is tolerated, the physical distance between people, the gender roles, and the norms for turn taking in any conversation.

By combining the above ideas we can identify a framework for analyzing qualitative data using a consistent approach across all data where the framework is used as a template to understand any source of data, whether it be an interview, observation or document. This is shown in Table II.1

Table II.1
Framework for Data Analysis using a "top down" approach to analysis

	Interview	Observation	Document

Setting
    Physical
    Psychological
    Cultural/social			

Participants
    Addressor
    Addressee
    Audience			

Purpose of
    Addressor
    Addressee
    Audience			

Key (tone)
    Verbal
    Non-Verbal			

Channels of Communication
    Oral
    Written
    Other			

Message Content
    Topic 1
    Topic 2
    Topic 3
    (And so on)			

Message Form
    Formal
    Informal			

Norms of Behavior Rule Breaking			

Norms of Interaction
    Turn Taking rules
    Category of Discourse			

Communication Function
    Literal
    Social			

Relevant Socio Cultural Knowledge being used
    Frames
    Scripts
    Scenarios
    Schemata
    Mental Models			

Inferences
    Automatic
    Constructed consciously (Who? What?
    Where? When? How? Why?			

if we are analyzing a piece of narrative, for example, this excerpt from a student study of interventions with abusive men by Walters (1995) where a probation officer is talking about the process for taking domestic violence cases to court; we can develop the analysis in table II.2 that gives us both an understanding of the meaning of the narrative and suggests further direction for data gathering. The narrative is reproduced first, followed by a top down analysis.

> *"The process goes as follows: the district attorney review the case form the police department, they must then decide if they even have a case. Sometimes there is not enough evidence, or maybe she hit him with a baseball bat before he hit her, or maybe the police officer wrote a lousy report; if the D.A. cannot make a case they send the file over to the person that handles the pre-filing diversions. The person there writes a letter saying "if you go to anger management, the case will be dropped" It's kind of a sucker approach because the D.A. isn't going to try to prosecute anyway. The rates of those who complete the classes as a result of this approach are low. These are called pre-filing diversions. It's frustrating because some of the cases sent for pre-filing are legitimate cases that should be taken to court. If the case is filed and goes to court, they can still be considered for the diversion program if they meet certain criteria. These are: they have no conviction for any offense involving violence within ten years, their record does not indicate that probation or parole have ever been revoked, they have not been diverted pursuant to this chapter within then years, and they haven't assaulted anyone with a deadly weapon. If they are diverted, I get their probation case and they have to go to 52 weeks of anger management classes. The deal here is that I have the leverage of the court, which is crucial, because if he doesn't go to anger diversion, the threat is that criminal proceedings will be reinstated. Let's say he doesn't fit into one of these categories, the case may be tried and he may go to jail. I'm afraid those cases are far and few between" (page 45)*

Table II.2
Analysis of excerpt from text of probation officer interview

Dimensions	Interview Narrative

Setting
  Physical
  Psychological
 	
  Cultural/social
	
	Courts, Anger Management settings, probation officer's office
	Abuser's denying guilt, court officials feeling inadequate, unable to prosecute or enforce law
	Notion that although abuse is illegal and prohibited, there will be no punishment for this offense since it is not serious enough.
	Need more data on settings for the abusive male and probation officer, perhaps through observation

Participants
  Addressor
 	
  Addressee
  Audience
	
	District Attorney, Diversion Officer, Anger Management Trainer, Probation Officer
	Abusive Male
	Victims of crime
	Need more data on audience.

Purpose of
  Addressor
  Addressee
  Audience
	
	To punish male abusers
	To avoid being punished
	To see that punishment happens?
	Need more data on times when the victims do not want to see abuser punished

Key (tone)
  Verbal
 	
  Non-Verbal
	
	There is an attempt to be firm with the abuser and suggest that punishment will happen but there is also a tone is a kind of tired cynicism. A regret that more is not done
	Need data on this, perhaps observation of exchanges between participants

Channels of
Communication
  Oral
  Written
  Other
	All participants have written and oral communication
	
	Need more detailed data on this, specific modes of communications between specific participants

Message Content
 	
  Topic 1
  Topic 2
  Topic 3
  (And so on)
	Process for taking domestic violence cases to court
	
	1. DA decides if they have a case, usually no case.
	2. Diversion officer threatens legal action if non compliance with anger management
	3. Labels diversion as "sucker approach"
	4. Completion rate low
	5. Process and criteria for diversion after pre-filing
	6. Probation's role in diversion
	7. Requirement for anger management
	8. Comment on rarity of jail time for offenders

Message Form
  Formal
 	
  Informal
	
	There are various formal messages between court and probation officials and the male abuser. There is the formal requirement for completion of anger management and the informal knowledge that the threats of punishment cannot be carried out.

Norms of Behavior Rule Breaking	 The official socials norm is that all these men have broken the law and that abuse of women is wrong. There is the unofficial norm that not much is done in term of punishment and the crime is not taken very seriously. This suggests that the norm is in fact only theoretical

	and not real. *Need more data on whether anyone ever breaks these norms and insists on prosecution and punishment*
Norms of Interaction Turn Taking rules Categories of Discourse	*Need data on how abuser interacts with other participants, perhaps direct observation or written accounts of interviews.*
Communication Function 　Literal 　Social	Communication between participants will involve legal mandates and required responses. The social function of these communications is to deter male abusers from continuing to abuse. However it appears that such a deterrent does not exist *Need more data on repeated offenders*
Relevant Socio Cultural Knowledge being used 　Frames 　Scripts 　Scenarios 　Schemata 　Mental Models	The probation officer is describing a sequence of activities that leads to minimal jail time or prosecution A sequence of actions is described regarding the processing of male abusers There is an official expectation that punishment will be carried out, people have roles, the offender moves through the stages without experiencing too much punishment Participants have a knowledge of the legal mandates and procedures and the anger management treatment. The overall assumption is that male abusers are committing a crime and are punished. Pragmatic descriptions tell us that this is not happening *Need more data on the abusers socio cultural knowledge of this process*
Inferences 　Automatic 　Constructed 　Consciously 　(Who? What? 　Where? When? 　How? Why?)	The automatic inference is that this process is not working and needs to be addressed. The constructed inference is that we need to no more about the participants, the constraints on the legal professionals, where and when the system breaks down, how it breaks down and why. *Need more data on each to the topics in message content.*

This framework for analysis of qualitative data gives us a set of dimensions that can be used to understand any piece of qualitative data, whether it is an interview narrative, an account of an observation or a document. The specific analysis in Table II.2 shows how the framework clarifies the meaning of what we have (a system that does not work effectively from the probation officer's point of view) and what we need (specific data that will show whether this perspective is correct and how others are experiencing the process). It shows us what we have and what we need in future rounds of interviews or observations. It gives us common dimensions that we can use for analysis for all our data and it gives us a structure for describing the meaning of our data.

A "bottom up" approach to analyzing qualitative data is much more inductive and open-ended and is rooted in the discipline of Sociology. It was Glasser and Strauss (1967) who introduced the idea that we can generate theory from empirical data. They suggested that research can be used to both test theory and create theory and they offered approaches to theory creation. Much later, Corbin and Strauss (2008) offered guidelines on the art of interpreting qualitative data when carrying out such theory creation. They suggested that various stages of synthesis should be applied with increasing complexity. Thus a narrative text is transformed from a series of words to a theoretical statement about regularities in nature. These stages of synthesis are described here in a sequential fashion but in reality we move back and forth between them as we develop the theory. We begin with **open coding**. Here the narrative of the interview or observation is broken down into themes or categories. Such categories guide refinement of future questioning and observation. At the next stage, **axial coding**, we propose relationships between themes or categories. We test these relationships in further rounds of data gathering. The third stage, **selective coding**, is when we develop a theoretical statement. We identify the conditions of the relationships between categories and themes and we include them in a comprehensive statement. The last stage is the **conditional matrix**, where we put the theoretical statement into the context of current knowledge about human interaction. In a study of gang life, for example, we might develop a theoretical statement linking "joining rituals" to acculturation for young people from immigrant families. This might then be included in the theoretical knowledge on acculturation for individuals, families and communities. This might also be added to social work practice knowledge on interventions with gang members.

Corbin and Strauss (2008) talk about this analysis process as sampling data. We begin by deciding upon a type, purpose and question for research and then choose a research site. We then immerse ourselves in the research focus at the site through interviews, observations and reviews of documents so that we can identify and sample concepts that are emerging from the data being gathered. Sampling, for these authors, is sampling of concepts to identify regularities that lead to theoretical statements. Sampling the correct group of people is not the major design issue, it is the sampling of observations, interviews, artifacts, and documents to explore emerging concepts and categories that is important when deciding whom to include in the study.

In our example student study of the insights of Parolees (Torres, 2007) the key players, the paroles, were interviewed and the resultant data was analyzed after each interview. Sampling was then continued, guided by all stages of the grounded theory analysis procedures. During **open coding** an inclusive process of gathering data from several key players, so that all relevant concepts were identified, was carried out. Then, during **axial coding**, where relationships between categories and concepts were being identified and articulated; the relationships between categories and concepts that emerged from the data dictated further data gathering from members of the parolee group who might have something to say about the emerging understanding of the data. The same was true at the stage of **selective coding** where the core theme was being identified. When the **conditional matrix** was built, data collection was mostly completed, since this is an overall reflective statement about where the newly created theory fits in the grand scheme of things.

Below are some examples of the results of such an analysis process in relation to the example study of Homeless Children (Young and Creacy, 1995) and the Torres (2007) study of Parolees

Open Coding

In the early stages of analysis, grounded theory researchers carry out microanalysis. This initial process is used to develop a routine practice of analyzing data with a frame of mind that is open to all potential interpretations. We may scan a narrative of an interview, for example, and pick an interesting segment. Then that segment is analyzed in detail. To do the analysis, we take chunks of the narrative that seem to hang together. This could be a word, a line, a sentence or a paragraph. For example we may find a statement such as,

"I'm glad we came here, cause before I was running the streets with hoods and going nowhere in life but now that I'm here, the rules are too strict and you can't go to the mall or 7-11 without your parents being with you" (page 21, Young and Creacy, 1995)

This might be divided up into chunks such as

- *"I'm glad we came here*

- *before I was running the streets with hoods*

- *and going nowhere in life*

- *now that I'm here,*

- *the rules are too strict*

- *you can't go to the mall or 7-11*

- *without your parents being with you*

We then use analytical tools to develop concepts, their dimensions, and their links with other concepts. Analytical tools include: asking sensitizing, theoretical, practical and guiding questions about the chunks of data; and making theoretical comparisons. Possible questions include: Who? When? Why? Where? What? How? How much? With what results? Questions about the above data might include:

- Where on the range of feelings does glad come?

- What are the range of places they have come to?

- How did they develop their assumptions about the direction of life?

- What rules do they mean?

- What range of rules have they experienced and what is their affect?

- What range of independent activities are they aware of?

- How do they understand parents' authority and its consequences?

Such questions and their answers identify concepts and theories as well as directions for further sampling and data gathering.

Techniques for making theoretical comparisons include the "flip flop technique, "systematic comparison" and "waving the red flag". They make us confront our values and assumptions about the data and re-assess any interpretations that we might be being taken for granted. In relation to the above data we might ask

- What happens to children who have feelings of unhappiness at being in a shelter?

- How do these statements compare to those of any teenager who is not homeless?

- How does the homeless adult react to being in a shelter?

- Is this appropriate developmentally for children at this age?

- Is there a situation where children would be better off homeless than in a shelter?

Usually, there is not enough time for all narratives to be analyzed in this detailed fashion. However, we should carry out microanalysis extensively with initial data and then later when new themes are emerging or we have noticed something that is puzzling.

Having used microanalysis tools to review and interpret the data we can sample appropriate study participants and gather data to facilitate "open coding", which is the process of identifying the social phenomenon's concepts, categories of concepts, properties of concepts, and dimensions of properties. Figure II.1 offers a visual illustration.

Figure II.1
Example of open coding

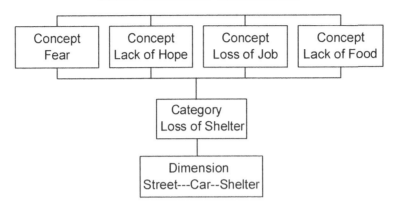

Social Phenomenon=Homelessness

| Concept Fear | Concept Lack of Hope | Concept Loss of Job | Concept Lack of Food |

Category
Loss of Shelter

Dimension
Street---Car--Shelter

In this illustration, after microanalysis of the narratives, the concepts of fear, lack of hope, loss of job and lack of food have emerged and the patterns in the narratives suggest that these concepts be grouped into the category of loss of shelter. One dimension of loss of shelter has been identified, type of shelter, and it ranges from none when the family is living on the street to living in a car to living in a shelter. To develop this analysis we take a piece of text or a transcript of an interview and using microanalysis techniques, review its possible meanings.

Writing memos in our research journal to explain our reasoning, we conclude that the four identified concepts are depicted in the text and that they can be grouped into a category of loss of shelter. One dimension of loss of shelter, the literal type of shelter, ranges from no shelter and living on the street, to living in a car, to living in a temporary homeless shelter. This process of open coding is repeated with other data so that a number of categories are identified that are included in the social phenomenon of homelessness. Study participants continue to be sampled according to their knowledge and connection with the open codes that are emerging. The next step is to identify the connections between these open codes or categories and Corbin and Strauss (2008) refer to this as axial coding.

Axial Coding

Axial coding is a procedure for linking the emergent categories and making statements about the relationship between categories and their dimensions. Moving forward with our example; as well as a category of homelessness we also have a category of "children's hope for the future" that has the dimension range of "hopelessness – a wish for a toy – a wish for a friend – a wish for a community of family and friends – an optimistic vision for the child's future life. When this is linked to the dimension of the lack of shelter category we have the following relationship

Figure II.2
Example of Axial Coding

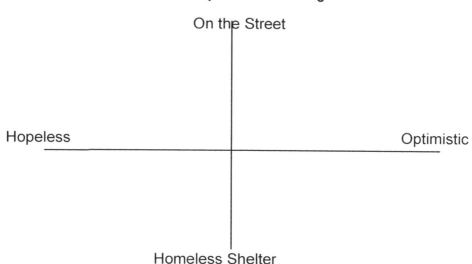

On the Street

Hopeless   Optimistic

Homeless Shelter

In this analysis four quadrants of possible experiences have been identified for homeless children.

- No Shelter/Hopeless (The child has nowhere to go and no wish for even a toy)

- No Shelter/Optimistic (The child has nowhere to go but still had hopes for a toy, a friend, and a community of family and friends)

- Homeless Shelter/Hopeless (Although having shelter, the child still does not have wishes for anything)

- Homeless Shelter/Optimistic (The child has shelter and wishes and dreams for the future)

Such dimensions having emerged from narratives led to a collection of more focused data on the characteristics of children falling into each of the four quadrants and why and how they reach those particular quadrants of homelessness. Another, more complex, example of axial coding can be found in the following excerpt from our example study of parolees (Torres, 2007)

"The following axial coding chart links the codes, discrimination, jobs and cops. The chart shows the dimensions of each of the codes and how these dimensions are connected. This chart demonstrates different codes within the theme, "label". The chart shows the different dimensions of the code, "discrimination". Some of the parolees reported that they did not experience discrimination as a result of their status as a parolee. Others reported that they did in fact receive discrimination. Finally, some of the parolees reported that they had not faced discrimination, however they described experiences that did in fact demonstrate discrimination against them. The codes where

discrimination was prevalent towards the parolees were, "jobs", "cops", "society", and "appearance". Within each of these codes, the parolees shared experiences that showed that they had dealt with discrimination, that they believed was related to their parolee status." (Page 77)

Figure II.3
Experience of Discrimination

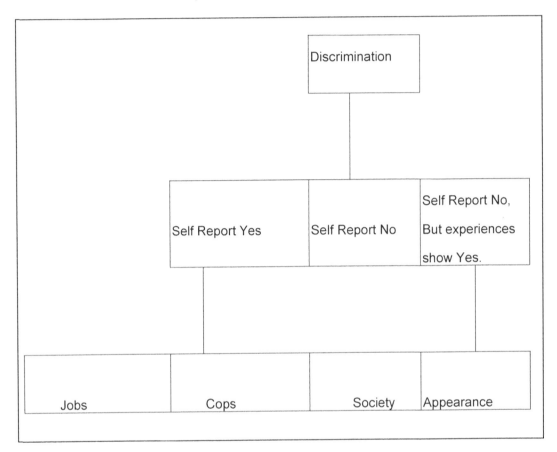

Selective Coding

Selective coding is the process of integrating and refining the categories and their dimensions to develop theory. According to Strauss and Corbin (1998) this process:

- is not based on romantic inspiration but is based on work;

- is created, not a solution to a puzzle;

- will not include everything there is to know about a topic in one version of the theory; and,

- will be brought together differently by different projects.

The first step is to identify the core category. This is the unifying theme that emerges from the data and the open and axial coding process. These authors (page 147) identify the following criteria for a core category:

- All the categories identified in open and axial coding can be related to it.

- It is a repeated pattern in the data.

- It allows the categories to be related in a logical and consistent manner without "forcing" the data.

- It is sufficiently abstract to be a term that could be used in research in other arenas

- It has explanatory power.

- It explains the main pattern in the data and variations of that pattern.

Strategies for developing the theory by identifying the core category and articulating its integration of categories include:

1. Telling the story by just spontaneously writing a few phrases that explain the findings. We can just give ourselves the freedom to take a blank piece of paper and simply write down what comes to mind when summing up the data and its meaning.

2. Using Diagrams to explain emergent connections between categories. If summing up findings in words is becoming a struggle, then perhaps drawing diagrams to illustrate major directions of the data analysis will come more easily.

3. Reviewing the research journal for patterns of reaction and decision-making.

4. Exploring patterns identified by a qualitative analysis computer program. These days there are a number of computer programs that can analyze languages and speed up qualitative data analysis. There is a discussion of the use of computers for qualitative analysis at the end of this chapter.

We now need to refine the theory that has emerged so far. We can do this by using the following strategies,

1. Identifying the properties of the core categories and filling in any dimensions that might be missing. In our example study of homeless children we may need more dimensions of hopelessness to fully describe the quadrants we have identified.

2. Both filling in poorly developed categories and eliminating categories that now are irrelevant. In our study the older children were resistant to talking about hopes and wishes for the future and it might have been possible, with

263

more of this age group in the study, to develop a more sophisticated category of hopelessness/optimism that was age appropriate.

3. Validating the emerging theory by comparing it with cases in the raw data. In our example study of homeless chidren there were 30 children. If the study had been on a larger scale with more resources, we could have included other shelters in the study and substantiated our theory as we studied children from these other shelters.

4. Building explanations for cases that do not fit the data. In our homeless children study, we would need to offer explanations for children who were optimistic while living on the street or hopeless while living in the shelter.

5. Building in variations. In our homeless children study, with additional resource, we could have looked at families that had been re-housed and moved on from the shelter to develop a broader dimension of the children's hopelessness/optimism.

When building theory we not only develop concepts, categories and their linking statements but we also describe the process that goes along with development of these statements. An analyzing process, according to Strauss and Corbin (1998), is "purposefully looking at action/interaction and noting movement, sequence, and change as well as how it evolves (changes or remains the same) in response to changes in context or conditions" (page 167). To identify the process, the analysis asks the following questions,

1. What is going on here? How does a child move from one stage to another and when? In our study, the process of being in group sessions at the shelter assisted development of self esteem and optimism.

2. What problems, issues, or happenings are being handled through action/interaction, and what form does it take? Who is involved in the children's transitions to various stages of hopelessness/optimism and what roles do they play? In our study, parents, shelter staff, social work students and other children all were brought together to promote self esteem in the shelter's children.

3. What conditions combine to create the context in which the action/interaction is located? Where does the child experience hopelessness/optimism, at school, with friends? In our study, this varied with the age of the child. The older teenage children tended to be pessimistic in all observed settings while the younger children were more open to expressing optimism in the group setting.

4. Why is the action/interaction staying the same? Are the children "stuck" at one stage and why? Again, in our study, the teenage children did seem stuck at a pessimistic stage but other arenas of their lives were not directly observed.

5. Why and how is it changing? Are the children changing and why? In our study this was related to the opportunity for shelter and the group sessions offered to the children in the shelter.

6. Are actions/interactions aligned or misaligned? Is it appropriate that the teacher, friend, stranger, plays the role they are playing in promoting or obstructing the child's hopelessness/optimism? In our study, it appeared that the school personnel were not able to play a stronger role in promoting optimism, since they did not always know the background of the shelter children.

7. What conditions or activities connect one sequence of events to another? Can we identity the usual process of moving from hopelessness to optimism, or optimism to hopelessness? In our study, this process was identified for young children as linked to the shelter and the prospect of a home and a "normal" life where friends come be invited home to play. For the teenage children, the process was unclear, even after nine months of study.

8. What happens to the form, flow, continuity, and rhythm, of action/interaction when conditions, or the usual patterns, change? Can we identify breaks in this usual process of moving from hopelessness to optimism, or optimism to hopelessness? Again, in our example study, the process of moving to optimism is speeded up by self-esteem focused group interventions in the temporary shelter.

9. How is action/interaction taken in response to problem or contingencies similar to, or different from action/interaction that is routine? How do we intervene with the children's process of moving through this dimension, what seems to be working? Again, we seemed to know how to work with younger children through art work and creative song writing but the older children made individual choices about whether they would be part of this. Their process was dictated by their own decisions rather than automatic acceptance of a program offered by a homeless shelter.

10. How do the consequences of one set of actions/interactions play into the next sequence of action/interactions to either alter the actions/interactions or allow them to stay the same? Can we build the more complete picture of the process combining, events, players and interventions?

A thorough example of selective coding is offered in the parolee study (Torres, 2007). The analysis is shown in Figure II.4.

The theory that the researcher discovered during the data analysis process was, that parolees may endure similar experiences before their incarceration period, during their incarceration period and after their incarceration period, which will reveal common personal reflections based on these experiences. The chart above shows the unifying social phenomena, before incarceration, during incarceration, after incarceration and personal reflection. Within these social phenomena are the themes, which were discovered in the data analysis process and are based on the parolee responses. Under the themes, the codes themselves are listed. The codes were defined by and directly related to the actual answers that the parolees shared during the interview process. (Page 111-112)

Figure II.4
The Experience of Parolees

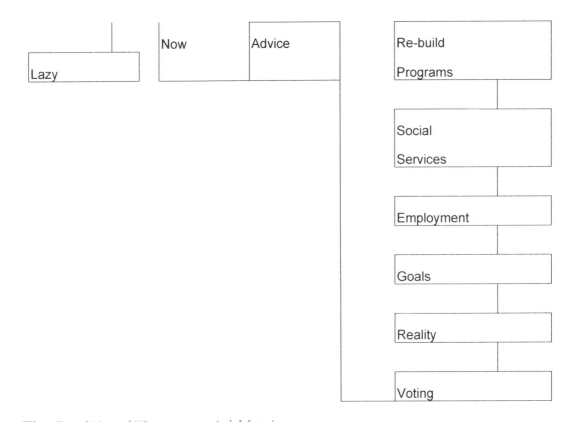

The Conditional/Consequential Matrix

The final stage of bottom up analysisis when we make a statement about how the newly developed theory fits into its societal context. To do this, Corbin and Strauss (2008) adopt social work practice's notion of micro and macro levels of human interaction. They have developed the **conditional/consequential matrix**, which prompts us to state where the theory fits in micro and macro levels of human interaction. We trace events identified in the process analysis through their spiral of impact on individuals, families, groups, organizations and communities at the local national and international levels. The matrix reminds us to link our findings to the human experiences and is particularly useful to social work researchers because it reminds us to consider, not only human interaction but also practice interventions at the various levels of human interaction. In our example from the homeless children study (Young and Creacy, 1995) it looks something like this

- **Individual level:** Homeless children in our study experience a transition from a feeling of hopelessness to a feeling of optimism as they move from the homeless state, to a temporary shelter. Younger children's feelings move more easily along this continuum than older teenage children. The movement to a more optimistic frame of mind is facilitated and speeded up by the provision of group session's encouraging artistic expression of hopes and dreams for the future for the younger children. For the older children, a personal choice has to be made to engage in such activities and some will choose not to be part of such programs.

- **Family level:** In this study, single parent families were the study sample. Children did express the wish for a "normal" family in a "normal" home but the single parent nature of the family did not seem to be a factor in developing optimism. The children accepted their family situations as a given and tended to blame problems on their homeless status rather than family issues. The fact that the family could be housed together in the shelter helped the process of building children's self esteem.

- **Group level:** The homeless children as a group tended to take care of each other and "watch out" for each other no matter what the age. The younger children were more adaptable and able to find hope while living in the shelter. The older children missed not being able to bring other teenagers home. They also were more conscious of being embarrassed about being homeless.

- **Organization level**: The organizations affecting these children were the shelter and their schools. The researchers did not have access to the school setting. A larger scale study in the future could explore this aspect of homeless children's lives

- **Community level:** At the local level, obviously the presence of homeless children is something that is addressed by shelters such as the one selected for the example study. It was clear that more shelters are needed in the local community but in addition, more child centered programs need to be developed in the shelters. At the national level, the phenomenon of homeless children clearly threatens the development of human potential and enrichment of life while making the nation vulnerable to the threats associated with having a class of alienated youth with low self-esteem. At the international level, the phenomenon of homeless children brings us into the arena of accepting responsibility for developing countries and the newer notion of links to terrorism where children with no hope see violence against their perceived enemy and martyrdom as the most optimist vision for their future.

To sum up, in this discussion of evaluation or interpreting the meaning of the data, two approaches to analysis have been described: a top down approach and a bottom up approach. The approach we choose depends on the questions we are interested in. If we want to understand how a process works in general and whether it relates to interventions at the micro or macro level, we probably should use the top down approach. However, if we simply have an exploratory question about "what is happening here" we will probably find the bottom up approach more useful. Important cross cuttings issues such as ethics, politics, diversity and technology are similar to those discussed in Part 1, Part 2, and Part 3. Additional important cross cuttings issues for the Evaluation stage are discussed in Chapter V. Below is a summary of this chapter and a learning assignment. We can now proceed to a discussion of Evaluation for the critical theorist.

- There are two possible procedures for evaluating the data and understanding its meaning. One is a top down approach using a common framework and the other is a bottom up approach where theory emerges from the data.

- The top down procedure uses a standard framework to analyze the data

- The bottom up approach utilizes open, axial, and selective coding to analyze the data. It uses the conditional/Consequential Matrix to give a context to findings.

Post Positivist Learning Assignments

1 Review the transcript of one student's comment on studying research methods using the four paradigms discussed in this book. Carry out an open and axial coding of the transcript. Discuss you analysis with your partner.

I think what I like about the alternative paradigms is that it gives us more social work knowledge, whereas regular research, and even papers we've done last year, like—I did one on Alzheimer's, and it's like we went and got—read journals and books. And this is what it is, and this is how it progresses. And it's just a lot of factual knowledge, but it doesn't really let you know how to work with somebody with Alzheimer's, whereas with the paradigms, it's like we can go—we're gonna talk to people that deal with them, that are providers, that are caregivers, that—and we're gonna get their experiences. And in presenting that, you get a better picture of—this is how to deal with it, how to cope with it, how to be a caregiver, how to be a resource provider, and you get a more dynamic picture of whatever you're researching. And so, I think that's more applicable to us. We're not—we don't need to know just straight data. That's a part of it, but that misses out on the whole bigger picture. So, I think that's what's neat about being able to do alternative paradigms.

The critical theory researcher completes three kinds of data analysis. The first is the analysis of data for developing the ideological position. The second is the analysis of data for developing the action plan. The third is the analysis of data to evaluate the effectiveness of the action

Ideological Analysis

Procedures for analyzing an ideology in the literature are offered in Part 1. However, we carry out an additional ideological analysis when we interpret the data gathered from key informants during the teaching learning process of "Looking". The goal of this analysis is to offer a synthesis that describes the oppression and empowerment experienced by study participants. For example, Hope and Timmel (1999), in their handbook for community workers, offer an instrument that can be used to carry out individual power inventories. We can give this instrument to study participants during the Looking phase. Then we can aggregate the data collected in these inventories to give a description of the power positions of the individuals, families, groups, organizations or communities that are the focus of our study. The instrument has been adapted below and basically it asks the following groups of questions.

1. *What job do you have? What jobs do your relatives have? What jobs do your friends have?*

   We can categorize the answers to these questions into socio-economic groupings and use them to describe the class position of study participants, their families and their social networks. In our example transportation study (Millet and Otero, 2011), participants were asked these questions and the results are shown in table III.1 and the qualitative explanation following it. In our other example studies, if time and resources had been available, these questions would have been asked in relation to university and school rather than work place. In the Riech (1994) study of Curanderismo, such questions would have shown the collaborating researcher and study participants who was best placed to effect change in the university and practice setting. The Christopulos (1995) study of eating disorders could have used this information to strategically negotiate with school districts.

2. *What organizations do you belong to? What organizations do your relatives belong to? What organizations do your friends belong to?*

   We can aggregate this data to show community links to power and action. In our example studies, the transportation study showed links to church and community groups in the U.S. and Mexico. The other example studies would have shown who was a member of a university or High school committee or organization that could have influence to affect change.

3. *What businesses do you use? What businesses do your relatives use? What businesses do your friends use?*

We can aggregate this data to show the economic power of study participants. In the transportation study we see limited economic power with participants reporting use of big box retail stores, restaurants, medical facilities and schools as described by Millet and Otero and shown in Table III.1

"...an overwhelming majority of the respondents work menial labor sector. These jobs do not provide opportunity for upward mobility. There is a low skill level required to work in this sector and a surplus of labor where the worker is dispensable by other unskilled workers. Employers are able to maintain low wages due to the surplus of low skilled laborers who are in need of jobs as a consequence of our current economic situation...

....The respondents were asked an open question about the organizations they belong to. Of the 66 respondents only 8 responded to the question. The distribution is as follows: 25% indicated they were affiliated with the North Shore Community Council, 12.5% indicated they were affiliated with The Knights of Columbus, 25% indicated they were affiliated with organizations in Mexico while 37.5% indicated they were affiliated with La Iglesia un Manatial en el Desierto. This category reflects the community's connection to power. The other 58 residents left the question blank and it can be inferred that they have little to no involvement with organizations.....Indeed the data shows that the North Shore Community involved in this study have a low level of organizational power...

...The businesses indicated by the residents reveal the challenges and limited economic power that hinder the empowerment process. The power analysis for this question suggests that the residents of North Shore are patronizing businesses thereby contributing to the economic sustainability of the region. As reflected through the analysis they frequent stores in Indio because the city of Coachella Valley does not have the larger retail stores such as Wal-Mart and Kmart which offer lower prices. In addition Wal-Mart has a superstore which provides commodities and food. This type of one stop shopping is ideal for the consumer who has limited access to transportation. It is a struggle for residents to travel to these establishments as they are relatively 20 to 30 miles outside of their community. The residents are in essences forced to use these stores that are far away to provide for their individual and/or family needs." (pages 79-85)

Table III.1
Example of Power Analysis (Excerpted from Millet and Otero, 2011, page 79)

Variable	n	Percentages
Employment:		
Student	2	2.6%
Unemployed	10	13.2%
Field Laborer	21	27.6%
Construction	1	1.3%
Homemaker	11	14.5%
Cashier	1	1.3%
Retired	3	3.9%
Handicapped	2	2.6%
Packing House	1	1.3%
House Keeping	2	2.6%
Pastor	1	1.3%
Nurse Assistant	1	1.3%
Organizations:		
North Shore Community	2	2.6%
Council Board Mexico	2	2.6%
Other, Knights Of Columbus and Barrio Unidas	1	1.3%
Iglesia un Manatial en el Desierto	3	3.9%
Businesses:		
Walmart in La Quinta	14	16.3%
Home Depot La Quinta	2	2.3%
Hospital Indio	1	1.1%
DMV Indio	1	1.1%
Food-4-Less Indio	16	18.2%
Cardenas in Coachella	8	9.1%
Social Security Bank	1	1.1%
Kmart in Indio	6	6.8%
Sunline	1	1.1%
Skip's Liquor In North Shore	1	1.1%
Gas Station	1	1.1%
Auto Parts	2	2.3%
99 Cents Store	1	1.1%
Rite Aid	1	1.1%
CVS	1	1.1%
McDonalds	4	4.5%
Coachella Valley Water Department	2	2.3%
Imperial	2	2.3%
Irrigation District Doctor	5	5.7%
Toro Loco	1	1.1%
Mecca Stores	1	1.1%
Stores	3	3.5%
Grocery Stores	2	2.3%
Schools	2	2.3%
All	1	1.1%
Dentist	3	3.5%
Chiropractor	1	1.1%
Medical	1	1.1%
Appointments	1	1.1%
Restaurants	1	1.1%

A further development of power analysis is to understand the roles that study participants play in each of these arenas. We can explore whether they and their relatives and friends have formal or informal roles and their levels of influence. This can be tabulated in a chart such as table III.2

Table III.2
Power Analysis of Roles

You and Your	Work Place/ School or University	Organizational Membership	Business Use
Roles 1. Formal Employed Leader 2. Elected Leader 3. Member/Worker/Customer			
Influence 1. Formal 2. Informal 3. None			

We can elaborate on this by asking about the kinds of power and influence that participants have and, again, tabulate the results, as shown in tables III.3 and III.4. In table III.3 participants are rating their own influence and in table III.4 participants are rating the influence of the organizations they are connected with. Participants can give a score of 1 (low), 2 (medium), 3 (high) for each of these dimensions.

Table III.3
Analysis of kinds of power

Your power over,	Work Place/School or University	Organizational Membership	Business Use
People			
Money			
Physical Property			
Various Skills (give list)			
Introducing New Ideas			

Table III.4
Analysis of Influence of Participants' Organizations

Entity's	Work Place/School or University	Organizational Membership	Business Use
Power over (people, money, property, skills, introduction of new ideas, other)			
Representation in Other Groups			
Representation in Gov. Groups			
Influence with Members			
Influence with other Groups			
Influence with Media			
Influence in Introduction and Control of New Ideas			

We can combine this data with Hope and Timmel's (1999) definition of power in relation to racism (page 126-127). In this definition they note that those who have power can have four kinds of power: **normative, hierarchical, resource and conceptual**

- Those with **normative** power set the standards by which they and others are judged; that is, they set the standards for appropriate behavior (normative power)

- Those with **hierarchical** power, have the capacity to make and enforce decisions that affect the lives of other people

- Those with **resource** power have access to resources and control the distribution of resources, and

- Those with **conceptual** power define the parameters of a discussion, determine the ideological framework within which debate takes place; that is, they define the problem and therefore determine the solutions that will be considered

We can summarize and analyze data from a survey of the items in tables III.5 to III.7 using these definitions to show the power of the individual, family, group, organization or community. We can develop charts aggregating the four kinds of power as shown in table III.5 for participants in the study and their relatives and friends. In each of the squares we would enter a numerical score as well as references to qualitative data. Such a power analysis of participants would develop further consciousness of the ideological message of the study. It would also suggest content for the teaching-learning phase and arenas for action strategies to promote empowerment.

Table III.5
Framework for reporting power analysis

	Normative Power	Hierarchical Power	Resource Power	Conceptual Power

Job/School or University:
    Your Role
    Your Influence				

Organization:
    Your Role
    Your Influence				

Business:
    Your Role
    Influence				

Job Site's/School's or University's:
    Power over (people, money, property, skills, introduction of new ideas, other)
    Representation in Other Groups
    Representation in Gov. Groups
    Influence with Members
    Influence with other Groups
    Influence with Media
    New Ideas, Intro. and Control				

Organization's:
    Power over (people, money, property, skills, introduction Ofnew ideas, other)
    Representation in Other Groups
    Representation in Gov. Groups
    Influence with Members
    Influence with other Groups
    Influence with Media
    New Ideas, Intro. and Control				

Business's:
Power over (people, money, property, skills, introduction Of new ideas, other)
    Representation in Other Groups
    Representation in Gov. Groups
    Influence with Members
    Influence with other Groups
    Influence with Media
    New Ideas, Intro. and Control				

In the transportation study (Millet and Otero, 2011), it became clear, very early, that participants had minimal power and influence and so the more complex power analysis described above was abandoned. In our study of eating disorders, the adolescent girls could have identified school based organizations in which they and their friends could or should have normative or conceptual power to influence development of school based programs to address female eating disorders. They may have also become aware of their lack of power in institutions that create their role models for eating and body types such as the media. In the Curanderismo study, the students, likewise could have identified campus based organizations and faculty with whom they had influential relationships who could lead initiatives to develop curriculum on folk healing. The students may also have become aware of their lack of power over curriculum development. However, any level of analysis is useful for understanding the group's situation and then moving on to the action phase of the study.

Action Analysis

Having assessed power, we can now move on to consider change strategies that have emerged from the ideological analysis. To do this we use a conceptual matrix to categorize each strategy and therefore understand the significance of the activity. Both dimensions of the matrix are the same; they are the levels of human organization that we intervene with as generalist social workers. Table III.6 illustrates this approach. If the target of action is an organization and the instigator of action is an individual, that individual will know his or her level of power and will work to increase that power and the power of the identified disempowered organization. If a community plans to intervene with an organization, the aggregate power inventory for that community is known and they will experience increased community empowerment as they negotiate with that organization. However, when an organization intervenes with an individual to address empowerment, for example county social workers addressing spousal abuse of women, the organization generally already has normative, hierarchical, resource and conceptual power.

Table III.6
Chart clarifying instigators and targets of action for Empowerment

		Targets of Action				
		Individual	Family	Group	Organization	Community
Instigators Of Action	Individual					
	Family					
	Group					
	Organization					
	Community					

The action strategies will depend on the results of the action planning. Much of this will rest with our social work practice skills. If the plan is for an individual to intervene with any of the targets of action, then that individual will need to be assisted with gaining the skills to intervene at the appropriate micro or macro level. If a family is to intervene with any target, then this is most likely to be a result of power and affiliation scores but they will still need guidance and support as they move forward with action. In our example Curanderismo study (Riech 1994), an influential family may have intervened with an individual or other family that they knew well who had power in the university setting. In addition such a family may have influence with the university trustees, or in local government. While taking action to enact empowerment, though, family members would need support and guidance on appropriate strategies. When the instigator of action is an organization or community, then the leaders of those entities will be using micro and macro practice skills to move action forward. Again, support and guidance is needed. In our example transportation study, the community built these skills becoming increasingly vocal and organized during a lengthy engagement phase and then an action stage that included various meetings with the local transportation authority, the circulation of a petition, and a community demonstration that was reported by the local media.

Analysis of Evaluation Data

As noted in Part 3, as critical theory researchers we may evaluate an action research project using positivist designsor constructivist designs. If we use a positive design then the quantitative analysis discussed in Chapter I of this part of the book would be utilized. If we use a constructivist design then the qualitative analysis procedures discussed in Chapter IV of this part of this book would be used. This concludes our discussion of critical theory evaluation. Important cross cutting issues of ethics, politics, diversity, and technology are similar to those discussed in Part 1, Part 2, and Part 3. Additional important cross cuttings issues for the Evaluation stage are discussed in Chapter V. Below is a summary of this chapter and learning assignments. We can now move on to a discussion of constructivist evaluation.

- Critical Theorists may well use the positivist and post positivist analysis techniques

- When understanding the power relationships being revealed in the data, the critical theory researcher can use three possible approaches: emergent, ideological and action analyses.

- Emergent analysis uses various strategies to inductively identify propositions.

- Ideological analysis facilitates a more specific statement of power relations and arenas for potential empowerment.

- Action analysis clearly identifies instigators and target of action. It also illuminates the practice skills needed to carry out action.

Critical Theory Learning Assignments

1. Think about your situation as a student. Either individually or in a group, make an ideological analysis and an action analysis of your situation. Share your analysis with other members of your class.

2. Decide how you would carry out your action plan?

As constructivist researchers our data analysis will depend on the sources of the data for the constructions developed from the hermeneutic dialectic circle. These are mostly qualitative interviews, documents, and readings. However, they could also be quantitative sources such as data included in reports and evaluations. Since our goal is not statistical prediction but comprehensive description, if we carry out any quantitative analysis, it will generally be descriptive rather than inferential. Qualitative analysis, however, will be our major form of analysis and we will do this in a similar way to the where we will engage in a continual interplay between data collection and analysis. This analysis is completed as soon as possible after each interview, observation or review of relevant documents. However, a difference between post positivist qualitative analysis and constructivist qualitative analysis is rooted in the difference between the constructivist's goal of identifying "units" of information and the post positivist goal of building a theory. When we develop the construction we identify "units" of information. Units are built into categories and then combined into a proposed joint construction that we share with all members of the hermeneutic dialectic circle at the "member check" meeting. Eventually the whole group agrees on the joint construction, which includes the group understanding of the research focus as well as agreed action strategies associated with the construction. The test of whether the analysis is correct is the degree to which the members of the hermeneutic dialectic attest to its accuracy.

Building and Modifying units

Erlandson et al. (1993) suggest that initial constructivist analysis should address a set of standard questions that are expanded upon here.

1. What did I learn from this interview, observation, artifact, or data source?

2. How will this shape my next interview, observation, review of artifact, or other data source?

3. What themes or suppositions were identified in this interview, observation, artifact, or data source?

4. Which other data sources were identified in this interview, observation, artifact, or data source?

5. Should I return to gather more information from this interview, observation, artifact, or data source? If so what am I looking for?

6. What are my emerging working themes and suppositions and how were they confirmed or challenged by this interview, observation, artifact, or data source?

7. How and where can I gather more information to confirm or challenge these working themes and suppositions?

Having used these questions to build summary data on the emerging constructions, we can carry out a more formalized process of analysis such as that offered by Lincoln and Guba (1985). They note that the first step is to identify "units" of information within the narrative descriptions. A unit has two characteristics, it must be heuristic (relevant to understanding or action in the research site and focus) and it must be the smallest piece of information that can stand alone (able to be understood without additional explanation). We record each unit separately in a data processing program that can sort columns and code with identifying information such as the source, type of source, and time and place the data was collected. For example, units developed in the HIV-AIDS study are shown in the table IV.1.

Table IV.1
Units of Analysis from HIV-AIDS Study

Unit (and category number)	Source	Type of Source	Date and Time Collected	Place data Collected
1. HIV-AIDS clients invisible	ID number of study Participant	Member of Client population	February 1st, 1995	Restaurant near participant's home
2. Social Workers need training in serving this client group	ID number of study Participant	Social Worker	February 10th, 1995	Agency Office
3. Fear of stigma associated with HIV-AIDS	ID number of study Participant	In Home Help Assistant	February 21st, 1995	In client home

Having created units, the next step is to group units into categories. We go back to the first unit and, for now, give it a number, say number 1. Then we review the second unit and decide if it looks like or feels like something similar to the first unit. If so, this unit is given the same number, "1", if not it is given the next number, say number 2. This process is repeated for all units of information. For any units that do not seem to fit with any other category, a miscellaneous category can be created for now. This is a time consuming process that combines rather than divides. The "looks like, feels like" process identified above builds categories rather than searches for repetitions of the same category. The core analysis question for the constructivist is, how does this unit enrich the category? In contrast, the core question for the post positivist is, how often is this unit repeated? For the constructivist, context is an essential influence that enriches and validates subjectivity. It as if the constructivist is building up the bones, muscle, blood and skin of a unique individual while the post positivist is searching for the common bone structure in each individual. Both are equally valid but they have very different analysis aims.

Having given a number to each unit, the units can be grouped into their categories. The AZ function in most spreadsheet programs will create this grouping if the number is in the cell at the beginning of the unit. This will bring all our units together into categories. All the units with the number "1" will be grouped together, all those with the number "2" and so on. Once the units are grouped in this way then we can start to develop criteria for inclusion of a unit in a particular category and give each category a name. This may lead to some re-sorting of units. However, now there are clear criteria that justify the creation of the categories that go beyond intuition. In the example study of spirituality in the African American family (Brown, 2011), a similar process, using a qualitative analysis software package produced the categories shown in Table IV.2 below where a sample from the final joint construction is shown.

Table IV.2
Major Categories in Brown (2011) study of spirituality in the African American Family.

Spirituality Religion and Parenting	Defining Spirituality / Religion	Spirituality /Religion And African American Culture	Spirituality/ Religion and Assessment	Spirituality /Religion and Placement	Spirituality/ Religion and Services	Concerns	Social Worker Skills
CWS needs to know client and child's religious background . Important for CWS to know values, beliefs on child rearing Important to ask families and youth about religious beliefs. Religion and parenting. Religious practices encouraged for children in foster care. **Personal Spiritual/ Religious Experience** Personal experience. Religious upbringing. Spirituality lived out. Spirituality part of my identity.	Belief in greater/high er power. Definition of religion spirituality. Definition of religion depends on the religion you practice. No distinction between religion and spirituality. Religion institutional. Religion involves practices. Religion is an organizatio n. Religion is formal. Religion is manmade. Religion is structure. Spirituality and energy humanness . Spirituality and reconciling good and evil. Spirituality and religion connected. Spirituality and religion go hand in hand. Spirituality beliefs without doctrines, regulations. Spirituality deeper than religion. Spirituality had depth, interactive. Spirituality	African American families bring up religious beliefs. African Americans often spiritual, not religious. Importance of church to African American families. Most African American families deeply religious. Reasons for misconcepti ons about religion for African Americans. Religion highly important to African American families. Spirituality a source of identity for African Americans.	Asking about religion helps establish community partners or supports. Asking about spirituality would increase sense of concern for client. Asking about support connection in assessment. Asking about spirituality would increase trust and comfort. Assessing for religion not offensive. Assessing for spirituality/rel igion at ER. Assessing for religion/spirit uality clients right. Assessing for spirituality is positive. Assessing religion for placement of youth. Assessment includes questions about supports. Assessment of religious/spiri tual beliefs may help establish connection. CWS did not ask about religious/spiri tual beliefs or upbringing. CWS needs	Assessing religion for placement of youth. Church as a placement resource. Concern with religious/spi ritual values of foster parents. Concerns about placement with non-believer. CWS staff didn't consider placement appropriate ness. Foster parent's religious beliefs different from youth. Knowing religious beliefs of children's family and foster family. Matching children with same religion foster care. Religious practices encouraged for children in foster care.	Agency flexibility in providing non-traditional services. Church partners at TDM changing attitudes. Church providing programs and tools. Concern that faith community services don't meet standards. Culturally relevant, culturally specific services. Faith based or spiritually driven service providers. Faith based organizations as a resource. Faith based services would increase level of trust. Faith community providing concrete supports. Finding out religious beliefs aid in service provision. Found own faith based services. Importance of praying in counseling. Knowledge of religious beliefs to refer to	Bad idea to include religion in social work practice. Concern some workers may find inappropriate to discuss spirituality. Barriers to prevent change in practice. Client complaints. Resistance to including spirituality in CWS practice. Careful not to put spirituality on others. Concern about liability as a barrier. Concern about assessing religious beliefs at ER. Concern about client' reaction to bringing up faith, spirituality. Concern for worker bias. Concern about religious beliefs that are against personal beliefs. Client's beliefs against workers beliefs. Concern of closing opportunities to faith partners.	Comfort in talking about religion. CWS staff didn't consider placement appropriate ness. CWS staff didn't really assess fully. Education/k nowledge about various religions needed. Effective use of spirituality/r eligion in SW practice. Impact of SW beliefs and values. Importance of tapping into clients support strengths. Knowing and building on families strengths. Need for

internal, religion external. Spirituality is personal. Spirituality is relationship to creator. Spirituality is relationship with God. Spirituality part of my identity. Spirituality provides moral support. Spirituality undisciplined belief. We are spiritual beings	to know about persons religious beliefs CWS didn't really assess fully. Expectation to ask or assess about religion. Holistic assessment. Impact of CWS asking about spirituality. Important to ask families and youth about religious beliefs. Inclusion of religious assessment part of assessing family. Relevance of religious questions for CWS. Religion/spirituality in assessment. Religious assessment increases social worker effectiveness. Social work experience impacts religious assessment. Spirituality assessment impact on placement. Spirituality questions would have improved assessment. Time barrier to asking additional questions about support.	religious support groups. Minister can't provide counseling unless licensed. Offer of faith based services. Referral to faith based services. Religious based counseling would have helped. Spiritual based services found effective. Work and support needed by faith based organizations	Concern religious assessment questions might open can of worms. Concern that many CWS workers don't have social work education. Concern that social workers not trained in spiritual assessment. Concern that social workers will use religion as a weapon. Concerns in incorporating religion or spirituality into CW practice. Don't bring up religion to clients. Proselytizing	guidelines. Relevance of religious questions for CWS. Role of social work education. Social work experience impacts religious assessment. Social workers lack of spiritual sensitivity impacts case outcome. System perspective to family should include spirituality. Ways to incorporate religion or/spirituality in practice. What social workers need

283

The next step is to search for relationships between categories. These relationships are not statements that predict repeated relationships between categories but bridges between categories that build a more complete construction. In our example studies they are the combination of units of information on the role of spirituality in the African American family that will assist child welfare social workers engaging with these families. They are the combination of units of information on the HIV-AIDS practice issues that give a complete picture or the factors that affect practice and identify the package of strategies that address those perceptions and barriers to practice. Or, in the homeless children study they are the combination of units of information on the characteristic problems of homeless children and then the grouping of action strategies set out by the member check meeting. These bridges, according to Lincoln and Guba (1989) are "Extensions" where "The inquirer begins with a known item or items of information and builds on them. He uses these items as bases for other questions or as guides in this examination of documents. Amoeba-like, he inches his way from the known to the unknown." (page 349). There is no list of rules to be followed to build these constructions, since every constructivist study is unique. The best way to illustrate the process is to show the results for our example constructivist studies: the study of spirituality, the study of HIV-AIDS, and the study of Homeless Children.

Study of Spirituality in the African American Family (Brown, L.E., 2011)

In this study, linkages were made between units and categories and they were presented in the following format for the member check meeting as shown in Table IV.3.

Table IV.3
Joint Constructions presented at Group Member Check

Major Categories	Constructs Agree	Construct Don't Agree
Spiritual/Religious Experience	⊙ Almost all those interviewed had some spiritual/religious upbringing. ⊙ That spiritual/religious upbringing impacted current spiritual/religious expression. ⊙ How that upbringing impacted current spiritual/religious expression varied by person.	
Spirituality/Religion and Parenting	⊙ Spiritual/religious values, beliefs and practices were seen as important in raising children. ⊙ These spiritual/religious values, beliefs and practices were seen as important in parenting in that they gave children; (Stability, security, strength, moral guidelines, sense of thankfulness.)	
Defining Spirituality/Religion		⊙ 3 major constructs ▪ Spirituality/religion the same ▪ Spirituality/religion connected

		▪ Spirituality/religion distinct

Functions of Spirituality/Religion	◉ Organized religion or the church serves several functions;
	 ◉ (Social support (connection, mentoring, nurturance), soft and concrete services (counseling, education, food, clothing, etc.) rules and expectations regarding lifestyle.
	 ◉ Faith or Belief;
	    ▪ strength, security, purpose, motivation, hope.
	 ◉ Spirituality;
	    ▪ Identity, internal resource, guidance, moral compass.
	 ◉ Religion;
	    ▪ Guides decision making, purpose, power and protection.	

Spirituality/Religion and African Americans	◉ The African American community is unique in terms of connection to the church (organized religion) ◉ African Americans even when not connected to organized religion tend to be spiritual or have a strong belief in God.	
Engagement and Spirituality/Religion	◉ Key to engaging families in CWS process includes gaining knowledge about the family, their strengths/needs, connecting with the family and building trust with the family. ◉ Asking the family about strengths, supports, values, which may include spirituality/religion, are some ways to engage the family.	
Assessment and Spirituality/Religion	◉ Asking about supports, strengths is important in making a good assessment.	◉ Asking about spirituality/religion should be part of a holistic assessment of the family. ◉ Asking about spirituality/religion crosses church/state and or personal/professional boundaries.
Placement and Spirituality/Religion	◉ Asking about the spiritual/religious beliefs and practices of the family of origin, youth and foster family may be important in making placement decisions.	

Services and Spirituality/Religion		⊙ Church or faith based services are preferred as these services are based on a similar belief system and established trusting relationships. ⊙ Church or faith based services may not be appropriate to provide formal services such as counseling, parenting, drug treatment. ⊙ Work needs to be done to develop and maintain understanding and communication between CWS and faith based community.
Concerns		⊙ No concerns about CWS including spirituality/religion in their practice. ⊙ Concerns about professional/personal and church/state boundaries. ⊙ Concerns about worker bias. ⊙ Concerns about system barriers(guidelines, policies, Court, admin support, liability)
Social Work Skills	⊙ Additional education, training and support needed. ⊙ Buy in regarding rationale, expectations, within and outside CWS. ⊙ Clear guidelines, procedures, direction. ⊙ Knowledge about available resources. ⊙ Administrative support and flexibility.	

We can see that a comprehensive set of major categories was developed and participants' attitudes towards those categories were clearly identified to facilitate discussion and action strategies in the member-checking meeting.

Study of HIV-AIDS (Hogan, P., 1995)

In this study, the following categories were built from units

- Definition: Agreement that HIV/AIDS is a medical condition

- Role of Social Work: Confusion among many key players about what a social worker is and what they do.

  - People living with HIV/AIDS were confused about what the unique social work contribution to their care could be

  - Social Work professionals were clear on their contribution and surprised by the literature findings

  - Volunteer workers with a range of credentials who were aware of and critical of social work's reluctance to play a key role in the field. They also suggested that, since the gay community was so active and the social work community in the eighties was focused on licensing, this may be an explanation.

- Image of Social Work: A consensus that the image of social work has been devalued and, since many of the respondents thought of social workers as volunteers who did charitable work, while those who with M.S.W. degrees were calling themselves psychotherapists.

- Who is doing Social Work: A belief that, since social workers were actually narrowing their roles to clinician only, nurses and other helping professionals offer the case management and support services and activism that used to be the social work domain.

- Social Work Leadership: Many noted that there was little social work leadership in the region

- Influence of Medical Context: There may be limited opportunities for social workers to get professionally involved, since the medical setting has most of the positions

- Influence of Work Place: Lack of funding for social work positions in HIV/AIDS settings. Mostly grassroots agencies, funded by grants, which cannot hire a social worker.

After these initial preliminary categories were developed a member check process via mail was conducted that identified the following constructions:

- Fears and Biases: Fear of Contagion, Stigmatization, Discomfort with talking about Sexuality, Morality, Discomfort with Death and Dying,

- Social Work Education: HIV/AIDS not addressed in many social work programs, lack of faculty expertise, not an institutional priority, political sensitivity

- Ideal Social Work Education: Should include HIV/AIDS information, inclusion in Substance Abuse and Sexuality Courses, and at all levels of micro and macro practice, could be issue of diversity or issue of oppression/empowerment

- Factors facilitating HIV/AIDS social work practice: change perception from death sentence to "living with" inspiration coming from working with this group, personal experience.

As noted above, this study did not proceed to a member-checking meeting. The above four joint Constructions (summarized) were developed via mail with members of the Hermeneutic Dialectic circle agreeing individually with their accuracy. They are an initial statement by the Hermeneutic Dialectic Circle of their understanding of social work practice with people living with HIV-AIDS and their suggestions for addressing issues related to social work practice with this client population. Since the group itself was not at a stage that permitted moving forward with building the joint construction and taking action, the case study reported the above constructions. This case study was shared with members of the circle and a general audience of interested readers. Readers of the report were invited to decide on the trustworthiness of the constructions and the need for action.

Study of Homeless Children (Young, M.L. and Creacy, M., 1995)

In this study, categories that were identified at the end of the first round of interviews in the first year of the study were:

- Homeless Characteristics:

  - Families: diverse, economic insecurity, living in a range of settings, affect depressed

  - Children: developmentally and academically delayed, had phobias, shame, anxiety and generally felt unsafe

- Scope of Service Delivery: shelters, health care services, school district services, social services.

- Lack of Continuity in Children's lives: inadequate network of services with gaps and duplications, needed regular meeting of those providing services to homeless children to better articulate and develop services. Quality of shelters variable, school's response not sensitive to homeless children's struggle to get to school and lack of continuity in education,

- Socialization: kids don't have network of friends

- Health Care: can't get records, physicians not willing to treat, no insurance, they don't want to use public health facility, difficult to get indigent status, children tend to by ill, therefore.

- Mental Health services: don't get assessments and interventions, substance abuse and general neglect, vulnerable to.

- Funding: services not funded, little low cost housing, slow getting welfare checks, parent education needed, employment needed.

- Major recommendation, Network of services.

In the second year of the study these categories were revisited with an expanded circle of respondents as noted above. Two rounds of individual interviews and sharing took place and the following categories were identified.

- Homeless Characteristics:

  - Families: low self esteem of parents, issues of substance abuse, child abuse as well as adult literacy

  - Children: Need for "safety net" in school system, teenage children embarrassed by clothing, need for outreach coordinator between school districts and service providers, need for a place where they can act normally

- Scope of Services

  - Shelters experiencing increased demand, increased programs re substance abuse for children and parents

  - Domestic Violence Shelter, increased demand, bureaucratic barriers to mainstreaming these families back into community,

  - Health Care Services, hard to keep immunization and children's general medical records as required by service providers

  - School Districts, now offering outreach educational services to children at motels, cars or wherever else children are living including shelters

  - Social Services, maintains food bank and makes referrals

- Lack of Continuity in Children's Lives: agreement with this problem and agreed to participate in networking conference

- Socialization: Commitment to outreach, especially mental health services

- Global Perspective: need for literacy training, affordable housing, employment opportunities, child care, change of bureaucratic barriers, break cycle of homelessness.

This circle revisited and further developed the constructions identified in the first year of the study. As a result of this development an agenda of action to address the issue of Homeless children was developed and a meeting of participants was held as described above. Thus we see that the constructivist implementation and evaluation processes develop from a general focus to a specific construction. Participants are engaged in both a process and a production of a product. Data is gathered and analyzed in partnership with participants and action plans are developed

To sum up, constructivist data collection builds the hermeneutic dialectic and analysis builds individual and joint constructions of the study focus. Constructions evolve from individual sources of data and the joint member checking meeting. This data is analyzed by identifying units and categories of information that describe the construction. A commitment to action associated with the construction is identified by the study participants who have been engaged in the hermeneutic dialectic process. This completes are discussion of constructivist Evaluation. Important cross cutting issues such as ethics, politics, diversity, and technology are similar to those discussed in Part 1, Part 2, and Part 3. Additional important cross cuttings issues for the Evaluation stage are discussed in Chapter V. Below is a summary of this chapter and a learning assignment.

Summary of Chapter IV

- The hermeneutic dialectic circle is developed from individual interviews and sources of data.

- Constructions are shared at a joint membership checking meeting where agreement is reached on claims, concerns and issues.

- Evaluation, or analysis, of the data requires identifying units and categories of data that should be included in the joint construction.

Constructivist Learning Assignment

1. Review the following quotes from staff members in Brown's (2011) study of spirituality in the African American family. Carry out an analysis developing units and categories. Describe the individual constructions and the joint constructions.

"The faith based community wants to help. It is part of their defining mission, at least the ones that I'm working with. Helping fellow man to better their lives is part of their defining mission... But then they can sort of surround the family, our families are isolated, they're in terrible neighborhoods, they are dysfunctional and they love their children and most of them want to get better. When the faith based group can come around them and offer support and invite them to dinner, or take them to church and they can be around other people that have been successful... they can get their heads going in the right direction and start being successful again, raise those children well. They don't feel so isolated, they have support, there's somebody to call at 10 o'clock at night if they don't call their sponsor, they can call another person and get that support. That's how I see it, little things that add up, little things that keep people sober, whatever it takes to break up the cycle. Sometimes they give them cribs cause poverty and child welfare, we can't get the two unhitched, baby clothes, maybe they pay for the kid to be involved in summer soccer."(CWS03) "To have those services, though not the traditional services, but services that are within the church and to maybe have a liaison from the church to us rather than us calling the parenting class about how are they doing, but somehow having more of a friendly connection and maybe it doesn't have to be a licensed therapist doing this, it doesn't have to be a

five week parenting class, but getting some of those services in the community in the church and being flexible and non-traditional services and they can be on our case plan."(CWS05) "My concern would be that social workers would really have to understand this. I think they would have to know the purpose; to understand how to engage the conversation and be consistent. I just think there needs to be some understanding of what, how and why we need to do this. So I think it would have to be a gradual, thoughtful kind of a roll-out, if it became division wide that we were doing this."(CWS05) "Well I think we'll definitely need some guidelines. Maybe this is what's appropriate, this is what's inappropriate. When you meet with the family, kind of like Social Work 101, be where the client is and it can help the client say this is saying this is a part of my life, that's the time to tap into it"(CWS11) (page 106)

Important cross cutting issues for the Evaluation stage are similar to those discussed in Part 1, Part 2, and Part 3. However, there additional diversity, and technology issues.

Diversity Issues

Debates about interpreting the meaning of data have taken some interesting twists and turns. Not only has there been the criticism of quantitative statistics as representing a patriarchal definition of "hard" facts but there has also been criticism of qualitative analysis of language as being too linear and still tied to patriarchal definitions of rational thought and synthesis. Alternatives, such as the use of poetry and drama to explain the meaning of qualitative data, have challenged usual definitions of analysis.

Feminist criticisms of quantitative statistics range from Betty Gray (1971) writing in the "Nation" magazine in the seventies about a "statistical industrial complex" that under counts women's participation in the labor force and over states women's progress in employment to Margaret Anderson (1983) writing in the eighties about under reporting of crimes against women and the Oakley's (1983) accusation of sexism in the ways data are collected, processed and presented referring to examples of how we understand terms such as "heads of households", "work" and "crime". The essential message of these critiques is that a statistic, once written on a piece of paper, becomes a "hard" fact even though there are questions about the biases that influenced the label given to a phenomenon.

The desire to create order out of the complexity of human experience, as well as the acceptance of probability theory, has led us to use rules of mathematics to manipulate numbers derived from a data collection instrument that measures constructs said to represent human experience. We use bivariate and multivariate analysis procedures to create statistical findings that dictate conclusions about the relationships between these constructs. However, any reservations about these conclusions that question the relationship between statistical manipulation of numbers and authentic human experience, are rarely expressed since this would suggest that one of the primary approaches to "science" in social science research rests on a shaky foundation. The pressure to be scientific and "get it right" embedded in the positivist approach to research discourages an open discussion of the limitations of quantitative measurement of human behavior. Numbers are quickly understood as summaries of a phenomenon. Words take longer to describe that phenomenon but may well offer a more complete representation of the complexity of a phenomenon. This is not to say that we should stop counting and measuring human behavior. However, we need to be open to admitting that the diversity of human experience cannot be fully understood with the production of a statistic.

Ironically, qualitative analysis of words that represent human experience has also been criticized as representing a linear, patriarchal thinking process. The top-down and bottom-up qualitative analysis procedures described in this book are said to be approaches to understanding data that fragment human experience and force its meaning into categories and theories of explanation that ignore the diversity of human experience. The more radical thinkers who have taken this position suggest that turning qualitative data into poetry, scripts for dialogues between key players, and the representation of people's ideas through art rather than words are analysis and synthesis procedures that are more true to the human experience. Coffey and Atkinson (1996) discuss the presentation of results through conversations between key players or the development of plays and sketches that outline and develop the alternative points of view that emerged from the data. This form of representative data analysis has developed to a point where it has been termed "ethnographic theatre" (Mienczakowski, 1994, 1995) and it is a vehicle for presenting data in a way that expresses diverse perspectives and experiences.

Technology Issues

When understanding and interpreting the data we can use computer software programs to do either quantitative or qualitative analysis. Quantitative analysis software packages can perform any kind of statistical analysis in seconds. Qualitative software programs can organize reams of narrative and assist in conceptualizing units of data and the connections between those units so that theory can be developed or the general meaning of data can be described.

Most students are familiar with computer programs that carry out quantitative data analysis. At the simplest level we have spread sheet programs such as Windows' Excel that permit us to lay out scores on items on a questionnaire for each member of our sample. In these programs we can create totals and mean scores and, in fact, any manipulation of numbers if we can create the correct formula. Beyond spread sheet programs, statistical packages such as SPSS (Statistical Package for the social sciences) and SAS (The Statistical Analysis System) have developed to such a user friendly point that we can, not only generate descriptive statistics (frequencies, means, medians and modes) and bivariate analysis but we can also, carry out the most complex of multivariate analyses with just a point and click of a mouse. It is not the province of this book to explain how to do this, merely to acknowledge that such packages are available and that we still have to understand the principles of statistics to use them appropriately.

Coffey and Atkinson (1996) have provided a helpful review of the use of computers for various stages of managing qualitative data: creating and managing data, coding and retrieving data, language meaning and narrative and theory building and hypothesis testing. Before discussing these topics it might be obvious but useful to remind ourselves that computers are very useful tools for the general organizational tasks associated with qualitative research such as: keeping lists of contacts; communication via email and the internet with experts, study participants and colleagues; management of bibliographies and reference lists; and preparation of reports, papers and presentations. These authors concluded that a word processing package can perform the functions needed for creating managing data such as: initial write up of notes: numbering of lines, paragraphs and pages; cross referencing and indexing; including contextual and other headings; and including summaries of longer data documents.

However, when it comes to coding and retrieving data, Lewins and Silver (2007) offer a helpful review of software programs. They show how each program has routines for attaching codes to chunks of data and then searching for the repeated occurrence of the code to identify the underlying regulatory mechanism that is emerging from the data. These programs also facilitate the insertion of memos linked to the codes that explain the reasoning for creating codes. This facilitates production of the content needed for both our journals. Since there is both the record of data collection and analysis and the reasoning behind coding and analysis decision required in post positivist, critical theory and constructivist research. Once data is entered and coded, these programs allow us to draw diagrams identifying the links between the codes (axial coding) and develop evidence for identifying the core theme (selective coding). All of this is done more quickly and efficiently than is possible by using index cards and paper notes. It is a very useful way of combating the data overload that often overwhelms qualitative researcher facing pages and pages of narrative. Drisko (1998) also gave an overview of various qualitative data software programs. He concluded that, if the researcher is careful to use a program that can fulfill the purpose of the chosen approach to research, such software is a great asset to managing and interpreting qualitative data. It is important, however, to remember that the researcher, not the computer, is in charge here. We need to use our own insight to build codes and their connections and dimensions and forge a most productive partnership between technology and humanity.

A final suggestion offered by (Coffey and Anderson, 1996) is the use of hyperlinks to make connections in the data. The researcher identifies the patterns of links between parts of the narratives by creating hyperlinks in the narrative that allow the reader to "click" on a word or phrase and be sent to its category, or core theme or other related category. This truly is the most flexible approach to synthesis of narrative and rescues us from the linear thinking represented in many discussions of qualitative analysis.

We have reviewed the quantitative and qualitative analysis procedures for each of our paradigms and considered associated diversity and technological issues. This completes our discussion of the Evaluation stage of our project and we can now move to the final stage of Termination and Follow Up.

Anderson, M. (1983). Thinking about women: sociological and feminist perspectives. New York: Macmillan

Austin,. J. L. (1962). *How to do things with words*. Oxford: Clarendon Press

Brown, L.E. (2011) Spirituality's Role in the Interaction Between Child Welfare and Black Families. San Bernardino: Loma Linda University, social work student doctoral dissertation.

Brown, G., & Yule, G. (1991) *Discourse Analysis*. New York: Cambridge University Press.

Coffey, A. and Atkinson, P. (1996) *Making Sense of Qualitative Data*. Thousand Oaks: Sage.

Cohen, J. (1994). The Earth is Round (p<.05). *American Psychologist 49(12) pp 997-1003*.

Corbin, J. & Strauss, A (2008) *Basics of Qualitative Research*. Thousand Oaks: Sage (3rd Edition)

Coulthard, M. (1985). *An Introduction to Discourse Analysis.* New York: Longman

Christopulos, J. (1995) Oppression through Obsession: A Feminist Theoretical Critique of Eating Disorders. San Bernardino, CA: Student research project

Drisko, J. (1998) Using Qualiative Data Analysis Software. *Computers in Human Services* 15(1), 1-18

Erlandson, D. A., Harris, E. L., Skipper, B.L., Allen, S. D. (1993). *Doing Naturalistic Inquiry.* Thousand Oaks: Sage.

Glaser, B.G. & Strauss, A.L. (1967). The Discovery of Grounded Theory: strategies for qualitative research. New York: Aldine De Gruyter

Gray, B. M. (1971) Economics of sex bias: the 'disuse' of women. *The Nation* June, 14th pp 742-747,

Hogan, P. (1995) A Constructivist's study of Social Work's Involvement with HIV-AIDS Unpublished Manuscript.

Hope, A. & Timmel, S. (1999). *Training for Transformation: A Handbook for Community Workers.* London, UK: Intermediate Technology (ITDG Publishing)

Hull, C. (1914) The Service of Statistics to History *Publications of the American Statistical Association* 14(105) pp 30-39

Karwell, N. and Meyers, E.D. (1983) "Computers in Survey Research" In Rossi, P.H., Wright, J.D., & Anderson, A.B. (Eds.) *Handbook of Survey Research.* Orlando, FL: Academic Press.

Lewins, Ann and Silver, C (2007) "Using Software in Qualitative Research: A Step by Step Approach" Thousand Oaks: Sage.

Lincoln, Y.S. & Guba, E. G. (1985) *Naturalistic Inquiry.* Newbury Park: Sage

Lofland, J., Snow, D., Anderson, L., Lofland, L.H. (2006). *Analyzing Social Settings: A guide to Qualitative Observation and Analysis.* Belmont, CA: Wadsworth.

Mienczakowski, J.E. (1994) Reading and writing research: Ethnographic theatre. *National Association for Drama in Education* (*Australia*), 18, 45-54

Mienczakowski, J.E. (1995) The theatre of ethnography: The reconstruction of ethnography into theatre with emancipatory potential. *Qualitative Inquiry,* 1, 360-375.

Millet, K. R., and Otero, L. R. (2011) The North Shore Public Transportation Dilemma: How Local Sociopolitical Ideologies, Ethnic Discrimination And Class Oppression Create Marginalization, And A Community's Quest For Social Justice. San Bernardino, CA. CSUSB, a social work student research project.

Oakley, A., & Oakley, R. (1979) "Sexism in official statistic" In J. Irvine, I. Miles & J. Evans (Eds.) *Demystifying Social Statistics.* London: Pluto.

Popper. K (1934) *Logik der Forschung.* Vienna: J. Springer. English Edition. London: Hutchinson (1959)

Popper. K. (1959). *The logic of scientific discovery.* London: Hutchinson.

Popper, K (1972). Objective Knowledge: An Evolutionary Approach. Oxford: Clarendon Press.

Riech, J. R. (1994). Psychotherapy Encounters Curanderismo: Implications for Clients Treated in the United States by Culturally Insensitive Social Workers. San Bernardino: Student Project, California State University San Bernardino.

Rubin, A. & Babbie, E. (2011) Research Methods for Social Workers. Belmont, CA: Brooks Cole/Cenage:

Sacks, H., Schegloff E. A., & Jefferson, G. (1974) "A simplest systematics for the organization of turn-taking for conversation" In *Language* 50: 696-735

Sinclair, J. McH., Coulthard, R.M. (1975) *Towards an Analysis of Discourse.* Oxford: Oxford University Press.

Stephan, F (1948) History of the Uses of Modern Sampling Procedures. In *Journal of the American Statistical Association* 43 (241) pp 12-39

Strauss, A & Corbin, J. (1998) *Basics of Qualitative Research.* Thousand Oaks: Sage (2nd Edition)

Torres, K (2007) *An Insight Into The Experience Of Parolees.* California State University, San Bernardino, M.S.W. Student Project.

Walters, R. M. (1995) *Treating the abusive male: a constructivist study.* California State University, San Bernardino, M.S.W. Student Project.

Weinbach, R.W. & Grinnell, Jr., R. M. (2010) *Statistics for Social Work*ers. Pearson, Allyn & Bacon: Boston

Young, M.L. and Creacy, M. (1995) *Perceptions of Homeless Children.* California State University, San Bernardino: Masters Research Project.

INSERT THE NAME OF YOUR

PROJECT ON THESE TWO LINES

_____

A Project Proposal

Presented to the

Faculty of

(Insert University Name)

_____

In Partial Fulfillment

of the Requirements for the Degree

Master of Social Work

_____

by

First, Middle, and Last Name

First, Middle, and Last Name

June 2006

Note: Spell out middle name NO initials

INSERT THE NAME OF YOUR

PROJECT ON THESE TWO LINES

_____

A Project Proposal

Presented to the

Faculty of

(Insert University Name)

_____

by

First, Middle, and Last Name

First, Middle, and Last Name

June 2010

Approved by:

Name(s), Proposal Supervisor and or Committee	Date
I.M. Encharge, L.C.S.W., Social Work Agency	

ABSTRACT

FINAL REPORT: TABLE OF CONTENTS

CHAPTER ONE

ASSESSMENT

In this section you address questions such as, what is your research focus or question? What is the perspective you are brining to the research focus, which paradigm did you adopt? Why was this one the most appropriate paradigm to use? What have you found out from the literature? How does a study of this research focus add to our knowledge of social work practice at the micro and/or macro levels of human organization? Use the following headings

Introduction

One paragraph outlining what will be covered in this chapter.

Research focus and/or question

Paradigm and rationale for chosen paradigm

Literature Review

Theoretical Orientation

Contribution of study to micro and/or macro social work practice

Summary

One paragraph outlining what was covered in this chapter.

CHAPTER TWO

ENGAGEMENT

In this section you address questions such as, how did you engage the study participants in the initial development of the research focus? How did you prepare yourselves to be sensitive to study participants? Which diversity issues did you prepare for? What are the ethical issues that your engagement of the study participants introduced? What are the political issues that your engagement of the study participants introduced? Was there a role for technology during this initial phase of engagement?

Introduction

One paragraph outlining what will be covered in this chapter.

Engagement strategies for Gatekeepers at Research Site

Self Preparation

Diversity issues

Ethical issues

Political issues

The Role of Technology in Engagement

Summary

One paragraph outlining what was covered in this chapter.

CHAPTER THREE

IMPLEMENTATION

In this chapteraddress questions such as, where and with whom you carried out this study? How did you gather data: interviews, observation, social artifacts, other? How did you select study participants? What were the phases of data collection? How did you record your data? Which procedures did you use to analyze your data: quantitative, qualitative, power analysis?

Introduction

One paragraph outlining what will be covered in this chapter

Research site

Study participants

Selection of Participants

Data Gathering

Phases of data collection

Data recording

Data Analysis Procedures

Summary

One paragraph outlining what was covered in this chapter.

CHAPTER FOUR

EVALUATION

This chapter explains how you analyzed your data, what you found out from your data, and what your findings have to say about micro and/or macro practice. If you used the positivist paradigm, state your questions and hypotheses and explain whether you were able to reject the null hypotheses and what that this means. Univariate statistics describing the important variables should be given, followed by bivariate analyses (and then, multivariate analyses if used). Enough data should be given to justify the findings. Tables, figures, and illustrations should be used to clarify, and facilitate economy in writing. Do not display all raw data or computer outputs. Briefly explain any tables and figures to show significant findings. The APA Publications Manual may be helpful in deciding how to present this section. Journal articles are also a useful guide.

If you used the Post Positivist, Critical Theory, or Constructivist paradigms explain how you developed your data codes or units and how you built your theory or joint construction. Use the entries from you journal to explain your decisions regarding joining codes for axial and selective coding or joining units to build constructions.

Introduction

One paragraph outlining what will be covered in this chapter.

Data Analysis

Data Interpretation

Implications of Findings for Micro and/or Macro Practice

Summary

One paragraph outlining what was covered in this chapter.

CHAPTER FIVE

TERMINATION AND FOLLOW UP

This chapter explains how your plans for either ending your relationship with the study site and study participants or continuing those relationships. Give justifications for your decisions regarding this. Explain how you plan to communicate your findings to the study participants. Give an overall evaluation of what your study achieved for the study participants and how you see things progressing in the future in relation to this research question/focus and these participants. Also, give a detailed dissemination plan for your study findings.

Introduction

One paragraph outlining what will be covered in this chapter.

Termination of study

Communicating findings to study site and study participants

Onngoing relationship with study participants

Dissemination Plan

Summary

One paragraph outlining what was covered in this chapter.

APPENDIX A
DATA COLLECTION INSTRUMENT(S)

Start appendix here

APPENDIX B
INFORMED CONSENT

Start appendix here

APPENDIX C
DEBRIEFING STATEMENT

Start appendix here

REFERENCES

Part 5

Termination and Follow Up

Ending the Study and Developing the Dissemination Plan that Translates Findings into Evidence for Social Work Practice

Contents

The final stage of our research project, **termination**, includes reporting findings (See Appendix A for a general report layout that can be used for all paradigms) and, in some cases, celebration as well as transforming our findings into evidence based practice via a dissemination plan. For the **positivist** researcher, termination is not a protracted process. Generally a commitment is made to report findings to the sponsor of the project, to present at a conference and to write a scholarly publication. The prime audience for the study findings, rather than being the participants in the study, is other social work researchers and practitioners. Study participants are informed about where a copy of the study report can be obtained and the researcher may well give a presentation of findings to key informants at the research setting. However, the aim is to present data rather than engage in a termination process. Generally, once the study is finished, positivist researchers do not have further plans to engage study participants. For the **post positivist** researcher, the reporting process is similar to the positivist. However, because of the more intense involvement with study participants and the research site(s), there is a stronger commitment to reporting back to study participants and key players in the research setting. For **critical theorists**, there is a major commitment to reporting back to the study participants and key players in the study as well as a need to celebrate achievements with study participants. For the **constructivist** researcher, some reporting back of findings happens during the study at the member check meeting but a more important need is to ensure that the hermeneutic dialectic practice will continue after the study is completed. For all the paradigms, **follow up**, or development of the **dissemination plan** involves understanding individual practitioners' attitudes towards change as well as the organizational culture regarding change. If our findings are to be transformed into evidence that affects practice, we need to convince individuals and organizations that our findings our worth their time and attention. We use the systems of communication at the research site to provide information on our findings and suggestions for incorporating these findings into micro and macro social work practice.

As positivists we can present our findings in the form of a poster at a meeting or conference, a presentation at a meeting or conference, a report, or a scholarly article.

Posters

A poster is usually an informal mode of presentation where we can display the key elements of our project. Members of the audience who are interested in the project can browse the display and discuss the project with us on a one-to-one informal basis. The poster simply and clearly describes the background to the study, the methodology used in the study, the study findings and the meaning of these findings. Of course it also includes the study title and the names and affiliations of the researchers. As part of the presentation, we also distribute one page handouts that include a summary of the project and a source for the full report of the project. According to Pellecchia (1999) a poster can be a time consuming project but is worth the effort if we can produce an attractive visual display using charts and graphs, as well a keeping things orderly and concise. The display needs to be interesting and eye catching, with minimal text and illustrative color pictures and charts. The text that is used should be in bullet list form and large and clear enough for a browsing person to read. There are a number of web sites we can visit that offer advice on constructing a poster including http://writing.wisc.edu/Handbook/ presentations_poster.html which is supported by the University of Wisconsin.

Presentations

The style of the presentation will depend on the size and nature of the audience. For a small group meeting, handouts summarizing the study by giving the background, methods, findings and interpretation of the findings are fine. In this situation, there can be an informal discussion and question and answer atmosphere. For larger audiences in a formal setting, presentation software such as "power point" offers a clear visual focus for the audience. Our presentation slides should just give key headings. More detail can be offered in handouts or by referring the audience to a web address where the full report or article can be found. As a minor piece of advice, some of the sound and visual effects that come with presentation software programs need to be used sparingly. At first they seem amusing but, if over used, they can start to be distracting and annoying for the audience.

Reports and Articles

The layout of the positivist report or article follows the requirements of a guide style such as that of the American Psychological Association (APA). It includes

Title: This is the first thing the reader will look at. It needs to be a simple clear description of what the report or article is about

Abstract or summary: This summarizes the purpose, methods, findings and interpretation of findings of the study. It is the next thing the reader looks at. It needs to be simply and clearly written if it is to convince the reader to read on. These days, abstracts are indexed "on-line" and thus they need to be doubly carefully written. Everyone in the world is able to read them.

Discussion of problem focus: This is a discussion of the information that was gathered as a result of the tasks described in chapter 2. It gives a background to the problem, it's significance and the specific research question(s) and hypothesis(es).

Discussion of literature: This is a discussion of the information that was gathered as a result of the tasks described in the "literature review" discussion in chapter 2. It should be organized under key topics that are the source of concepts and variables that were operationalized in the study.

Description of research methods: This is a discussion of the information that was gathered as a result of the tasks described in chapter three and four. It should include a description of the design (causal or correlational), the study participants, the data collection instruments that were developed, the procedures for data gathering and the analysis procedures

Description of findings: This describes the information that was gathered as a result of the tasks described in chapter five. The results of each analysis procedure that was described in the research methods should be given with the tables of data, the significance test values, the degrees of freedom and the probability levels.

Discussion and interpretation of meaning of findings: This interprets the information that was gathered as a result of the tasks described in chapters 4 and 5. The *Publication Manual of the American Psychological Association* (APA) suggests that this section should address the contribution that the study has made to new knowledge, the contribution this study has made to the resolution of the original research problem, and the overall conclusions and theoretical implications of the study findings.

References: This is listing of all books, articles and reports cited in the main body of the research report or article. It is not a bibliography, just a listing of citations. The function of a reference list is to give the reader the information needed to find that citation. Most social work publications use the APA publication manual guidelines for creating reference lists.

This structure can be incorporated into the generalist model discussed in this book where:

- Assessment and Engagement is parallel to the discussion of the problem focus and the literature review;

- Implementation is parallel to the description of the methods;

- Evaluation is parallel to the discussion of results; and

- Termination and Follow is parallel to the Discussion of the interpretation of the Findings.

With so much qualitative data to mange, post positivists approach a major writing task when reporting on findings. In his paper on writing up qualitative research, Wolcott (2008) offers some entertaining, playful and very useful strategies for getting started on writing as well as making writing a personal habit. He begins by offering some tips for getting started. This process of convincing ourselves to get to work might commence with a ritual of having to do other "essential" tasks before sitting down at the desk. These might include: washing the kitchen floor; vacuuming the house throughout; or, in one of my colleague's time of resistance, making granola from scratch. We need to recognize, embrace and compress this ritual of avoidance as far as possible. With so many games on the computer, social networking and email to pick up, we could get to the computer quickly by intending to have some fun and communicate with friends. We could put out some snacks on the desk. Once there though, we need to bring up the blank page and start typing some words. However we do it, let's recognize our human frailty and move forward.

Once we have got to the blank page, Walcott (2008) suggests the following preliminary writing exercises to get us moving:

- Write down the Plan. Write a statement of purpose. Write the sequence of events. Writing a "pretend" table of contents can help with this. Come up with phantom chapter headings and page numbers. Put sub headings within the chapters. The generic structure might be:

  ○ Introduction and Overview

  ○ Focus of Inquiry

  ○ Methods of sampling and data collection

  ○ Approaches to evaluating the meaning of the data

  ○ Results of top down analysis, using dimensions of framework for headings

    or, concepts and categories identified in open coding process and rationales.

  ○ Theoretical statements developed and overall statement of theory in context of human activity

  ○ Implications for social work practice with individuals, families, groups, organizations or communities

  ○ Strengths and Limitations of the study and its findings

- Recommendations and Implications, statements about the meaning of the study and future potential of this study and its findings (without veering into opinion and rhetoric).

- Start writing as soon as the study begins. There is a proposal, start rewriting that with a final product in mind. One possible start could be to write about the methods being carried out as the study progresses. Another way to start would be to give a simple narrative description of the project and its setting.

- Write the problem focus. This may require several drafts and turn out to be a thinking and refining exercise that results from trying to explain the project on paper and talking to other people about the project.

- Write drafts of each of the chapters identified in the pretend table of contents. This will go through stages: scattered notes and thoughts at first, then an outline, a rough draft, and finally a polished draft.

- Take a break from writing and draft the acknowledgements and dedications and possible title.

These are ideas for getting started and staying motivated. When the first draft is written, then the task is to refine the product and write a report with a formal structure. To do this we can get feedback from colleagues or those who took part in the study, but be careful, as Wolcott warns; a little feedback goes a long way.

The final structure of the report can follow the generalist structure offered in this book, with major chapters being Assessment, Engagement, Implementation, Evaluation, and Termination and Follow up. The headings and sub headings for each chapter are developed during the study. For example, in the chapter on Evaluation, they can either be the headings offered in the "top down" approach to analysis or they can be the components of the theory that emerged during the "bottom up" approach. There are no strict guidelines on what to include. However Coffey and Atkinson (1996) report six possible levels of generalization that help organize our thinking. They suggest that we decide whether we are making,

1. Universal statements: An overall summary statement about everything we observed, the people, the activity, the processes,

2. Cross-cultural descriptive statements: Comparative statements about individuals, groups, families, organizations or communities we observed

3. General statements about one specific individual, family, group, organization or community we observed.

4. General statements about the context of the activity we research

5. Specific statements about the concepts and categories and their relationships that we developed

6. Specific statements about one incident.

When the report is finished, to check that it is complete, we can use the questions created by Drisko (1997) for assessing qualitative research as guidelines. Has the report described the paradigm being used, rationales for the paradigm, procedures for each stage of the research process, and study findings and implications?

As post positivists, like positivists, we report our findings at conferences or in journals in the form of posters, presentations and papers. However, we would also tend to be committed to reporting findings back to the setting that was the focus of the inquiry. In preparing for this very different audience, we need to think about communication with the audience. A community audience will generally be a novice audience when it comes to knowledge about research methods and tolerance for abstract discussion of their own experiences. They are interested in the presentation because the topic is real and alive for them, thus our presentation of findings needs to build on this motivation. Coffey and Atkinson (1996) when exploring alternative forms of presentation address visual presentation of data and offer some useful thoughts for those who are preparing to present to a community audience.

- Use diagrams and tables to summarize narrative

- Use photographs and images to bring the data to life

- Show social artifacts from the setting (in our homeless children study, reproduction of drawings, poems and songs written by the children about their experience of homelessness were included in the final report)

- Also in community presentations it is helpful to give study participants a role in the presentation. At the presentation of the findings of the homeless study to the community and other students, the researchers displayed children's drawings and poems around the walls and invited them to sing a song they had written about homelessness. There wasn't a dry eye in the house.

Not only do post positivists need to present findings to colleagues and to the research setting, we also need to develop a process for terminating with the research site. The presentation is the formal procedure for marking the end of the study but since there has been such an intense involvement with the research site, an informal disengagement is needed. This could simply be an informal discussion over coffee about how the study went and plans for the future. It could be a more elaborate event with food and congratulations and thanks given to participants and study sponsors. However it is done, there needs to be acknowledgement of closure at both the formal and informal levels.

For critical theory researchers, this final stage of the project includes not only reporting and distributing findings, but also reflection and celebration. The first audience for reporting findings is the people who were the targets for empowerment. We collaborate with these study participants to jointly develop a statement on the progress made on empowerment. This might be a statement to the media, a community meeting, a more personal private communication at a group or individual meeting; or individual letters, emails and phone calls to those for whom empowerment was promoted. In addition, we develop a formal report for the sponsors of the project and, like any other researchers; we will publish research findings for the audience of professional colleagues, generally in academic settings. One function of reporting, for the critical theory researcher, is not only communicating findings but also disengaging from the community. The project would not have been successful if the community was not now able to carry on the work that had been started. At the end of the study, we carry out disengagement, termination and celebration in a thoughtful careful manner where control of the product is ceded to the study participants.

As noted above, our primary responsibility is to ensure that study participants and the target entity (whether it be individuals, families, groups, organizations or communities) are informed about the study and its impact. So we need to package the results of the study in ways that communicate most effectively with these entities. For communication with individuals, families and groups, informal phone calls, emails and personal conversations may be enough. However, if formal communication is expected, then, we are responsible for organizing meetings and developing presentations and handouts that explain the study and its impact. We should invite key informants to contribute to the presentation, giving their perceptions of the impact of the project. This is an important phase of disengaging with the participants in the study, since the goal is to convince the participants that they can lead future empowerment activities.

Formal methods of presentation include: developing a "power point" presentation, distributing handouts summarizing the project, and organizing joint panel discussions with researchers and participants. Media representatives may well be invited to such presentations as well as appropriate organizational leaders. The presentations should include the following items with variations in sequencing as seems appropriate:

- Summary of problem and ideological orientation to problem

- Description of teaching-learning engagement with community and key player participation (if confidentiality is requested, then the role can be listed, e.g. a local teacher, community activist, social worker)

- Summary of analysis of data from key informants

- Overview of action plan

- Description of action taken

- Review of impact of action

- Statement of celebration and reflection on action and suggestions for future action

Millet and Otero (2011) note the following termination meeting:

Disengagement from the study was initiated in the form of a celebratory community reunion. A total of 80 community members were contacted via telephone and invited to attend the community celebration. The researchers intended the reunion to serve as a symbolic farewell party as well celebration of the hard work of the dedicated community participants and community leaders. It was also an opportunity to reflect on how the community journeyed through the empowerment process starting from a voiceless and politically uneducated community to having participated in active community organizing and actually dialoguing with pertinent local politicians. The celebration commenced with an opening speech from the researchers. A visual chronological timeline with the steps of action and events was displayed and reviewed. The researchers presented four community leaders with a framed certificate of acknowledgement of their hard work and dedication to the positive development of their community. Two families were also presented with certificates of acknowledgement of their dedication as they attended every community meeting and actively participated by bringing food and diffusing pertinent study information throughout the year. Each person acknowledged was given the opportunity to reflect on the events of the study or offer any personal sentiments.

Other community members followed suit and spoke about how the study and how the events affected their lives. Many people were overcome with emotion and expressed great gratitude at the experience to participate in such a movement. After the certificate presentation the researchers presented the results of the study. The community members were then welcomed to mingle. Music was also played on the researcher's laptop. The community members brought food such as pozole, carne asada, pasta salad, cookies, chips, soda, and water. The celebration was quite festive and emotional. (page 138)

We also need to formally report to sponsors of the study and communicate findings to the wider social work academic and practice community. This raises the question of who would fund such challenging, and perhaps controversial, research. In this era of poverty action centers and empowered women, minority action groups and gay rights groups; the infra-structure is developing that can sustain such projects. Given a clear proposal and methodology, such projects have the potential to be sponsored by various action groups. For such groups, as well as the academic audience, a traditional report and/or article should be written. Lofland and Lofland (2006) offer helpful guidelines to structuring the report or article. These are modified and reorganized here for the critical theory need.

1. Title: This should reflect the overall ideological orientation and the topic that is the focus of the study. For example, "Psychotherapy Encounters Curanderismo: Implications for Clients Treated in the United States by Culturally Insensitive Social Workers" or "Oppression through Obsession: A Feminist Critique of Eating Disorders.

2. Abstract and Table of Contents that gives an overview of the content and organization of the report

3. First Paragraphs that lay out the ideological orientation, the topic or issue being studied in the form of a proposition about power relations and the need to promote empowerment. For example, the statements from our example studies:

> *The research project adopted a critical theory paradigm since it seeks to expose the issues of the voiceless by exploring the systemic complexity of sociopolitical ideologies in society, and by revealing the ways in which current attitudes fail to acknowledge the effects of ethnic discrimination and class oppression. This approach also enabled the community to voice the need for a public transportation system due to a lack of political education and inability to participate in the political change process that apparently originates from their invisible existence within the larger context of society. Education on the political process ultimately transformed the community from a powerless people to an empowered community that permitted them to actively participate in the political change process.*

> or,

> *"The United States is made up of many races, creeds, cultures and ethnic groups that have come together, each with their own social constructs. Therefore, social workers involved in direct practice need to be aware of their clients' or patients' worldview. This study examined the worldview of the Mexican immigrant living in the United States, or Mexican Americans, who participate in the phenomenon of folk healing. The particular type of folk healing addressed in this study was Curandersimo, which is the folk beliefs about illness, herbal medicine, curative practices, and psychiatric therapy. The preceding is a positive definition...the actual dictionary definition of a Curandero is, 'Quack, Medicaster, an artful and tricking practitioner of physic'"*

> or

> *"This research project asked how obsession with weight and body image preoccupies women and adopted and ideology that suggest that such obsession renders women powerless. The ideological position of this critical theory study is that eating disorders in women, brought on by the oppression of women and confusing messages delivered to women by*

society and the media, can be eliminated by re-socializing women's perspectives at the high-school level.

4. Early Overview. As we all were taught in English classes, when writing an essay, "…say what you are going to say, say it, and then say you have said it." This is the essence of the summary given in the overview. What was the study intended to do? What did it do? What was its impact?

5. Literature Review. Give an integrated review of both the literature on the ideology and the literature on the specific issue or problem that is the focus of the study.

6. Describe Data Sources. In this section discuss the selection of the key informants, approaches to gathering data from them, the sources for action strategies and the approach to evaluating the action. Talk about the partnerships with participants, strategies for engaging participants, and the practical details of interviewing and observing

7. Subdivided Main Body. Organize discussion of the study under the stages that have been discussed here. (see alternative layout in appendix A)

8. References

Of course, when writing the report or article it is important to follow appropriate conventions regarding style and layout. In social work this is usually the APA (American Psychological Association) style and sometimes the Chicago style. Make sure the report flows logically and the reader can easily understand the organization of the report.

Alternative Forms of Presentation

There are many critical theorists, particularly feminists, who have challenged the traditional methods of reporting to the academic community as simply an arbitrary set of rules that have been accepted as the correct way to represent reality (Wolf, 1992; Mascia-Lees et al., 1989; Clough, 1992). Mulkay (1985) has experimented with different forms of presentation including presenting the results of data analysis in the form of conversations between ideal type characters discussing the concepts and categories being developed in the form of a one act play or sketch. For some authors this has gone as far as developing drama and theatre out of data (Mienczakowski, 1994, 1995). Such dialogues have been presented to study participants with the aim of giving them a voice regarding the issue of oppression being addressed in the study. Such approaches combine both the written and oral presentation of information. This approach to reporting by combing the arts with research has been expanded into writing fictional stories and poetry based on the data that has been collected and analyzed (Krieger, 1983; Richardson, 1992)

Reflection and Celebration

In his article on self reflection in research, Bell (1998), suggests that as critical theory researchers we need to reflect on our personal context, our social context and the complex environmental context of the research setting when understanding and reflecting on a research project. He concludes that researchers are fallible and vulnerable people who, rather than impose their view of the world on the research setting, can partner with others to develop an understanding of a particular research project and its findings and mistakes. He advises that the non reflective researcher will experience: unrealistic quality standards, doubt, a fear and need for self-preservation, incessant self-expression, undue self-assertion, and a feeling of being out of his or her depth. A reflective practitioner will experience: realistic expectations, tolerance, humility, self-giving, listening, a feeling of being part of the project rather than outside the project. The overall idea of reflection is to establish a norm that no research project is the perfect project and that we can all learn to do better the next time. Such a norm frees us to approach a research project with the idea that we will do the best that we can but always assume that we will make unanticipated mistakes. When our study is found to have shortcomings, as all studies are, we celebrate our learning rather than apologize for our incompetence.

For both Stringer (1996) and Finn and Jacobson (2003) an important part of evaluation, reflection and termination of a project is "celebration" of the project and its accomplishments. Finn and Jacobson note that celebration of achievements keeps us focused on our vision for the project and for a just world (page 359). They suggest that celebration includes:

- Celebrating learning, not just winning

- Creating a celebratory spirit with, for example, decorating a meeting room and providing food and snacks

- Celebrating our adversaries as well as our allies

- Including personal touches during the research project such as remembering peoples' birthdays or celebrating project milestones

- Celebrating symbols of and milestones in resistance to oppression, such as taking time to celebrate national women's day or a cultural holiday in the middle of a project

- Celebrating to bring joy into work.

To sum up this discussion, for the critical theorists there are both internal and external audiences for the final report of the project and there are many dimensions to terminating a project that include not only communicating information but the spirit with which information is communicated. A democratic partnership is essential and reflection and celebration is mandatory.

The structure of the final report suggested in Appendix A is a starting point for writing the final report on our constructivist study. The structure of the evaluation chapter has been emerging throughout the study by means of the ongoing analysis of each interview, observation, or social artifact. Throughout the period of data collection, we have been using qualitative analysis procedures to organize and synthesize the data into a shared construction. Individuals' constructions have emerged and been compared and contrasted with other individuals' constructions. Units, categories and constructions have been built. Claims, concerns and issues have emerged; i.e. areas of agreement have been identified, areas of disagreement have been identified and issues requiring action have been identified. In our example study of homeless children, there tended to be agreement on the claims and concerns during the meeting but opinion varied on action issues and strategies. Since this was the first meeting of a network, such disagreements were recorded and identified as possible agenda items for later network meetings. In the study of the role of spirituality when intervening with African-American families in the child welfare system, areas of agreement and disagreement on claims, concerns, and action were clearly identified and stakeholders committed to continue working on the issues identified. In the HIV-AIDS study, there were claims and concerns but a there was a hesitancy to broach issues and action strategies. Some stakeholders had a vulnerability to a perceived stigma associated with the HIV-AIDS issue. So much so that the member checking meeting was not feasible. Thus reflection on how to move forward in the face of this reticence was considered by individual stakeholders but not by the group as a whole.

The final constructivist report should include the following:

- The initial research focus

- A detailed description of the research site

- A description of the final membership of the hermeneutic dialectic circle with explanations of how they were identified and why they were selected. If confidentiality is an issue, the roles or agency names can be given rather than names of actual participants.

- A description of data gathering techniques, interview and observation. This should include a summary overview of the processes identified in the research journal and changes from the initial focus to the final foci

- A description of the units, categories and final construction as identified and agreed to at the member check meeting that includes claims, concerns and issues.

- A plan of action addressing the issues that were identified at the member check meeting (Who? What? When? Where?).

The constructivist researcher is committed to creating a dynamic discussion regarding a research focus and its context. The member check meeting and the final report is not seen as the end of the research but the point at which participants take over their own process and continue the ongoing development of the joint construction with all its claims, concerns and issues. Thus the final report is simply a statement on the joint construction at that point in time. It is assumed that the group will move beyond the findings contained in the report.

When we organize the member check meeting, we should be clear that this is the time when we will be handing responsibility for the project to the group and ending our involvement in the project. By the end of the member check meeting we will have engaged in a process of terminating with study participants that includes a commitment from the circle of participants to leading and implementing the plan for future action. The goal is for the hermeneutic dialectic process to have engaged the stakeholders in the knowledge generation process to the point where they have taken ownership of the future development of the project. For social work researchers this is the same as termination with any other client. The NASW code of ethics tells us that termination should happen when goals are accomplished. In this case we have facilitated a process and product that now have a life of their own. Again we can take some advice from the social work practice field. Kirst-Ashman et al. (2012) note that at the end of a project where change has been implemented in systems such as organizations and communities it is important to

- *Routinize procedures and processes*: encourage the stakeholders to continue the constructivist approach to discussion of claims and concerns and to move forward with action to address issues.

- *Clarify policies and procedures*: encourage stakeholders to prepare memorandums of understanding with each other regarding future tasks associated with the project (Who? What? When? Where?)

- *Reduce the Availability of the Researcher to the Stakeholder Group*: in our study of homeless children, the researcher agreed to organize the follow up meeting as her last task. She did not intend to attend the meeting and encouraged the group to select a chair or facilitator at that next meeting.

- *Inform Stakeholders of other resources to address the issues that may come up*: leave stake holders with resource lists and researcher contact information if they should need consultation as they move forward.

An integral part of Termination and Follow Up, no matter which paradigm we adopt, is to develop a dissemination plan that translates the findings of our study into evidence for social work practice change. To do this, we need to think about practice knowledge that social workers are willing to incorporate into their micro and/or macro interventions with clients. In other words, we need to transform our research findings into guidelines for evidence based social work practice. What are the criteria for deciding that a study and its findings contribute to **evidence based social work practice**? Also, what do we need to do to convince **individual** social workers and social work **organizations** to change their interventions at the micro and macro levels of practice?

Evidence Based Social Work Practice

According to the web site for the Social Work Policy Institute (2010), evidence based practice (EBP) is

"…a process in which the practitioner combines well-researched interventions with clinical experience and ethics, and client preferences and culture to guide and inform the delivery of treatments and services. The practitioner, researcher and client must work together in order to identify what works, for whom and under what conditions. This approach ensures that the treatments and services, when used as intended, will have the most effective outcomes as demonstrated by the research. It will also ensure that programs with proven success will be more widely disseminated and will benefit a greater number of people." (Evidence Based Practice Page)

The NASW code of ethics notes that

Value: *Competence*

Ethical Principle: *Social workers practice within their areas of competence and develop and enhance their professional expertise.*

Social workers continually strive to increase their professional knowledge and skills and to apply them in practice. Social workers should aspire to contribute to the knowledge base of the profession.

It also notes that:

4.01 Competence

(a) Social workers should accept responsibility or employment only on the basis of existing competence or the intention to acquire the necessary competence.

(b) Social workers should strive to become and remain proficient in professional practice and the performance of professional functions. Social workers should critically examine and keep current with emerging knowledge relevant to social work. Social workers should routinely review the professional literature and participate in continuing education relevant to social work practice and social work ethics.

(c) Social workers should base practice on recognized knowledge, including empirically based knowledge, relevant to social work and social work ethics.

And also:

5.02 Evaluation and Research

(a) Social workers should monitor and evaluate policies, the implementation of programs, and practice interventions.

(b) Social workers should promote and facilitate evaluation and research to contribute to the development of knowledge.

(c) Social workers should critically examine and keep current with emerging knowledge relevant to social work and fully use evaluation and research evidence in their professional practice.

(NASW website http://www.socialworkers.org/pubs/code/code.asp)

Not only is there a logical reason to understand evidence for best practice but there is also a professionally ethical reason to do this. We need to understand the definition of "well researched interventions". The usual, definition, which relates to positivist research only, has been offered by Roberts and Yeager (2004) who suggest the levels of evidence that should be used to reach certain levels of rigor. The highest level is randomized two group designs, as discussed in this book in positivist approaches to research, and the lowest level is anecdotal case reports.

Table V.1

Levels of Evidence

This approach to rigor, as we now know, assumes only one paradigm: positivism. However, with our four paradigms in mind, we can develop a very different chart of rigor. All our paradigms offer scientific rigor when implemented completely and correctly. However, if we use these criteria: then, the post positivist approach becomes less scientific as sampling, data gathering, and data analyses become more limited; the critical theory approach becomes less scientific as teaching/learning is reduced, action is limited, and empowerment is not assessed; and, the constructivist approach becomes less scientific as key informants are limited, development of the joint construction is partial, and a change process for action is partially developed. To address this limitation in defining scientific rigor, additional criteria for levels of evidence are shown in Table V.2. These criteria accommodate the assumptions of post positivism, critical theory, and constructivism.

Table V.2
Levels of Evidence for Positivism, Post Positivism, Critical Theory and Constructivism

Scientific Level	Positivism	Post Positivism	Critical Theory	Constructivism
1	Meta-analysis or replicated randomized controlled trials (RCT) that includes a placebo condition/control trial	Data collected in naturalistic setting using appropriate purposive sampling and rigorous interviewing, observations, and is analyzed using open, axial and selective coding.	Ideological Position clearly articulated and rooted in literature. Empowerment and action based on rigorous teaching learning, empowerment is assessed to have been achieved	Key players are identified before and during study as a result of the developing joint construction. Individual Constructions are confirmed with participants. All interview data is analyzed using open coding. Joint construction is developed in membership checking meeting, Change process evolves as a result of the study (*Study of Spirituality)*

2	At least one RCT with placebo or active comparison condition, evidence obtained from multiple time series with or without intervention, or national consensus panel recommendations based on uncontrolled studies with positive outcomes or based on studies showing dramatic effects of interventions	Data is collected in naturalistic setting but sampling is stopped before full redundancy is achieved. Interviews are rigorous, analysis is not all the way to selective coding *(Study of Homeless Children, study of Parolees, study of GLBT parents))*	Ideology is fully developed. Teaching/Learning process is ended prematurely, action is implemented but not evaluated *(Study of Transportation)*	Key informants are identified but not all constructions are represented, member checking is completed and action for change identified but not implemented *(Study of Services for Homeless Children)*
3	Uncontrolled trial, observational study with 10 or more subjects or opinions of respected authorities, based on clinical experiences, descriptive studies or reports of expert consensus.	Data collected in naturalistic setting. Interviews time limited and semi structured. Analysis open coding only	Ideology fully developed, limited teaching/learning, action designed and evaluated by researcher only. *(Study of eating disorders, study of Curanderismo)*	Limited number of key informants, individual constructions developed, limited membership checking for joint construction, action identified mostly by researcher
4	Anecdotal case reports, Unsystematic clinical observation, descriptive reports, Case studies and or single subject designs	Data collected in naturalistic setting, with convenience sample using structured interview instrument, descriptive analysis	Ideological Position rooted in literature, no teaching/learning, action designed and evaluated by researcher only	Limited number of key informants, individual constructions developed, action plan not developed in membership checking meeting, suggested not implemented *(HIV-AIDS study)*

Now we have an expanded definition of "well research interventions" that assumes a range of approaches to developing evidence for evidence based practice and we have criteria for showing that both quantitative and qualitative studies can be at level 1 science. If we combine this with our generalist model and consider levels of practice, we have a framework for identifying the aspect of practice that our studies affect. The interesting insight here is that our post positivist, critical theory, and constructivist studies, because they stress both the ongoing process of the study as well as the findings of the study, offer us evidence, not only from their findings but also from their methodologies. These studies' methodologies tend to unfold as they are implemented and so when translating the studies to evidence for practice we see examples of implementation of each stage of the generalist model in the descriptions of the methodologies and the findings of the study.

In tables V.3, V.4, and V.5 are brief summaries of the contributions that the examples student studies in this book have made to social work practice. They are all level 2 science and so the practitioner considering these studies would note the study limitations. However, we can see that the combined findings of the studies give us evidence for practice at each stage of the generalist model and for all levels of micro and macro social work practice. For the post positivist studies the evidence tends to be at the individual, family and group level. For the critical theory studies it tends to be more at the organizational and community level and for the constructivist studies it tends to be at the individual, family, organization and community levels of practice.

Post Positivist Studies

1. Young, M.L. and Creacy, M. (1995) *Perceptions of Homeless Children*. California State University, San Bernardino: Masters Research Project. (level 2 science)

2. Torres, K (2007) *An Insight Into The Experience Of Parolees*. California State University, San Bernardino, M.S.W. Student Project. (level 2 science)

3. Study of LGBT Parents (level 2 science)

Table V.3
Post Positivist Studies' contribution to evidence for Social Work Practice

	Individuals	Families	Groups	Organiz ations	Commu nities
Engagement					
Study 1	Examples of how to engage homeless children using visual, musical and written art projects	Examples of how to engage homeless families using visual, musical and written are projects	Examples of how to work with homeless children in groups using visual, musical and written art projects		
Study 2	Examples of how to engage parolees in individual interviews about their personal experiences				
Study 3		Examples of how to engage LGBT parents in parent interviews about their children's interactions with schools and other children and families			
Assessment					
Study 1	When assessing homeless children we need to be aware of the children's stage of homeless and the differential impact of homelessness on children according to age				
Study 2	Need to assess, individual, family, and life history, examples of characteristics that need to be noted.				

Study 3		When working with GLBT families, be aware of dynamics of disclosure according to age of children.			
Planning					
Study 1	When planning an interventions with homeless children, be aware of age and stage of homelessness				
Study 2	When planning an intervention with parolees, a theory has been developed that explains pre, during and post incarceration behaviors				
Study 3		When planning interventions with GLBT families, be aware of heteronormal assumptions that may make about who might be the children's parents			
Impleme ntation					
Study 1	One way to intervene with homeless children is through art and music				
Study 2	Interventions with parolees need to address identified personal characteristic, experiences and history and be aware of the theory of pre,	Identifies a range of family experiences that can affect interventions with parolees			

	during and post incarceration parolee experiences				
Study 3					
Evaluatio n					
Study 1	When working with homeless children, art work, poems, and songs can be evidence of the impact of homelessness on the children				
Study 2					
Study 3					
Terminati on and Follow Up					
Study 1	At the end of the homeless children study, these children were brought to campus on the student research poster day. They displayed their art and performed their poems and songs.				
Study 2					
Study 3					

Critical Theory Studies

1. Millet, K. R., and Otero, L. R. (2011) The North Shore Public Transportation Dilemma: How Local Sociopolitical Ideologies, Ethnic Discrimination And Class Oppression Create Marginalization, And A Community's Quest For Social Justice. San Bernardino, CA. CSUSB, a social work student research project.

2. Riech, J. R. (1994). Psychotherapy Encounters Curanderismo: Implications for Clients Treated in the United States by Culturally Insensitive Social Workers. San Bernardino: Student Project, California State University San Bernardino.

3. Christopulos, J. (1995) Oppression through Obsession: A Feminist Theoretical Critique of Eating Disorders. San Bernardino, CA: Student research project

Table V.4
Critical Theory Studies' contribution to evidence for Social Work Practice

	Individuals	Families	Groups	Organizations	Communities
Engagement					
Study 1				Describes strategies for engaging political interests and transit authority.	Gives detailed description of several phases of community engagement and teaching/learning re oppression of low income, minority, immigrant community
Study 2			Describes Teaching/Learning sessions with social work students regarding Curanderismo		
Study 3			Describes Teaching/Learning sessions with high school girls re eating disorders		
Assessment					
Study 1					Shows how to develop ideological analysis of power relationships for low income, minority, immigrant community regarding public transportation
Study 2				Shows how to identify need for organizational change, through describing need for change in social work schools re curriculum content on traditional healing methods and biases	

				towards western approaches to mental health.	
Study 3	Shows how to developed ideological position regarding gender and eating disorders				
Planning					
Study 1					Gives description of developing plan for campaign for public transportation in low income, minority, immigrant community
Study 2	Gives description of pre and post testing social work students before and after seeing video on curanderismo				
Study 3	Gives description of pre and post testing high school students before and after seeing presentation on sexual stereotypes, body image, and eating disorders				
Implementation					
Study 1					Gives detailed description of both teaching/learning sessions and campaign to bring public transportation to

					low income, minority, immigrant community
Study 2	Gives description of developing materials on curanderismo and implementing pre and post tests of students on awareness of the values of traditional healing methods				
Study 3	Gives description of developing materials on eating disorders in teenage women and implementing pre and post tests of students on awareness of the impact of sexism on such eating disorders				
Evaluation					
Study 1					Gives description of informal community assessment
Study 2	Gives results of pre and post test showing effectiveness of presentation				
Study 3	Gives results of pre and post test showing effectiveness of presentation				

Termination and Follow Up					
Study 1					Gives description of ongoing community commitment to public transportation campaign and celebration of achievements.
Study 2				Describes presentation of results to one social work program	
Study 3				Describes presentation of result to one social work program	

Constructivist Studies

1. Brown, L.E. (2011) Spirituality's Role in the Interaction Between Child Welfare and Black Families. San Bernardino: Loma Linda University, social work student doctoral dissertation.

2. Becker, J. E. (1994) *A Constructivist study of the social and educational needs of homeless children.* San Bernardino, CA: CSUSB, a social work student research project and Kelly, G. (1995) *A Constructivist Second Year Study of the Social and Educational Needs of Homeless Children.* San Bernardino, CA: CSUSB, a social work student research project.

3. Hogan, P. (1995) *A Constructivist study of Social Work's Involvement with HIV-AIDS.* San Bernardino, CA: CSUSB, a social work student research project.

Table V.5
Constructivist Studies' contribution to evidence for Social Work Practice

	Individuals	Families	Groups	Organizations	Communities
Engag ement					
Study 1	The study has findings explaining how a discussion of spirituality will further engage African American parents				
Study 2				Studied described how agencies working with homeless children engaged each other during study	Study show how to join organizations that work with homeless children into a community or practitioners working with this client group
Study 3	The study has descriptions of issues related to engaging HIV-AIDS workers.				
Asses sment					
Study 1	The study explains how spirituality can be included in assessment of African American children and families	The study explains how spirituality can be included in assessment of African American children and families			
Study 2				Study shows how gathering the constructions of key players working with human services identifies strengths and gaps in services	
Study 3	Develops individual constructions that suggest				

	how personal bias affects assessment of HIV-AIDS clients				
Planning					
Study 1	Builds individual and joint constructions of how spirituality can be included in intervention plans with African American children and families	Builds individual and joint constructions of how spirituality can be included in intervention plans with African American children and families			
Study 2				Builds a joint construction identifying a plan for inter agency collaboration	
Study 3	Builds individual constructions of how social workers can plan interventions with HIV-AIDS clients and be aware of biases.				
Implementation					
Study 1	Offers joint construction showing how interventions with African-American children and families can include faith based resources	Offers joint construction showing how interventions with African-American children and families can include faith based resources			
Study 2				Describes how agencies serving homeless children can work together to coordinate more	

				efficient service delivery	
Study 3	Builds individual constructions of how to intervene with HIV-AIDS clients without bias				
Evaluation					
Study 1				Builds joint construction of need for training in discussing spirituality with children and families	
Study 2				Builds an interagency process that caused participant to commit to ongoing contact with each other.	
Study 3				Builds individual constructions suggesting that social work agencies can assess their biases regarding HIV-AIDS clients	
Termination and F.U.					
Study 1				Builds joint construction of how workers can include faith based agencies in long term planning for children and families after they leave he child welfare system.	
Study 2					
Study 3					

To sum up, when we assess our example studies using the criteria in Table V.2, they are all offering evidence for an aspect of social work practice at Level 2 science. Our post positivist studies gave us findings on micro practice for each stage of the generalist model. Our critical theory studies gave us findings for mostly macro practice with the eating disorders study (Christopulos, J. 1995) offering micro practice findings. Our constructivist studies gave us findings for all levels of practice and each stage of the generalist model. To guide social workers making a decision about whether to incorporate the findings of our studies into their practice we need to return to the concept of **transferablily** which was discussed in Part 1 of this book We should advise social workers to ask themselves two questions when they read the description of the study and its findings:

1. Does this process of data gathering transfer to my practice setting?

2. Do these findings transfer to my practice setting?

If the answers to these questions is yes then social workers can begin to consider incorporating our findings into their practice. This is the focus of the next section

Changing Social Work Practice at the Individual and Organizational Levels

Encouraging individual practitioners to change the way they intervene with clients is a challenging goal. Changing the organization in which they work is even more challenging. It is common to become comfortable with the way things are done and to be a little resistant to suggestions that things need to be modified or transformed. So it can be a struggle to translate research findings, such as those noted above, into practice. The health arena has been addressing this issue for some time, since medicine, public health and nursing have been implementing an evidence based approach to practice since the 1980s. According to Green et al. (2009) the National Institutes of Health (NIH), the Center for Disease Control and Prevention (CDC) in the U.S., the Canadian Institutes for Health (CIHR), the Medical Research Council in the UK and several other major health research funders have recently shifted to an emphasis on studies of translation of scientific findings to practice, sometimes referred to as "bench to bedside". These authors note that there is evidence to suggest that, in the public health arena it takes 17 years to turn 14% of research findings into patient care. One can only wonder what happens to the other 86%.

So how can we improve the situation? Gladwell (2000) suggests that for any idea or product to be accepted by a large number of people, it needs to be promoted by three kinds of people, connectors, mavens and salesmen. Connectors have good social skills and are networked well into the practice group, mavens are experts who like to share their ideas, and salesmen (or salespeople) are people with strong personalities who are good at persuading people that they like an idea. When we reflect on this, we realize that these are qualities that we would expect any social worker to have. Social work researchers should be well equipped to be champions of incorporating new evidence into practice.

Rogers (2003) in his discussion of diffusion theory notes that there are five stages to the process of adopting a research process and incorporating it into practice: knowledge, persuasion, decision, trial and adoption. Green et al., (2009) when discussing this process in terms of knowledge utilization list the following influences: **source of the new knowledge**, **content of the new knowledge**, the **medium by which the new knowledge is communicated, characteristics of the user of the new knowledge** and **the context in which the user of the knowledge is operating**. These are discussed below in relation to social workers.

Source of the New Knowledge

For the social worker to be willing to consider practice changes suggested by a particular research study, the **author** of the research project that created the new evidence for practice needs to:

1. Be credible: the researcher and/or the research advisor needs to be somebody that social workers respect as having an understanding of the practice arena and not someone who is out of touch with the realities of the work place.

2. Build Relationships with potential users: It is helpful to include the practice community in the development and implementation of the project. This partnership is built into the methodologies for post positivist, critical theory, and constructivist research.

3. Have realistic expectations of use: It might not be necessary to wait 17 years for the study findings to be incorporated into social work practice but it would be useful to understand that there is a process of individual and organizational change that must take place for this to happen.

4. Build an expectation of use into the design of the study **"even engaging the users in the research—even letting them control it"** (Green et al. page 164, my underline and bold) Even traditional researchers are acknowledging the need to adopt methodologies associated with post positivism, critical theory, and constructivism.

Content of the New Knowledge

For the social worker to be willing to consider practice changes suggested by a particular research study, the **findings** of the study must be perceived to be

1. Accessible: the study and its findings need to be easily understood and perceived as easily implemented. The social work practitioner, generally, sees research as something that it too complex and difficult to understand. The study author(s) need to acknowledge this and present the study and its findings in a way that engages practitioners.

2. Adaptable to the social worker's approaches to practice: The social worker must feel that the new knowledge will not radically change the approach that she or he has developed over time through practice experience

3. Advantageous to the social worker: The new knowledge will need to be seen as improving a social worker's practice or making aspects of practice more easily or clearly implemented

4. Compatible with the social worker's values, concerns and expectations: the new knowledge will, of course need to abide by the NASW code of ethics as well as social workers' own understanding and expectations regarding ethical practice

5. Challenging the status quo: the new knowledge needs to be seen as something that is indeed new and not just an old idea that is being recycled to look like new knowledge.

6. Have quality, trustworthiness, and soundness: the report on the research study must describe a rigorous approach to the study using the appropriate methodology for the approach taking and giving a thorough description of both the process and findings of the study.

7. Emphasize positive behavior with clear, low cost, action implications: The new knowledge needs to be presented in a way that does not suggest that the practitioner is intervening incorrectly with clients but rather that the new knowledge suggests even better ways to intervene with clients. Also, the changes need to be on a scale that is realistic for the social worker's practice setting.

Medium by which the new knowledge is communicated to social workers

We generally present the findings of studies via presentations or poster sessions at conferences or specific university research days and staff or community meetings in the agency or community setting in which the study took place. It is important the medium through which the study findings are communicated to social workers:

1. Provides opportunities for open and equal partnership discussion of the findings

2. Provides opportunities for intermediaries between the researcher and the practitioners to assist with dissemination of the study findings

3. Includes personal interaction between the researcher(s) and practitioners.

4. Is timely; i.e. be knowledge that the social work practitioner sees as immediately useful

5. Is communicated in language that is, "simple, clear, brief, reinforcing, more concrete than abstract, andenriched with analogies that can be understood in the local language" (Green et al, page 164)

When preparing a poster, presentation, or discussion of the study findings we should consider the setting and set it up so that we encourage discussion rather than passive listening to the presenter. We should also consider attendees. Are friendly supervisors or well respected opinion leaders willing to attend and be intermediaries between the practitioners and the researcher(s)? We need to consider presenting the knowledge in a way that makes it useful, perhaps developing examples case examples of how the new knowledge might be used. We might also want to show some of the presentation to one or two of the social workers before the presentation to check if the language makes sense to them.

The User of New Knowledge and their practice context

For social workers to adopt the new knowledge suggested by a particular research study, they need to be:

1. Involved in the research project from the beginning,

2. Willing to make changes to their practice,

3. Networked with other users who are interested in the research topic,

4. Willing to put an effort into understanding the findings of the research study, and

5. Interested and have a practice philosophy that goes with the research project

For organizations within which social workers practice to adopt the new knowledge suggested by a particular research project they need to:

1. Have the resources to consider implementing the findings of the research project and supporting long term relationships between researchers and practitioners that might be necessary,

2. Be supportive of considering changes to practice and considering new knowledge,

3. Have no strong bureaucratic or political opposition to considering the implications of the study findings,

4. Provide incentives for considering changes to practice; and

5. Model acceptance of change in the leadership style.

Johnson and Austen (2006) offer some practical strategies for creating a culture willing to consider and adopt evidence for changing practice.

At the Team or Unit Level:

- Develop and disseminate an in-house newsletter on relevant research

- Form and support monthly journal clubs to discuss an article or book of relevance to practice and to encourage knowledge sharing among practitioners

- Include research on the agenda of supervisory meetings, unit meetings, and departmental meetings

- Involve students in agency field placements to search for, summarize, and share relevant research

- Create a library in every supervisor's office of relevant research articles, reports, and books

- Help staff to access existing databases (Cochrane and Campbell Collaboratives)

At the Department or Agency Level:

- Develop an organizational environment that recognizes the importance of research in making decisions at all levels of the organization

- Identify champions for evidence-based practice (chief information officer, knowledge manager, etc.)

- Demonstrate ownership of evidence-based practice by senior and middle management (may require special orientation sessions)

- Provide resources for evidence-based practice (internet access, training, library materials, etc.)

- Establish a steering committee responsible for implementing evidence-based practice

- Support the design, implementation, and utilization of service evaluations

- Create a climate of continuous learning and improvement (learning organization)

- Promote evidence-based training and evidence-based decision-making

- Develop system of email alerts of recent, relevant articles

- Create a policy on supervision that includes evidence-based practice

- Consider mandatory in-service training on evidence-based practice and lobbying forsimilar content in local pre-service university programs

- Promote protected reading time for staff to review relevant research

- Structure student placements around evidence-based practice

At the Researcher's Institutional Level:

- Provide clear, uncomplicated, user-friendly presentations of research findings

- Conduct research relevant to the service mission of the organization

- Develop research and evaluation partnerships between agencies anduniversities/institutes

- Utilize multiple methods of dissemination. For example, posters, well produced reports, power point presentations, web based discussions, provision of web based resource materials, informal discussions

- Build dissemination strategies into all research projects

- Engage practitioners in research topic identification and development

At the Senior Management Level

- Develop and circulate a policy statement that clearly identifies the value-added qualities of adopting evidence-based practice including:

  - An approach to assessing service effectiveness

  - A way of finding promising practices for adaptation/incorporation

  - Evidence of support for decision-making about evidence based practice at the line and management levels

  - An approach to making decisions about the effectiveness of contracted services

- Develop an orientation program whereby senior staff become thoroughly acquainted with evidence-based practice and begin to redesign the organizational culture to make it possible to install this new approach to service delivery

- Identify a champion from the rank of either senior management or middle management to serve as the agencies chief information officer (knowledge manager) to guide this organizational change (based on a well-defined job description or work portfolio)

- Identify a university/institute partner to conduct systematic reviews of existing evidence by involving agency staff in:

  - selecting the areas for review,

  - reviewing the results of the reviews and recommendations,

- ○ designing the strategies for incorporating new knowledge into ongoing practice and evaluating the outcomes,

- ○ coordinating all agency efforts to promote evidence-based practice through the agency's chief information officer or knowledge manager.

(These strategies adapted by Johnson and Austen (2006) from Center for Evidence-based Social Services (2004). Becoming an evidence-based organization: Applying, adapting, and acting on evidence – Module 4. *The Evidence Guide: Using research and evaluation in social care and allied professions.* Exeter, UK: University of Exeter)(These strategies adapted for this book from Johnson and Austen (2006) Figure 6 pages 92-93)

This leads us to a starting point for our dissemination plan. if these strategies exist in our research setting then we can connect to them and use them.

The Dissemination Plan

Our dissemination plan is not another report it is our planned strategy for effectively communicating our findings to our research setting. To develop our dissemination plan we should follow these steps:

1. Make sure we did indeed follow the correct methodology for the approach that we adopted and make sure that we give a clear thorough description of the research method and the findings in our report.

2. Make a chart of the evidence we have found using levels of practice and the steps of the generalist model as our guidelines as shown in Tables V.3, V.4, and V.5

3. Review the setting in which we would like our findings to be adopted and see if the characteristics listed above for propensity for individual and organizational change are present.

4. Consider these individual and organizational characteristics when preparing to present our chart of findings to the practice settings. For example

   a. Target practitioners who are likely to respond positively to adopting our findings

   b. Use the meetings, newsletters, and other forms of communication that the practice setting already uses to communicate innovation.

5. Develop suggestions for policy change proposals in collaboration with practitioners in the practice setting.

And so now we have come to the end of our research project. We have terminated appropriately with our research setting according to the paradigm we adopted and we have implemented strategies that give us the best likelihood that our findings will make a contribution to social work practice. It has been a long and rigorous journey. As we sigh with relief, we can also celebrate the work that we have done and the contribution that we have made to new knowledge in the social work profession.

Summary

- For **positivists**, termination and follow is a reporting of the findings

- Findings can be reported by means of posters, presentations or written reports

- For **post positivists** termination involves writing a paper, making presentations and disengaging with the research site and research participants.

- Writing is a habit that needs to be formed from the start of the study using various strategies to get to the "blank page" and then fill it.

- Make sure that the intense personal engagement is honored by appropriately saying "goodbye" to the people who have contributed to the success of the study.

- For the **critical theorist** the goal of the final stage of the project is to give the study participants ownership of the project

- This is done by reporting findings in user-friendly modes, reflecting on the strengths and weaknesses of the study and celebrating both the achievements of this project and the potential for future empowerment.

- For **constructivists,** termination with the hermeneutic dialectic circle happens as the members of the circle take charge of the project and its further development.

- Rather than end our project with data analysis, we need to consider strategies for transforming our study findings into evidence for social work practice

- There are both logical and ethical reasons for integrating new evidence into social work practice.

- The criteria for well researched evidence depend on the approach that was taken in the research project

- The stages of the generalist model and levels of practice can be used to chart the evidence that a study has provided for practice

- Translating research findings into changes in social practice requires a consideration of the characteristics of the individual practitioners and the practice settings

- A dissemination plan should acknowledge and work with those individual and organizational characteristics.

Learning Assignment

1. Find a research article in a scholarly journal on a topic that you are interested in. Review the article and evaluate whether it includes all the sections described above under reports and articles for positivists. Is anything missing?

2. With your partner have a brief discussion of reporting as the method of terminating with study participants. What are the advantages of this approach to terminating with study participants and what are the advantages?

3. With a partner, role-play different ways you might terminate with a study site where you have carried out a post positivist study.

4. How is post positivist termination different from the termination you carry out with clients in practice situations? Write in your journal about these differences.

5. Plan a presentation and celebration for the critical theory project you identified at the end of chapter two.

6. Discuss with your group how you would report and celebrate a study of student empowerment.

7. Write a case study of your experiences so far in this research course using the journals you have been keeping and the outline for case studies described above.

8. Think of the study that you are proposing and develop a dissemination plan for the study findings. Include

    i. Individual practitioners to be targeted

    ii. Meetings to be targeted

    iii. Newsletters and publications to be targeted

    iv. Style of presentation (formal slide presentation, informal discussion, poster, etc)

    v. Strategies for developing a policy change in the targeted practice stetting.

Bell, S. (1998) Self-Reflection and Vulnerability in Action Research: Bringing Forth New Worlds in Our Learning. In *Systemic Practice and Action Research, Vol. 11, No. 2,*

Becker, J. E. (1994) *A Constructivist study of the social and educational needs of homeless children.* San Bernardino, CA: CSUSB, a social work student research project

Brown, L.E. (2011) Spirituality's Role in the Interaction Between Child Welfare and Black Families. San Bernardino: Loma Linda University, social work student doctoral dissertation.

Clough, P.T. (1992). The end(s) of ethnography: From realism to social criticism. Newbury Park: Sage

Coffey, A. and Atkinson, P. (1996) *Making Sense of Qualitative Data.* Thousand Oaks: Sage.

Drisko, J. W. (1997). Strengthening Qualitative Studies and Reports: Standards to Enhance Academic Integrity. *Journal of Social Work Education*, 33, 1–13.

Finn, J.L. and Jacobson, M. (2003). *Just Practice: A Social Justice Approach to Social Work.* Peosta, Iowa: eddie bowers publishing.

Gladwell M. 2000. The Tipping Point: How Little Things Can Make a Big Difference. New York: Little Brown

Green, L. W., Ottoson, J.M., Garcia, C., and Hiatt, A. (2009) "Diffusion Theory and Knowledge Dissemination, Utilization, and Integration in Public Health" in *The Annual Review of Public*

Health (publhealth.annualreviews.org), January 200910.1146/annurev.publhealth.031308. 100049

Hogan, P. (1995) *A Constructivist study of Social Work's Involvement with HIV-AIDS.* San Bernardino, CA: CSUSB, a social work student research project

Johnson, M. & Austin, M.J. (2006). Evidence-Based Practice in the Social Services: Implications for Organizational Change. *Administration in Social Work*, 30 (3), 75-104.

Kelly, G. (1995) A Constructivist Second Year Study of the Social and Educational Needs of Homeless Children. San Bernardino, CA: CSUSB, a social work student research project.

Kirst-Ashman, K. K. Hull, G.H. (2012) Understanding Generalist Practice. Florence, KY: Cenage.

Krieger, S. (1984). Fiction and Social Science. In N.K. Denzin (Ed) *Studies in symbolic interaction 5* (pp 269-286) Green which, CT: JAI

Lofland, J., Snow, D., Anderson, L., Lofland, L.H. (2006). *Analyzing Social Settings: A guide to Qualitative Observation and Analysis.* Belmont, CA: Wadsworth.

Mascia-Lees, F. E., Sharpe, P., Cohen, C.B. (1989) The postmodern turn in anthropology: Cautions from a feminist perspective. *Signs*, 15, 7-33.

McNevin, M (2011) How Do Heteronormative Perspectives Affect Same-Sex Parents? California State University, San Bernardino: M.S.W. research project

Mienczakowski, J.E. (1994) Reading and writing research: Ethnographic theatre. *National Association for Drama in Education (Australia)*, 18, 45-54

Mienczakowski, J.E. (1995) The theatre of ethnography: The reconstruction of ethnography into theatre with emancipatory potential. *Qualitative Inquiry*, 1, 360-375.

Millet, K. R., and Otero, L. R. (2011) The North Shore Public Transportation Dilemma: How Local Sociopolitical Ideologies, Ethnic Discrimination And Class Oppression Create Marginalization, And A Community's Quest For Social Justice. San Bernardino, CA. CSUSB, a social work student research project.

Minkler, M. & Wallerstein (2003) *Community-Based Participatory Research for Health.* San Francisco: Jossey-Bass

Mulkay, M. J. (1979). *Science and the sociology of knowledge.* London: George Allen & Unwin.

Mulkay, M.J. (1985) The word and the world: Explorations in the forms of sociological analysis. London: George Allen and Unwin.

Pellecchia, G. L. (1999). Dissemination of Research Findings: Conference Presentations and Journal Publications. *Topics in Geriatric Rehabilitation.* 14(3) pp 67-69.

Prevent Child Abuse American, Literature Review on Evidence Based Practice (2006)
http://member.preventchildabuse.org/site/DocServer/EBP_Literature_Review.pdf?doc ID=162

Richardson, L. (1992) The consequences of poetic representation: Writing the other, writing the self. In C. Ellis & M.G. Flaherty (Eds) *Investigating subjectivity: research on lived experience.* (pp125-137) Newbury Park: Sage

Roberts, A. R. and Yeager, K.R. (2004) Evidence-Based Practice Manual: Research and Outcome Measures in the Health and Human Services. Oxford: Oxford University Press, Inc.

Social Work Policy Institute web site, Evidence Based Practice page (2010) http://www.socialworkpolicy.org/research/evidence-based-practice-2.html

Rogers E. M. 2003. *Diffusion of Innovations*. New York: Free Press. 5th ed.

Stringer, E.T. (1996). Action Research: A Handbook for Practitioners. Thousand Oaks: Sage.

Wolcott, H.F. (2008). *Writing up Qualitative Research*. Newbury Park: Sage

Wolf, M. (1992) A thrice told tale: Feminism, postmodernism, and ethnographic responsibility. Stanford, CA: Stanford University Press.

Made in the USA
Middletown, DE
26 January 2022

59722539R00199